Become The Woman of Your Dreams

Grace Harris

Copyright @ 2020 by Grace Harris
All rights reserved.
Published by Dutch Global

No part of this book may be reproduced, stored in a retrieval system or transmitted in any way or by any means, electronic, mechanical, photocopying, recording or otherwise, without the prior written permission of the publisher, except in the case of brief quotations embodied in critical articles and reviews.

www.BecomeTheWomanofYourDreamsAcademy.com

First edition

Contents

PROLOGUE 1

PART ONE 7
    Chapter 1 Omen 9
    Chapter 2 That I will live, in spite of death 19
    Chapter 3 The Silent Apprentice 24
    Chapter 4 Seeds and weeds build a jungle 27
    Chapter 5 At peace in my high 34
    Chapter 6 Shadows of rage 37
    Chapter 7 The orgasm of cruelty 42
    Chapter 8 If you bite me 47
    Chapter 9 Magic 54
    Chapter 10 Once upon a time, a shithouse 60
    Chapter 11 Slave, deprived 64
    Chapter 12 Touch us no more 69
    Chapter 13 Ain't no communion for broken people 75
    Chapter 14 Indifference breeds the darkest evil 80
    Chapter 15 Just another high school weirdo 84

PART TWO 89
    Chapter 16 Truth Seeker 91
    Chapter 17 Queens have hearts, not crowns 99
    Chapter 18 Who invented the treadmill 110
    Chapter 19 Goodbye, mother 116

Chapter 20 Sovereign beings above the mud 123
Chapter 21 Impostor breeding transitions 133
Chapter 22 Blue-eyed monster 140
Chapter 23 Moral prostitution 146
Chapter 24 Crystal Tunnel 157
Chapter 25 No Deal 163
Chapter 26 Tidal waves make me sink or swim 166
Chapter 27 Sober comeuppance 175
Chapter 28 Walking away with an army of angels 182
Chapter 29 The last Tango 187

PART THREE 193
Chapter 30 My beloved, demonic self 195
Chapter 31 The shadows are full of piranhas 202
Chapter 32 Classic, elegant fear 211
Chapter 33 Fatal Resurrection 214
Chapter 34 Showdown 222
Chapter 35 Personal Revolution 231
Chapter 36 Strip me bare but my dignity 237
Chapter 37 Opening up to my higher self 242
Chapter 38 London – Resilience and Teamwork 245
Chapter 39 Rome - Becoming the woman of my dreams 251
Chapter 40 Venice - Prophecy 255
Chapter 41 Paris - Razzle Dazzle 260
Chapter 42 Strong 269
Chapter 43 New Friendships 273
Chapter 44 Inner Child 277
Chapter 45 Kindred Souls 289
Chapter 46 Self-love 294

EPILOGUE 299

PROLOGUE:

This book has been written as a testament to a journey of healing from the inside. A spiritual odyssey that is both tumultuous and transcendent, it chronicles my own stories and stories of other people, who have been involved in the spectrum of abandonment, abuse, and indifference.

My intention is to honour men and women, who were once children, and were silent victims of neglect, abandonment, emotional, physical, mental and sexual abuse; and to help open the gates to their endless source of unbounded personal power. An inner light that will truly heal their life, and the lives of their loved ones.

Yes, I am speaking to you, and with you.

For so long, the epidemic of child abandonment had become so common around the world, especially in poor, third world countries, that we, the abandoned children, have been swept under the rug, as remnants; and compartmentalized as only the periphery of mainstream problems, such as drug abuse, terrorism, global warming, and many more eye-catching, thought-provoking, world issues. The spotlight shines on the most stunning decays of civilisation, as we remain mostly suppressed and unaddressed. Many of us have fostered a good enough life where we appear to be doing great on the surface, while millions of others are still living in the dark, nursing their deep-seated wounds with their substance of choice, to numb an unaddressed, nameless pain. We are kindred souls, made of beautiful mosaic, art pieces. Every little piece gives a glimpse of a shining, but never quite a glimpse of the source, of the shining. We were scattered, but we are beautifully whole, if only we gave ourselves a fearless chance.

In the Philippines, there are two million abandoned and neglected children strewn around the country, at the time of writing. These children's fates were largely due to poverty, where their parents believe that they have no means to feed themselves, let alone others, including children that they have sired. That being said, there is a fraction of neglected, abandoned and victimised children, who have come from middle class families, whose mothers or fathers were financially and physically capable to care for their children, but somehow made the decision to move on with their lives, by first getting rid of the unnecessary baggage, that is the child. I speak from experience, and I know that the difference between an abandoned child from extremely poor parents, and an abandoned child from 'can afford' parents, is the blatant, unadulterated indifference of the parent, toward the child - which is the biggest epidemic that I see.

I was abandoned due to indifference, I was raised in a houseful of indifferent people, at their very best. The indifference in our society is so prevalent, that it becomes part of our own self-limiting beliefs. We come to live with indifference not only to others, but indifference to ourselves. It becomes the way that life seems to be, and the reason why many of us don't bother looking for deeper answers, as to who we really are and why are we really here?

BECOME THE WOMAN OF YOUR DREAMS

I wrote this book for all the men and women who raised themselves as abandoned and abused kids, through hell and high water. I see the grit in you, and I love you for that. What I would like for you to do with me now, is put that grit away, and be vulnerable with me. Open your heart, as I open mine to you, and let's look at the one real thing that will surpass the test of any sorrow and loss. Let's talk about what it takes to find unapologetic and radical self-love.

"Always remember that beneath your shattered pieces is a mosaic of tranquillity, wisdom, and power.

Never forget that your strength and tenacity were birthed by your courage and vulnerability.

Be faithful to the knowing that whatever came your way, whatever is in the way, and whatever will block your way - you will continue to soar with your wounded wings; as your healing is bestowed upon you, through the protection of the divine, which is your unshakeable belief and Self Love.

You are infinitely beautiful and powerful in ways that your human self will ever be able to comprehend.

Believe In You."

PART ONE

Chapter 1
Omen

There was an old billiard hall around the corner from my kindergarten school. It was so brown and so ancient that it looked like it had been half toasted and narrowly survived a fire, yet it was very popular. The same bunch of men hung out and played billiard all day every day, that I often wondered if there was anyone waiting for them to come home. They would poke and push the coloured balls for hours on end, repeatedly, patiently and joyfully, occasionally cheering and cajoling one another, as if there was not a care to be had in the world.

Thirty-five years later, I drove past my old kindergarten school and saw the billiard hall around the corner, looking exactly the same as I remember it, dilapidated, dusty and very popular. This blast from the past made me realize that no matter how far I've travelled in life, some things, places, and people, will always be the same. The dichotomy of my existence was inescapably clear, that no matter how much I've changed, I will always be me.

This epiphany triggered me to look deep, and way back into my early life, and inspired me to illustrate my journey, so that others may find some valuable lessons in my experiences; that they may be able to create bigger, better and stronger opportunities for themselves, no matter their current circumstance.

My first memory was a surprise meeting with a big, slick, and indifferent, reticulated python, at the age of three. We were then living in a small compound of three households in South Osmeña Street, when my big brother and I were playing with some kids from the neighbourhood, and I wandered curiously by myself, towards a stack of tyres sitting idly at the far end of the fence. There were four used rubber tyres piled on top of each other, and they towered over me, making me feel even more interested.

I gingerly pulled myself up towards the top of the pile, determined to conquer its challenging height. Halfway through climbing, I heard some of the kids yell, *"Panaog! Mahulog ka!"* (Get down! You will fall!) I tried to consider their suggestion, but I was already in the awkward stage where going down or going up, would be equally challenging. I kept climbing. Then finally, I got to the top and without preamble, I began to jump up and down the pile like they were a trampoline.

While jumping, I looked down on the gaping hole in the middle of the pile, and there was a black snake with saucer sized white spots on its skin, quietly looped inside of the tyres. It was staring at me. Shocked, I locked eyes with the snake and froze in my position. It flicked its tongue a few times, but its body remained very still. I tried to yell out for help, but I couldn't find my voice, so I just kept eyeballing the snake, afraid that if I ever took my eyes off him, he would pounce out of the tyres and sink his fangs on my cheek. After a minute of tongue flicking and eyeballing with the python, I felt my body slowly climbing down from the four-tiered tyres, feeling like I was about to faint in anticipation of a snake biting my face. I never once took my eyes off the snake, who looked rather bored, but nevertheless still a snake. Once down on the ground, I bolted, albeit my legs felt like led, that I couldn't seem to run fast enough. I told the first adult I could find, who then alerted other people. They told everyone to stay clear of the rubber tyres, and all of us kids were sent back inside our houses.

Afterwards, I never really thought much about that snake encounter, but as I grew older, I noticed that unlike most people who cringe at the sight of snakes, I found them fascinating and eerily beautiful. Over the years, a snake would visit my dreams and although it never posed any sense of danger or fear for me, it always exuded a certain sense of ponder and caution. Like a nagging thought that sits at the bottom of my mind.

I was born as the second illegitimate child to my parents Gregorio and Teresita, in a small, quiet town called Dadiangas, in Southern Philippines. Named after a shrub that matures into a small tree at its fullest glory, Dadiangas would become known as "boomtown" General Santos City or *"Gensan"* for short, for its significant economic contribution to the country through fishing and agriculture. By the turn of the twenty-first century, its population had quadrupled from a hundred thousand to half a million people.

As a child, I've always felt a sense of exclusivity about Gensan. It was a town where everyone was originally born and bred there. Decades later I would go back to Gensan and find that the exclusivity of the town and the originality of its people were gone. It had transformed into a major city with an international airport, shopping centres, sports cars, hotels and resorts, thousands of scooters on the roads, and people from other towns migrating to make a living and raise their families in General Santos City. The small town that I remember dearly as a child, was no longer. Almost everything was unrecognisable. Almost.

After living in the quiet neighbourhood of South Osmeña Street, we moved to Cagampang Street, a busy road that led to the one and only Public Market in town, which we simply called *"Palengke"*. The Palengke had a fish, as well as a meat section. I liked the fish section better because it was clean and fresh. Tons of fish were stocked in iceboxes and the entire area was always wet from clean, running water which kept them nice and shiny; whereas in the meat section, the floor always seemed dry and unwashed. Rows of unrefrigerated dead animals hung above the vendors' butcher tables. Flies flew everywhere and the meat gave an unpleasant stench that sometimes made me dry retch. Along the stairways were hundreds of vendors selling organic vegetables, spices and dried seafood at low prices.

Aside from being so close to the Palengke, our house was across the road from the most beautiful building in town, during that time. A four-storey brick building called *"Yap Mabuhay Enterprises"*. Its exteriors were beige with a coarse, sandstone like texture that always felt cold to touch and defied the heat of the sun.

In the hustle and bustle of Cagampang Street, my mother opened a *"sari-sari"* (assorted) store at the front of our house. Sari-sari stores usually sold items like candy, cigarettes, biscuits, paracetamols, sugar, soda and alcohol. Other sari-sari stores would also buy comics subscription and rent them out to comics readers. This was the most common entrepreneurial endeavours of household owners in the Philippines wanting to earn money from home.

My mother's sari-sari store was well positioned, being in such a busy neighbourhood. She sold all the general items that people needed, plus more. She had comics available for readers, as well as home-made delicacies and home-made ice-candy for sale. Compared to others, my mother's store looked like a high-end sari-sari, which I was quietly proud of.

From what I've been told, my father worked in a pesticide company, as the area manager for sales. He drove a company car, which was a rare perk in the tiny town of Dadiangas, back in the early '80s.

The first memory I have of my parents was of them having a heated discussion. One day shortly after we moved to Cagampang Street, I was sitting on the corner of a bed, in the bedroom that we shared as a family. My mother sat next to me and my father was sitting across from her, on the corner of another bed. I was flipping through what would have been a picture book, as I was too young to read, when my mother told me to turn away and *"just read"*. My tears fell through my face and landed on the book pages, as I did exactly what I was told: I flipped through the pages religiously, as their discussion elevated to an intense argument. I willed the pages to drown their voices and my mind to hear only the flipping of the pages of the book. I cannot remember what they were saying, but I remember the pain in my little chest.

After this point, there was a void in my memory and then I found myself looking at broken glass that fell from the door of a clothes cabinet. The cabinet itself looked as if something strong went through the middle of it, and then I saw my father wrapping a piece of white cloth around his bleeding hand.

I don't remember him getting up and punching the glass, nor did I hear the noise of the glass breaking; but I remember the grief and fear I felt, as I looked at the blood-soaked cloth on my father's hand and the broken furniture.

The second and last memory I have of my parents being together, was on a rainy afternoon. My mother was sitting behind the counter in our store and my father was standing across from her. They were on a heated argument again when my father lost his cool and slammed his fist down on the counter so hard, that the *"garapons"*, (clear, plastic candy jars with red coloured lids) levitated from the counter like jumping jacks. I was scared. At the time a woman named Vicenta worked for us, as a helper. Vicenta was a tall woman with beautiful, dark brown skin, short hair and broad physique. She had an aura of maturity about her and when she sensed my fear, she took me away from the scene of my parents fighting, and out into the rain. Together we walked two houses down the semi-industrial neighbourhood of Cagampang Street. We stopped out the front of a metal sheets manufacturing shop, its doors were made of brown, imposing, folding steel. I pressed my body against the corner of the cold brown steel and grey concrete, and tried not to get wet from the rain, sobbing away in sadness for my mother and father fighting.

That day, my parents decided to separate, and I didn't see or hear from my father again until ten years later. Shortly after he left, I learned the truth about me being a bastard child, something that I'd suspected for years. Gossip was rife in our neighbourhood and I heard that my father only lived one hour away from our town with his 'original' family. Some kids used to ridicule me and my big brother for being *"anak sa labas"* (kids borne outside the marital home). We were bullied not so much for being illegitimate but more so because we were seen as easy targets, with no father to defend us, nor a mother who cared to deflect bullies away from her children. Being a child in Cagampang Street was tough. Bullying was rife amongst kids, and hardly any parents took any notice. Indifference seemed like an ingrained way of life.

I was four years old when I discovered that I can read. My mother was sitting behind the counter in our sari-sari store, holding a Filipino comics in her hand. She told me to come over to her, then she pointed to the words in the speech bubbles, syllable by syllable. I was surprised and very pleased that I could read every syllable she pointed to. Immediately I connected the syllables and understood the words I was reading. It was a happy moment for me as I smiled up to my mother's face; but she had never been one to commend, celebrate or congratulate me for anything. She simply nodded her head in approval, as well as to signal that I was dismissed.

Every now and then, people would come over late in the evening when the store had closed, and they would stay all night playing cards with my mother. They always played *"piyat-piyat"*. A seemingly complicated game where each of the four players took thirteen cards and they would arrange their cards in a tower of three, five and five, similar to Chinese Poker. I tried to understand how this game worked but it never made sense quick enough to keep me interested, so I resigned myself to thinking that it was an "adult card game".

There was a round tin that roved around the table, and the players slipped money in it for the *"tong"* (notes and coins donated by the winning players, as tokens of their appreciation to the host of the night's session). Often, I was in charge of making sure that the tin for the tong was safely moving around, and that it was never too full nor too empty; steadily enticing the winners to keep the tong flowing in, all night long. These game nights ran till the wee hours of the morning, and I never stayed awake long enough to see them finish.

When my father left, my mother essentially became a single woman. She was beautiful, with porcelain like Chinese skin, high cheek bones, purt lips and big, doe like eyes. Her black hair was always a short bob which showed off her slender neck on a slender body. Sometimes I would watch my mother dance in front of the mirror. She would see me watching her and she never asked me to dance with her, making me feel like I was gawking at my own mother, which was really awkward. As a young girl, it was uncomfortable to see my mother being pretty and sexy, without being escorted by a respectable man. Sometimes she would get all dolled up and disappeared for two days, leaving me and my brother with the helper, wondering where she went or who she was with. It stirred feelings of confusion inside my young mind.

One very cool thing that my mother did as a home-based entrepreneur was starting up a Chess Club. She set up a couple of long, wooden tables, with three laminated chessboards on each one, allowing for six games running simultaneously at any given time. The set-up was complete with professional sets of wooden chess pieces and wooden chess clocks. People, mostly young men, would come and pay to play chess. It didn't take long to pick the best players from the regular patrons. Some of them were total geeks and shared stories of people like Russia's Anatoly Karpov and Garry Kasparov, the two strongest chess players in the world during the '80s. I found chess to be a lot of fun. I would sometimes play with one of the good players, bravely using a chess clock. I think that they may have given me a whole lot of handicap without me knowing, so that I could have a chance at beating them, which I did fairly often, making me feel like I was a chess prodigy. Those were fun times.

Crown Bookstore was an iconic retail shop in Gensan back in those days. On the way to school one day, I recall walking into this store to buy crayons. I was only five years old and may not have been by myself as a customer, but I clearly remember a feeling of free enterprise. The sensation of looking at the things I needed to get, so that I can create my school projects, was one of intense focus. There was an array of thick crayons, thin crayons, boxes of eight, twenty-four, thirty-six crayons. The best brand was Crayola, they always smelled sweet and gave me a feeling of softness and joy. The rare freedom to be able to choose and have what I needed – sparked a circuit in my young brain. The circuit of self-sufficiency. I would find out much, much later in life, that the freedom and independence to support myself for my own needs, was one of my strongest inner drivers.

On Mondays during flag raising ceremony at school, pupils and teachers must attend the school grounds to sing the national anthem and recite the *"Panatang Makabayan"* (Pledge of Patriotism). Afterward, the school Principal would call out selected pupils' names and acknowledge those who have done well in the last week, academically as well as behaviourally.

One particular Monday, I had a funny but strong feeling that I was going to be called over for some kind of recognition. Having worked diligently in the classroom, I thought I was going to receive an academic praise; but instead I was called out for a good behaviour award. I stood there listening to them calling out my name, but I hesitated to move, thinking that they had made a mistake in calling me out for a good behaviour recognition. This hesitation infuriated my teacher, and she hurried me along in her shrill voice. I rushed over to the stage, walking as fast as I could with my little legs, and up to the podium to accept a ribbon. Dumbfounded by the 'good behaviour' award, I took the ribbon in my hand and then quietly turned to leave the stage. As I gingerly walked back to my place in the queue, the microphone boomed behind me, it was the school principal commentating on the fact that I may have received a good behaviour recognition, but I didn't have the right manners to say, "Thank You."

There was muffled laughter in the crowd. I was so embarrassed, and the feeling of humiliation was potent. Unbeknownst to me, I was building a character in a subliminal but chronic fashion. Little did I know that the constant niggling of criticism and negativity around me, coupled with my introverted nature, and fuelled by the absence of role models in my life, was going to shape the next thirty years of my journey.

Chapter 2
That I will live, in spite of death

The term of endearment for grandma in Filipino is *"Lola"*, but my grandmother never wanted to be addressed as "Lola" because she felt it was only for 'old' people. She preferred to be called "Mommy".

Mommy's house was on the east side of town some twelve kilometres from my mother's house. In the early '80s, the main mode of public transportation were tricycles. These iconic, three wheeled vehicles were made of Kawasaki or Honda motorcycles, attached to a custom built, six-seater, tin car with two passengers at the front and four passengers facing each other at the back. The size of the seats were designed for passengers with an average weight of fifty kilograms, making tricycle rides a close encounter for the majority of the population. Back in those days, private cars were only for the wealthy citizens.

One day when I was six years old, my mother took me to my grandmother's house to visit. It was a bright, sunny day and I was wearing my one and only going out frock, a blue dress with puffy sleeves, swirly skirt and ruffled hemline that went down to my knees. I felt quite pretty and excited to be going out with my Mama. But then shortly after we arrived at my Mommy's house, Mama said to me *"You stay here, and I will be back this afternoon."* I nodded and didn't think much of it, trusting that when my Mama said she would come back that afternoon, then that's exactly what she was going to do. Little did I know that my mother's promise would ignite unimaginable grief and puzzle my soul for many years to come.

By mid-afternoon I felt bored, so I went out the front of my grandmother's house to await my mother's return. There was a stationary tricyle parked nearby my Mommy's front yard and when I saw that it was empty, I leaned on it while staring at the top of the street some two hundred yards away, ready to see my Mama.

Restless, I stood on the backside of the tricycle and began jumping up and down as it wobbled and bobbed like a trampoline. I stopped when I saw the first tricycle from a distance, travelling towards me. I knew it was my Mama coming to fetch me. I watched the tricycle in anticipation and excitement, but it didn't stop. It wasn't my mother. I whispered, *"That's okay."* And told myself that my mother will be in the next tricycle. I resumed my trampolining and stopped again when I saw a second tricycle coming. I squealed *"Yay! That's Mama now!"* But just like the first tricycle, it sped past my Mommy's house. After the fourth tricycle, I began to feel worried, but I told myself to be patient. I knew that my Mama was going to be in one of these tricycles, coming to pick me up.

But dusk quickly came and there were no lamps on the street where my Mommy lived; darkness began to set. My childish energy was quickly waning and there was a moment, after what felt like twenty tricycles driving past without my mother in it, when I looked up to the dark grey and fading blue sky, and noticed the faint hint of what was a glorious sunny day. This gloomy colour combination had given me a moment of realisation that my mother was never coming back, at least not like she said she would. My chest tightened and the world momentarily stood still, like a lifeless, black and white static on a broken television screen. She left me. This was the moment when faith and hope bowed their heads in defeat, and gave birth to a spirit that did not have capacity to trust.

There's something about kids and jumping, perhaps this is why someone had invented the trampoline, because jumping is the channel of expression of a child's joy. As a kid I just loved to bounce and jump in my uncontainable, innocent and happy energy; and I never had to hide how I felt, because I was a happy child.

Until I felt the need, and consequently learned, to disguise feelings that caused me pain.

As a young girl, I adored my mother. I clung to her wherever we went, and I did everything she would tell me to do because she was my Mama and I loved her. The shock of finding out that she didn't want me, was a feral experience.

In this defining moment at my grandmother's house, I transitioned from child to adult. At the age of six, my spirit split in two alternate manifesting personalities, completely misaligned and incongruent with each other. This was the day of death of my childlike innocence, and the birth of an unwilling but tenacious warrior, who took on the responsibility to help me cope with what was about to transpire in the next two decades.

I've become two people in one body.

There was the inner child that remained hopeful, hoping that my mother will come back and take me home, because I thought she loved me like I loved her.

Then there was *Pandora*, a spirit that loomed in the crevice of my mind, just looking, and watching out for the inner child that remained in me. The one who did not believe in faith and hope, borne from the death of trust and the savage pain of abandonment. An entity who, for decades to come, did a very good job of obliterating trust and faith that came its way.

I was six years old. But the alter spirit that split from within me was ageless. It wasn't six years old, nor was it ninety-six. Pandora was not born from a linear perspective. She was born from a pain perspective. Her power and strength came from pain. Over time, the more pain I was subjected to, the more powerful *she* became. She took away my ability to trust, as a strategy to steer me clear of anymore anguish. She was a warrior, gifted with the superpowers of dangerous independence, lack of forgiveness and sheer stoicism. She would fuel my dark emotions so that I would often become most evocative in my writing when I was melancholic, lonely or extremely sad.

The birth of Pandora shielded the child within me, and locked away the abandoned, unloved, confused little one into safety. For most of the time, Pandora functioned in my behalf, because life from that day forward, was almost always unhinged.

Manual labour was my first assignment at my grandmother's. Two days after my mother left me, I found myself sitting on a low, wooden seat, washing clothes with my bare hands. To wash and rinse clothes, I had to fetch water from a metal pump with a stand-up lever mechanism. It was a rigid set up, about one foot taller than me and responded to pure force and strength only. A mighty task, it took all of my strength to just pump the handle down so I can squeeze some water out. Fetching water was a killer, while vigorously rubbing my little fists in harsh detergent was taxing, as it was sad. I felt like my life was an upward avalanche, where I wish I could be buried and forgotten, but instead I was summoned for something that I wasn't big enough to do. Like a cruel explosion that did not crush me to death but instead spat me out to an open battle. I was still grieving and somewhat confused, as to why my mother never came back for me, when I noticed my grandmother watching my progress, and then she said, almost in mockery, *"Ano, nahirapan ka?"* (It's hard, isn't it?)

My thoughts raced, trying to come to terms with the reality that I am all alone now, telling myself I should quickly learn to fend for myself to survive. Suddenly, as if in a trance, I got up from my sitting position and walked away, and then I turned to look back. As I turned, I watched myself, there, sitting on that little wooden seat, rubbing her fists in the detergent water, half choking as she held her tears back so ferociously. At six years old and under enormous mental and physical stress, I had my first out of body experience, borne from a profound moment of sadness and terror.

Chapter 3
The Silent Apprentice

My grandmother had a two-storey house that sat on a land that was shaped like a trapezoid. Downstairs was made of brick with two bedrooms, bathroom, toilet, kitchen, shopfront, hallway, and a receiving room. Upstairs was made of wood with another two bedrooms and a living room. Built by my Chinese grandfather, it was considerably bigger than most regular houses back in those days.

The house being sizeable and having several different sections, also served as a shop front and stockroom for my uncles who ran a highly lucrative TV Repair shop business. It was the age of analogue technology when TVs contained a picture tube, in boxlike casings.

My grandma's house was filled with hundreds of TVs. TVs that customers dropped off for repair, TVs that have been repaired and waiting to be picked up, as well as TVs that were broken beyond repair and abandoned by their owners. While there was a scattering of TVs in almost every section of the house, it was the living room that resembled a TV museum, with TVs in every corner, some of them stacked from floor to ceiling. The main shop front had a four- metre foldaway door that served as a parking space for my uncles' motorcycles, as well as the pick-up and drop off point for customers' TVs.

I had six uncles working in the business. Two of them went out of town every so often for training and development, always coming back with what looked like giant, baking papers with intricate, blue diagrams that I could never decipher. Today, my teenage son could probably study those blueprints and work out how to build a picture tube TV within a day's work. But back in those days, my uncles were definitely ahead of their game.

The house was always full of male customers coming and going for their TVs. My uncles themselves were very territorial and even if they didn't live with my grandparents, their authority in my grandmother's abode was definite. They were constantly pacing the hallway, kitchen and backyard, like lions quietly observing, always ready to pounce on prey. No one paid attention to me except when I got told to wash the dishes, sweep the floor or do some work, either by my grandmother, or by one of my uncles. Just like any kid, I sometimes didn't do as I was told, so that I would get a stern talking down to, but I never pushed the limits beyond getting yelled at. I was obedient for the simple reason that I had nowhere else to go. Unwanted by my own mother and having been dumped at my grandmother's place, I could only be thankful that at least I was not out living in the streets. There, was better than being homeless. Or was it?

My uncles' TV Repair shop was the only TV Repair Service in town. The importance of getting a broken TV fixed, was high up in the must dos of wealthy households, the television being the only source of home entertainment for Gensan residents at the time.

It was obvious to me that my uncles had command of their craft. They were perpetually dismantling TVs, extracting picture tubes from their casings, endlessly soldering what looked like circuit boards, and continuously testing channel receptions. Picture tube TVs seemed to have four major problematic areas. Either they didn't have sound, the screen is blank, the screen is fuzzy and hissy, or it didn't pick up channels.

My uncles also fixed pre digital movie players starting with the Betamax in the early '80s and then the VHS players. Being the town's home entertainment repair gurus, they had the power to name their price for their services. The customers who came to have their TVs fixed were not poor. Most of them came by in their own private cars and were either working class or cashed up businessmen.

I once overheard one of my uncles charge a customer four hundred pesos for the repair of their TV. While the minimum daily wage in the Philippines in early 1980's was four pesos per day, my uncles used timing and scalability to leverage their business and make as much money as fast as they can, potentially generating daily revenue that would have been equivalent, or more, than the poor man's annual income. As pioneers of the TV repair industry in our town, they were able to use their Chinese connections to build their customer base. Strategic, innovative and forward thinking.

Chapter 4
Seeds and weeds build a jungle

Growing up, I often questioned the things I heard about the bible. As much as I loved going to church to admire the high ceilings and vivid paintings of Jesus and his disciples, I was puzzled about the priest who never failed to make me feel like I was born a sinner, and should spend all of my life repenting sins that were questionably mine. I never really understood why the church was so hung up on educating me about mortal, immortal and original sins. These ideas were rather uninspiring at best and totally depressing most of the time. I was obligated to worship, yet I was unworthy of esteem. I was secretly ashamed for questioning the priest and the bible, so I never expressed my opinions to anyone. Perish the thought of an insignificant child critiquing the church!

One of the most intriguing biblical verses I've ever come across as a child, was the idea that "the love of money is the root of all evil". I wondered, if it were true, why did my mother and her siblings forever fought and bickered over money, accusing one another of greed, convinced that there was never enough to get around? It seemed to me, that the root of all evil was not the love of money, but the lack of money. In my young, naive brain, it was logical to think that if scarcity made them fight with one another, then abundance would make them love each other.

But then again, over the years it was shocking to see that no matter how much money was available, none of them ever felt a sense of abundance. Money remained the number one reason for the eternal disparity between my mother and her siblings. As I grew older and became more independent of the church's teachings, I came to understand that the "love of money being the root of all evil" looks more like "scarcity mindset" and "fear of not being good enough".

My grandfather, Kim Tong Tan, was born in Fujian, southeast China. From what I heard, his parents sent him away in a boat to escape their country during the second world war, so that he would avoid getting enlisted as a soldier and spare his life from the perils of war. Once in the Philippines, a marriage was arranged between him and my grandmother who was only fifteen at the time, effectively saving my grandmother from the risk of becoming a 'comfort woman' for the Japanese soldiers. Together they had seven surviving children out of nine.

My grandfather's trade was buying and selling Copra. He used to own a truck for his business, but he sold it in the early '80s to retire and become a member of the local Chinese Club. Chinese folks gathered together in this air-conditioned hotel conference room, three hundred and sixty-five days a year to play Mah-Jong, and simply hang out with one another.

Effectively, my uncles who used a good half of my grandparents' residence as their principal place of business, became my grandparents' main source of income and sustenance. Which meant that whatever my grandmother received from my uncles in form of money, was used to feed the mouths that lived with her, including myself.

Aside from my uncles, the other source of money for my grandmother was my aunt Ellie, who lived abroad, but whose son, my cousin Mark, also lived with my grandmother. Aunt Ellie was the most generous person I've ever met. Not only materially but more so compassionately. However, her indiscriminate generosity fuelled jealousy and greed between her siblings, which unfortunately she was never privy to, being that she lived so far away. Her siblings constantly squabbled over monies that she wired from Europe. They fought verbally, aggressively and sometimes legally. I stayed inconspicuous in and amongst the constant bickering and feuds between my grandmother's grown up children, as I did not want to risk being ejected once again and end up totally alone and homeless on the streets. The fear of not belonging was slowly etching its way into my character.

Like most children in my grandmother's neighbourhood, I loved to play. But more often than not, playing usually involved a lot of chasing and competing with other kids, which was all a little too much for me. My favourite game was *Piko* (Hopscotch), but the most popular and rather robust game was *Tumba Lata* (knock the tin over).

The object of the game was to hit the tin can as many times as possible with our rubber slippers. We would go out to a pile of rubbish on some vacant land to find an empty tin of sardines. About thirty kids including myself, would then gather outside the front gate of the richest neighbour, Doctor Auguis. Tons of little black and white pebbles were laid out the front of her property to cover the dusty soil. Doctor Auguis happily allowed the neighbours' kids to play on it. But the pebbles made it so difficult to run without skidding, and we were always guaranteed to graze and cut ourselves from the impact of Tumba Lata. We would form two groups, each one standing on opposite sides while the little old tin can was placed in the middle. We would hold a rubber slipper in our hand and throw it to the tin, to knock it over as many times as possible, then running over to pick up the rubber slipper, and back again to hit the tin some more. In all of the madness, some kid who can run very fast would have been in charge of placing the tin back in the middle, just as quickly as it had been knocked down.

It was a fast and furious game, with slippers flying all over the place, hitting not only the rusty old tin, but also our faces and heads. There were lots of screaming and hollering, and I could never figure out how the game concluded, because I always ended up quietly resigning and sitting back to watch the rest of them destroy each other over Tumba Lata.

Every so often, I would get invited to friends' houses to hang out, celebrate a birthday or do homework together. My friends' houses, regardless if they were big, small, old or new, always had an air of warmth and safety. I loved hanging out in a real *sala,* (family living room) without strangers walking briskly in and out. At my friends' houses, we would be greeted by a parent or a sibling who would offer food or simply strike a nice, friendly conversation. My friends lived in *homes.* There was love, and care, and peace. A feeling that I never had, and constantly yearned for, at my grandmother's house.

My grandmother was a simple woman. She could read and write a little, as well as count simple Maths for the purpose of basic trade; but beyond that, she did not demonstrate any faculty capable of nurturing or caring for a confused and orphaned grandchild such as myself. She was simply there to ensure that I was still breathing and physically visible.

Consistency was the only quality I saw from my grandfather. Every morning he would get up, cook his *lugaw* breakfast (soft boiled rice with sugar and salt), brew his tea and leave immediately after his breakfast, to hang out with his fellowmen at the Chinese Club. He would return before dark to eat supper by himself. He never ate with anyone, nor asked any of us to join him. He made no effort to strike a conversation with anybody, not even to my grandmother, except when he needed to ask questions like, "Where is the salt?" or "Is the food cooked?" or "Is this pot clean and ready for me?" After supper, he would wash in the bathroom and change into his night clothes, and then settle himself in his room to read one of his Chinese pocket-sized books. Then he would fall asleep and do it all again tomorrow. He did this every day of the week, three hundred and sixty-five days a year, including Christmas and New Year's Days. It was as if his life with us was nothing but a shadow that he felt no need to pay attention to. Watching this kind of unrelenting repetition and utter lack of care, I couldn't help but see that it was possible for someone to do something meaningless and repetitive, and not die from it. Which ironically, made me think that I would in fact, rather die, than do something meaningless and repetitive.

My grandparents slept in separate beds in the biggest room upstairs. *Lolo* (grandpa) had the larger bed, and next to his bed were a cane chair, a reading lamp, and a small bookshelf that also served as the night table. The bookshelf was filled with pocket sized Chinese books which read vertically from top to bottom and the pages flipped from right to left, so that it was like reading from back to front. I was curious what stories were in those books, but I never did ask my Lolo, because it was obvious that he didn't like talking to any of us. Instead, I was content with just being able to touch the pages of the book, they felt like slithers of bark with strange looking characters. Most of them were so old that they didn't have covers; and what's left of the ones with covers were faded images of people wearing traditional Chinese garments. I wondered where those books took my Lolo back to, each time he read them. A question that I hope someday I could find the answer to.

Once a year my aunt Ellie came home from Europe. Half the time she came home with her husband and the other half just by herself; in which case she would sleep in my grandmother's house, instead of the hotel. As luck would have it, I was designated to sleep in the same room with her, perhaps because I was the smallest and the least privacy invading human being in the house. So, I got to spend quite a lot of time with my aunt, who was so generous in every way. She let me touch her things, like her makeup, perfume, clothes, camera and jewellery. Everything about her was beautiful and smelled so divine. She used exquisite fragrances like Anais Anais, and Lancome makeups. She always had top of the range technology like a Nikon for her camera and Sony for her Walk Man. She told me stories of her life abroad where she worked in her husband's business, and how they had freedom to travel anytime and anywhere they wished. She told me about her friends, showed me pictures of her beautiful garden, tennis games and amazing architecture from European countries. In my mind she painted a life of freedom, comfort, cleanliness, joy, laughter and soft, beautiful clothes.

One day, we were at the only supermarket in town, which was called Kimball Plaza, to buy groceries. It was an expensive but super fun thing to do. We pushed a metal shopping trolley, and as we walked together along every aisle, she allowed me to have whatever I liked. I chose items like the Tang powdered juice, peanut butter, Anchor butter, jelly cups, and Sky Flakes biscuits. There was a moment when we paused and my aunt Ellie said to me, *"Ging, one day, you will love the life abroad. It's really nice."* Ging-ging was my nickname. I didn't say anything back to her. I just stood there, savouring every word of her prophecy. In that moment, I believed. In that moment, a seed of hope was planted in my heart that one day, I will live a nice life too. One day, I will have a comfortable home and the freedom to buy everything I need and want from the supermarket.

Little did I know how much I needed that prophecy, so that I could hold on to a hopeful heart and open mind. My Auntie's words served as a thread of sanity that twined between my inner child and Pandora. The ability to hope, was definitely my antidote to total self-sabotage.

Chapter 5
At peace in my high

I was seven years old when I first heard the poignant song "Romeo and Juliet". One evening, three of my uncles were in my grandmother's kitchen drinking Tanduay Rum and smoking odd shaped cigarettes that were too short, too thin and crinkled on the tip; while they listened to a Dire Straits album on the family cassette player. The air was thick with some potent smell, and there was a strange feeling of calm in the room, even though the music was fairly loud. I sat on a chair in the kitchen, passively observing the scene and listening to the lyrics of the song from the cassette.

"Juliet... The dice was loaded from the start..
And I bet..
And you exploded in my heart.."

My uncles weren't talking to each other, their eyes had a dreamy look, void of the usual tension they carried on their faces. Although it was a calm situation, I couldn't shake the feeling that the calmness was induced. Then I wondered why it couldn't be the other way around. Why couldn't calmness be their usual way of being, and grumpiness be their induced way of being? But just as quickly as the thought entered my mind, I felt the induced calmness take over my own body, just as it had taken over my uncles'. There was not much that I could remember after that, except that I happily surrendered to the calmness as I sat on the chair in my grandmother's kitchen, enjoying the song, and simply being.

Thirty-two years later in Australia, on a sweltering summer day in January of 2014, I was driving along the stretch of Kirra Beach listening to an FM station when I heard a familiar melody, just as I saw a rare parking space overlooking the beach. I turned the volume on high and pulled over. The melody picked up as the song crescendoed into a doleful ode. Romeo and Juliet by Dire Straits.

Suddenly I was seven years old again, in my grandmother's kitchen, high as a kite on second-hand marijuana smoke, innocently watching my uncles get their fix as I unconsciously float in a fix of my own. Flashbacks of memories flooded my mind. The black colouring of the cassette, the smallness of its buttons, the cracks on the edges of the linoleum covered table, and the blaring, one metre fluorescent light that dangled like a trapeze from the tin roof above me. After all these years, the momentary freedom from pain, fleeting as it might have been, had stayed in my memory. Hearing the song unexpectedly after such a long time, had once again liberated me.

"A love-struck Romeo…
Sang the streets of serenade..
Laying everybody low…
With a love song that he made…
Finds a street light.. steps out of the shade..
Says something like, 'you and me babe, how about it?..'"

"Juliet! the dice was loaded from the start ..
And I bet..

And you exploded in my heart,
And I forget.. I forget…
The movie song..
When — you're gonna realize it was just that the time was wrong…
Juliet…?"

The lyrics and melody opened up a gateway to a part of my heart that seemed otherwise disabled — the place of simply being — with no emotional walls to guard, no defences to keep or fears to act out on.

Listening to Romeo and Juliet again was so profound that it almost felt like my feet lifted off of the ground, defying the gravity of life as I had lived it so far. Who's to say if it was my biological makeup working for me, or Pandora, my alter ego doing her thing to protect me, or God and his angels watching over me; but that night when I was a child under the influence of second-hand cannabis, I could've gotten into all sorts of trouble. Yet somehow something had helped me transcend its chemical influence, so that I could attach the feeling of deliverance, purely to the song, and then retrieve it decades later, for me to use as a much-needed pacifier.

On the same day, I downloaded the song on my iTunes and listened to it for months, night after night, before I went to sleep. It became the lullaby that I'd never had as a child, cocooning my soul into a loving slumber. Life has the strangest ways in giving you solace when you really deserve it.

Chapter 6
Shadows of rage

It was easy to understand that I had no significance to anybody. The way that my grandmother treated me was opposite to the way she treated my cousins, whose parents supported her with monies. When my cousins and I misbehaved all at the same time, I copped a beating on my bum with my grandmother's slipper, or a slap on the face if I was being a back chatter. My cousins were never deemed to ever be at fault, so that they were never punished nor disciplined.

One night when I was seven years old, my cousin Mark and I started a childish argument on who had the weirdest name between the two of us. He said that my name *"GRACITA"* was ugly. I snapped back and said *"I'd rather have an ugly name than be you. You are Satan's disciple!"* Mark is five years my senior and he was a foot taller. He raised his arm and then whack! His backhand landed on my left cheekbone with such force that the whole world had gone so peaceful and quiet, and I couldn't hear anything.

As I recovered some of my hearing through my right ear, the left side of my face began to sting. Trying to move my face muscles made the stinging worse and then a sharp ringing sound started to come out from inside my head. I shook my head to try and stop it, but it only grew louder, like a massive microphone feedback. I felt shocked by the blow, and acutely aware of how scared and angry I was at the same time. I knew that physically I was no match for my cousin, nor could I run to my grandmother for help. It would be too much to take if I had to listen to her blatantly condone my cousin's violence on me. I was scared to confront the unfairness of my circumstance, because there was nothing I could do to change it.

Without thinking, I bolted out of the house and into the dark streets, running as fast as I could. I ran along the main roads, keeping as close to as many houses as possible. As upset as I was, I was still aware that I was putting myself in more danger, by running away. But then again, running away seemed like a safer option than not running away. I felt so confused, angry and all alone.

Soon enough, I began feeling tired and slowed down to a walking pace, still mindful to keep myself on the main streets. I stopped to catch my breath, crouching over as I leaned on my knees. The town was dead except for a lone tricycle passing by with its driver throwing me a curious look. In a split second I remembered my grandmother's horrendous stories of tricycle drivers kidnapping their passengers into the wilderness and leaving them dead after raping them. In a state of defiance, I decided that I would prove my grandmother wrong so that whatever happens, I wasn't going to be kidnapped, raped and left for dead by a tricycle driver. Having been whacked in the head by my cousin was not enough for me to waste my life into a tragic kidnap and murder ending.

For all I knew, the tricycle driver who passed me by may have been a good Samaritan, concerned about a stray child out in the streets in the middle of the night. But I had already learned that I cannot trust anyone nor rely on anybody's help. I picked my pace up and started running again.

With the sobering thought of wanting to stay alive, I headed back to the direction of my grandmother's house. As I got to the top of the street, I saw a wooden bench bolted in between two trees. I was getting close to my grandmother's house, but deep inside, I really wished I could be somewhere else. So I sat on the bench feeling cold and tired, wondering what to do next.

I don't know how long I sat there for, but after some time a lady came out of her house and sat on the space next to me. She asked what my name was, but I was unwilling to participate in the interview, and refused to take kindness from anyone. Kindness was what I really needed at the time, but I felt like if I opened up to kindness, it would break me, and I certainly did not want to break. I became so familiar with anger, fear and loneliness that I could not recognize genuine compassion even when it slapped me in the face.

The lady gently urged me to answer her questions. *"Unsa'y ngalan nimo dai?"* (What is your name young girl?)

I said *"Wala ko'y ngalan, wala'y nakaila nako."* (I don't have a name. I'm a nobody.)

She pressed, *"Asa ka nagpuyo? Taga asa man diay ka?"* (Where do you live? Where is your home?)

I said *"Wala ko'y balay gipuy-an."* (I don't have a home.)

We went through this question and answer repeatedly, the lady never tired of asking me my name and where I lived, and I never tired of telling her that I was a nobody and didn't live nowhere.

The truth was, I was secretly hoping that someone would show me a better place to go home to.

A while later, my 'rescue' team arrived. It was my mother and a few of our next-door neighbours, walking side by side. Rumour has it that as soon as my grandmother realized I ran away she immediately went to my mother's house to tell her what happened.

Now that they found me, my mother stood in the middle of the crowd and said that they've searched for me all over the town and had been so worried. Fatigued and jaded, I did not believe her story. If they truly 'searched all over' they would've spotted me hours earlier because I never wandered away from the main streets. Clearly, they weren't worried enough nor did they search much. But I, like everybody else, was prepared to accept her rescue story because it didn't matter. She was more concerned for her reputation than anybody's business, including her own beat up, runaway child.

I was reprimanded for making them so worried, and I was told to do no such thing again. My mother and her rescue team walked me back to my grandmother's house. I tried to explain to her, privately, why I ran away, but she wouldn't hear any of it.

Back at my grandmother's house, it was like nothing had happened. People went about their usual ways, and I wasn't fussed over by anyone. Not that I wanted to be fussed over or anything, but I silently waited for any discussion about the whack in the head that I copped, and the lingering ringing in my ear. Nothing. My mother left once again, dumping me without any explanation or promise of return.

That night as I lay in bed, my cheek was sore, and I could still hear the faint ringing in my left ear. But there was no greater pain than the stinging of my sore heart. Having been whacked in the head, and then seen my mother again tore me apart. Inside of me, I battled with the strongest of conflicting emotions, like loving and longing for my mother, hating her for her cold heartedness; and all at the same time, my mind was frantically building defence mechanisms by anticipating the worst of people.

I was hurting, yet I was getting sturdier. I was lonely, but I never wanted anyone to get close to me. I knew I was vulnerable, but Pandora had built me a safe box in which to tuck away my vulnerability. She was building me up for the battle that she was born for. I was aching so much inside of me that it felt like my spirit would break, but could not quite break. Rather, it was slowly and painfully mutating into something ugly. Being so young, I couldn't quite name those ugly and unpleasant sensations that were growing inside of me. Little did I know that my anger would fester so much, and it would take over my life in the next few decades to come.

Chapter 7
The orgasm of cruelty

One day we were all invited to my uncle Andy's house to celebrate his daughter Beth's birthday. I liked going to my uncle Andy's house, because his wife Anet was a kind and pretty woman.

The party had lots of food plus a big, beautiful birthday cake, and colourful helium balloons. When the party was over, my auntie Anet allowed me to pick the balloon that I could take home with me. I chose a baby pink coloured balloon, with little white floating balloon prints on it. It was so pretty. To stop the helium balloon from flying away, she tied it on a miniature plastic balloon shaped toy, and then she handed it to me with a heart melting smile.

A group of us began walking home, including a third-degree uncle and auntie, with their child Rudy, who would be my third-degree cousin. A particularly hyperactive and demanding kid, Rudy was four years younger than me. We used to call him *"Terror"* because he would carry on crying and screaming if he didn't get what he wanted, until he got what he wanted.

As we all walked together, Rudy saw how happy and excited I was for my beautiful pink balloon. He started screaming and crying for my balloon.

While his parents were there to make decisions in his behalf, I had no one to defend me and my balloon. Rudy's parents cooed and gently appealed to me saying that we might as well just give Rudy my balloon, because he will not stop crying otherwise. In my mind, I screamed *"No, this is my balloon!"* I wanted to say it out loud, but I couldn't. I had no guts to stand up for myself against this trio of mother, father and son, who were making me give up my balloon just because Rudy wanted it.

In desperation I started to run away from them, but little Rudy was not only spoilt rotten, he was also highly energetic and fast. As quickly as I conceived the thought of running away, he sensed it so that before I could even gain momentum, he lunged behind me and wham! He landed his little fist, right in the middle of my back and his knuckles made a crunchy contact on my spine, as I fell down to my knees. The shock and sharp pain took my breath away, and I could not scream or cry, no sound would come out of my throat.

I was afraid of what else Rudy could do, and of what else his parents would let him to get away with. Against every fibre of my being, I let him take my balloon, and they all went happily away. I limped my way back home, and upon reaching my grandmother's house, I went straight to the bathroom and reached for a basin where there was some stagnant water. Without checking if it was clean or not, I gratefully scooped the water with both hands and splashed it on my face, and again, and again, and again, as I cried. I didn't want anyone to hear me crying, but I was too sad to stifle my gut wrenching tears, so I used the sound of splashing water to camouflage my pain and anguish. I stayed there until darkness set in, just splashing water on my face and crying as quietly as possible. And then I went upstairs and slept.

My Uncle Roy bought a block of land around the corner from my grandmother's house and immediately started building his home. The construction site became a playground for the kids around the neighbourhood. It was a novelty walking on gravel and using rusty scaffolding, crumbling hollow blocks, and half-finished rooms, for a game of maze.

One afternoon, a group of kids, including myself, wandered to the back of the building site. We stood on top of the slab that was going to be the septic tank, and adjacent to it was the skeleton of what was going to be the toilet and bathroom. Looking up, we were surrounded by high scaffolding; while looking down, an assortment of sharp, triangular pieces of scrap timber scattered everywhere.

A boy who lived across the road from my grandmother named Luloy, and I, began shouting and fighting with each other. Luloy was a chubby kid with curly hair and sported a rounded belly, which meant that his family had money to buy plenty of food. We were getting into a heated verbal fight, while the rest of the kids didn't pay too much attention to us. Annoyed, I stepped down from the septic slab to distance myself from him, but he simply amped up the ante, and began calling me ugly and *itom* (black), insinuating that my dark skin was a symbol of inferiority. I heard myself think *"I am going to pick up a rock and throw it at him"*.

As if in a trance, I bent my knees to a squat without taking my eyes off him as I wrapped my hand on an object; and then with amazing trajectory, I hurled it to his direction, approximately four metres in front, on a one metre elevation point. I had never hurled anything in my entire life before that. And unfortunately for me, the object was not a rock, it was a triangular, scrap timber, and its sharp end landed right between his eyes, splitting soft tissue just above his nose. Blood spurted out of his forehead, forwards and sideways, like a mini shower. The sight of its pressure and pinkish quality, made me woozy.

Suddenly, everyone was running and screaming for help. Luloy was taken to the hospital. I didn't know what to do. But I knew one thing, that I did something terrible, and I was so sorry. So, I went to Luloy's family compound where him and his relatives lived, and waited for his parents to come and flog me for what I've done to their son. I felt truly scared and sorry that I hurt him so bad, and I worried that I could have caused him some serious damage. I was shivering in disgust of what just happened, and I wanted to be punished. I felt so guilty and I berated myself, that I didn't have the right to hurt anyone like I did, no matter what they did to make me feel angry. But a couple of hours passed, and neither of his parents came to speak to me. Instead, my mother made an appearance.

She gave me a tongue-lashing in front of what seemed like the entire neighbourhood, plus all their dogs and cats; that if I did anything like that ever again, she would call the police to report me and send me to jail. I nodded to agree with her, and all I could think of was, *"Thank God, this means that Luloy is going to be okay, because no one is saying that he is still bleeding or going to die."*

I was relieved.

As for my mother saying that she would send me to jail if I hurt anyone again, was no surprise. I figured jail wouldn't be any more difficult and torturous than what my life already was anyway. Besides, a voice in my head said, *"I will never express my feelings in that way, ever again."* It was a great lesson as far as Pandora, and I, were concerned. For the first time, my alter ego and I had joined forces towards a unified mission of survival.

My mother dismissed me after her tirade, and I was once again left to my own devices. It dawned on me that if I was ever desperate for some attention from her, all I had to do was something gravely wrong, then I would be rewarded with her precious conniption. But on a second thought, I would much rather that she left me alone. Her presence, was slowly beginning to enrage me.

Chapter 8
If you bite me

Every child has a natural sense of resourcefulness. I used mine to find things that could make me feel free. Free to be myself, free to laugh, free to smile, free to be happy without fear of punishment. Freedom for me, came with nature, where I could unleash my unbounded imagination, and no one can make me feel rejected.

My grandmother's house was on an intersection right next to a zoned, squatters-free land called *Bulaong Subdivision*. It was a very quiet part of the town back then, which I loved. On the corner across from my grandmother's house was a huge block that had rusty, barbed wire fences. Inside the property was a small, tumble-down wooden house where an old man lived as the caretaker. I called him *Manong*, which is a respectful way to address an elderly gentleman. Manong was very kind, always smiling and happy, and he always allowed children to trespass the property and play.

Inside the block there were hundreds of giant, concrete pipes that took up most of the space in the property. I spent many hours playing hide and seek with my neighbours through the labyrinth of those pipes. But where my heart really sang with joy and freedom, was not inside of those fun, giant cylinders, but on top of them. I hopped, skipped, and ran all along these pipes endlessly. I jumped as far and wide as my legs would let me, and I felt like I could fly. The wind caressed my face and blew my hair free, and I opened my arms wide and twirled round and round and squealed delightfully. I felt welcomed and belonged. Surrendering to the open space gave me a feeling of unspoken hope and possibility.

The East side of the block was lined with *Madre De Cacao* trees, which were strategically planted to intertwine with the barbed wires and help hold them up, instead of using wooden posts. Madre De Cacaos grew to a medium size and their trunks were sturdy and pliant. When I needed rest from flying through the pipes, I would grab a friend and together we would climb the Madre De Cacaos, and take a rest, up in the trees.

We climbed through the barbed wires to get up high, and because we were little kids with small hands and feet, it was easy to hold and step in between the barbed wire spikes without incident. We were old enough to understand the danger of tetanus, so we never rushed the climbing process and amazingly, we were never injured by the barbed wires.

The trees were two metres apart, so we would each take a tree for ourselves and once up high, we would relax, and talk, and rest, for hours. I loved looking down from a five to ten metre height and have always been fascinated by how comfortable it felt up in the tree. This was my happy place, and I truly believe that sitting up on those Madre De Cacaos and looking back down on the ground, have given me a subconscious perspective that things can possibly be more than how they were down below. Again, there was that unspoken hope.

Those beautiful days spent in that block of land with the concrete pipes and Madre De Cacaos were part of my saving grace. I have managed to subconsciously lodge a self-belief, which I daresay I have birthed on my own. It was a belief that wasn't given to me by anyone; a self-belief that even I didn't really understand for myself for a long time to come. A self-belief that would be challenged, and totally obliterated, before it would resurrect itself again, in decades to come.

One day, my mother decided to also 'relocate' my older brother Larry, to come and live with my grandmother. I wasn't totally surprised by this, although I remained puzzled why she chose to dump me first. Was it a coin toss decision? A short end, long end of the stick consideration? Was I a useless child?

Unlike myself, my brother was fully informed that he was coming to live with our grandmother, and he would then be nine years old and on fourth grade. Whether he asked questions as to why he was being left to live with our grandmother, I don't know. Larry was the golden child for my mother. Gifted with a very high IQ and a flair for phenomenal academic achievements, Larry was also light skinned, which easily showed off his fair, Filipino-Chinese profile. My mother used to say that he had taken after her physical features and intelligence.

As for me, I have heard my mother explain to people, that I've taken my looks from my father's side, with my dark skin, curly hair and all; and in fact, she thought that I was a spitting image of *Inday*, my father's sister, whom I have never met. I was confused because I had seen photos of my mother and her siblings back in grade school at the local Chinese Academy, and I was a spitting image of her. Her declaration that we looked nothing alike made me feel that she must really dislike me, and I wondered what I had done, for her to feel that way.

People also asked my mother about my two front teeth, and why they were permanently rotten. She once explained the story to someone, that when I was a baby, she and my father hired a nanny to take care of me. This nanny fell in love with a man who eventually left her for someone else. Unbeknownst to all, my nanny was so heartbroken that she stopped eating and never told anyone. She fell so sick but still pretended to be okay, while taking care of me as a baby. One day they found my nanny in the bathroom with blood on her face. They took her to the hospital where she soon died due to advanced and untreated tuberculosis.

A little while after my nanny died, they noticed a growth under my right chin, which kind of started as a boil and just kept getting bigger and softer, which gave the baby, yours truly, so much pain and discomfort. I was taken to the hospital, and the doctor immediately performed an operation to open the massive growth and extract all the pus that had accumulated inside of it. The pus was a toxic load of Tubercle Bacilli, the causative agent of Tuberculosis disease, which of course, I had contacted from my late, heartbroken nanny. Afterwards, the doctor prescribed some strong antibiotics to help eradicate the TB in my system. The side effects of these medication were my rotten teeth.

I have no recollection of this experience whatsoever, but I have a scar under the right side of my jaw where the doctor had cut me open as an infant, to remind me that I was a warrior, long before I could even walk.

One day we had another one of those birthdays at my Uncle Andy's house for his second child, my cousin Vince. On this occasion my mother was in attendance and when the party was over, we started walking. Knowing that my mother would be hailing a tricycle to go back to her own place at any minute, I turned to her and bravely said, *"Ma, why can't I come home with you?"* I was almost eight years old and had longed to ask this question many times. *"I would if I could. Right now, it's not good for me."* Was her response, and that was the end of it. She was so curt and cold that it made me feel mad deep inside. Mad at my mother for her lack of care but also mad at myself for asking the question. Someone, or something inside me did not appreciate my show of weakness. *"Well, what did you expect she was going to say? That she loved you and she missed you and she wanted to take you home?"* A voice inside me was taunting my mind and messing with my feelings. It was bizarre, like listening to another person who lived in my head. I shut the voice off as best I could, but not before I could hear it say one more thing: *"Whatever made you think that you were special?"*

I attended the local public school for free, and I was halfway through Grade two when my big brother came to join me at my grandmother's house. Instantly, Larry took on his role as a caring and protective big brother. For a change, it was really nice to know that I had an ally, someone who cared about me.

There was this one time when Larry and my cousin Mark discovered a 'shortcut' way to get to school. It would cut our walking distance by one kilometre, but we had to climb a hollow block fence, crossover some stranger's backyard, and then run for our lives to complete the shortcut via the front gate; dodging the dog who barked, chased and no doubt wanted to eat us. This was not my idea of a shortcut by any means, but because I was one girl and outnumbered by two older boys, it didn't occur to me to contribute logical thinking and veer them away from such a crazy idea. It was like blind faith where the dumb was following the dumber.

The shortcut route was fine for a couple of weeks. Climbing the hollow block fence was tricky, as it was higher than me, and I constantly nursed cuts and bruises from pulling myself up to it, and jumping down from it. Running for my life between the fence and the front gate, I must admit, was quite exciting. I dreaded the thought of getting bitten by the dog, especially back in those days when there was no way to tell if a dog had rabies or not, and it would just be pure luck if you got bitten by one who did not have rabies; otherwise, anyone was one dog bite away from death by rabies. A dog barking and chasing me was definitely not my cup of tea. However, when it was time to run from the hollow block fence to the front gate of whoever's property it was that we trespassed every day, I wasn't only running from the dog; in my mind, I was also running away from adult punishment. It gave me such an adrenaline rush knowing that I was about to defy someone's rules and I could get away with it. And that's exactly how I got through those crazy times of shortcutting to school.

One unforgettable morning, the three of us were on our way to the shortcut route, when two stray dogs came hurling towards us. I was so surprised, and froze like a rabbit, while the boys have started sprinting to save themselves. Suddenly I had a vision of me running, and the dogs jumping at me and then devouring me; and then I had another vision of me crouching down in a foetal position, while the dogs stood inches from me, barking and salivating to eat me. I quickly chose the second vision, and then I slowly curled down to a sitting foetal position, shaking and crying in fear. One of the dogs stopped inches away from me growling and barking, but not quite trampling me down. I looked at his eyes and pleaded silently not to bite me, which he obliged. But the other one was a lot less mindful of my feelings; it was a smaller dog, and he rushed to me and started chewing on my bum, shredding my skirt into pieces. This feral puppy was about to take his first bite off of my flesh when suddenly, I saw my brother and cousin running back to me, hurling stones to the dogs until they skiddadled.

After that day, we stopped taking shortcuts to school.

Chapter 9
Magic

Towards the end of Grade Two, a girl named Selina moved in with the neighbours who lived across the road from my grandmother's house. She had fair skin and beach blonde hair, and although she would've only been nine or ten years old, she was the kind of girl that received crude and salacious innuendos from boys and men. One day Selina and I were playing *Takyan* at the front of my grandmother's house. Takyan is a household sport using an improvised shuttlecock made with flattened bottle top and plastic straw. The object of the game is to kick the shuttlecock using one leg, in an inward, repetitive motion, without the shuttlecock ever touching the ground.

While we played, my uncle Cris, the youngest of my mother's siblings, and our neighbour Lito, watched. When it was Selina's turn, my uncle made a comment saying, *"Watch out! Your IUD is falling off to the ground!"* and then he and our neighbour laughed, like as if it was some kind of a funny joke. I wasn't quite sure what an IUD was, at the time, but I was old enough to sense that they were sexualizing Selina. Selina just ignored them and didn't seem fazed by it.

Like myself, Selina was 'sent' to live with other relatives, through a decision imposed upon by her parents. The difference between her experience and mine was that Selina was fully aware of the drill of being abandoned: The parents would warn and tell the child that she or he was being sent somewhere else to live. There may or may not be any explanations as to why, and there may or may not be promises of return and reconciliation, but the bottom line would be that the child was a burden that had to be relocated to ease the load off his or her parents. This wasn't Selina's first time to be relocated to a relative. In fact, she almost exuded an air of expertise in her circumstance, taking me in under her wing as a *protégé abandonee*, if there was such a thing.

One day she told me that she had a secret to reveal to me, and that I must keep it a secret for myself. I was so intrigued and immediately agreed. The secret was that she had found *Magic*.

I said, *"Magic? What Magic?"*

Her eyes grew big and her voice softer as she whispered, *"Magic! You see, you can do anything you want! You can create anything you can imagine! Just think, everything that you want to happen, you will make it happen, with Magic!"*

My chest opened up with hope and joy. There is Magic and I can make anything happen!

With my heart beating faster by the minute, I asked, *"Show me!"*

She squealed, *"Show you?! I will give it to you! You can have Magic! First you must follow some important events. If you don't follow the events, Magic will not come to you."*

I said *"Yes, tell me what to do! What events?"*

Selina said that the first *event* was to give her Two Pesos. I had confided in her earlier that I have been saving money for many months. Monies that my uncle Roy would literally throw at me, whenever I watched him count wads of notes and handfuls of coins, which he usually did on the kitchen table, not caring that I was sitting there and watching. At the end of counting money, my uncle would then acknowledge my presence, as if in an afterthought, and throw a fifty-cent piece over my way. I saved all of these fifty cents, and over time they started to add up.

At first, I was a little perplexed that Magic needed money in an event. I thought that Magic itself should be able to make as many pesos as it needed or wanted, for any event. But on a second thought, maybe this was a test, and if I didn't pass the test, Magic wouldn't come to me. So, I better follow the events and pass Magic's test. I went home and fetched Two Pesos from my savings and gave it to Selina, who then told me that the next step was to wait three days for the next instruction.

I spent the next three days trying to think about the possibilities, when I would finally get Magic. At the age of eight, I found it a little confusing trying to imagine a world of magical and wonderful things. In my mind, I knew what I wanted, a big house with my own bright, big room filled with things that I loved, like a big bed and a beautiful tiled, clean kitchen with so much food. But I found that I couldn't put feeling into my imagination. I had the "what it looks like", but I struggled imagining "what it would feel like".

I also tried to imagine my mother taking me back, but then I worried if it was right to change other people's feelings without their consent. What if my mother reunited with me, but only because of my magic spell, and not because she really wanted to? I worried about what would happen to the rest of the world, when I have Magic. Was Magic bad or good?

That night I stayed up feeling so torn between excitement and fear. My heart did little bursts of palpitation when I thought about how much my life was about to change, and at the same time, I felt frozen with so much fear worrying, what if it doesn't work? What if Magic was not real? What if I was so close, only to realize that I was so far?

The third day came, and I sought Selina out and reminded her that it was the third day. She said she hasn't forgotten, and that Magic had given her the *instruction* for the next *event*. She told me that I now have to give her *ALL* of the money that I had. I was upset by this instruction because I didn't understand the logic behind it. I lied to Selina and said that I would go home and *"see if I have any money left."*

I went to bed that night thinking about how close I came to getting Magic. It was almost in the palm of my hands, and then I would have had the power to make anything happen, to make everything I ever wanted, appear in front of me. My mind became obsessed by the possibilities that Magic can bring. I wanted it so badly. Under my pillow was Twelve pesos. All of my savings. I started rationalizing to myself that I didn't really know what I would have used them for anyway, and I certainly never thought I would ever be in a position to trade money for Magic.

Suddenly I had a lightbulb moment, *"That's it! I'm trading Money for*

Magic! Why wouldn't I? Then I can just magically make more money when I get the magic in exchange for my money!"* Desperation has taken over me and the next day, I took all of my Twelve Pesos and gave it to Selina. She then said that the next step was to wait one week.

This time I knew I had nothing left to give in terms of money, so I was relieved thinking that one week will be the last instruction, and then I will have Magic.

The week passed and when I asked Selina, she tried to tell me again that more money was needed for the next "event" - this time I was a little pissed off and told her that there was no way I could give her any more money, because I've already given her everything I had. I meekly protested that she never told me Magic would require so much money, and that if I knew, then I wouldn't have put myself in the position of giving away all of my money, only to find out that I would never have enough to fulfil all of the "events"; and God knows how many more money events Magic was going to require down the line!!

Selina looked at me piercingly and said, *"Ok. I'll tell you what, I will ask your big brother Larry and see if you really deserve to have the Magic."*

With that, I started to feel that I couldn't trust Selina and retreated away from her. There's something about people pushing me around and palming my fate off into other people's hands, instead of just being honest and telling the truth, that really turned me off. I became subconsciously discouraged, and so disenchanted by the whole Magic thing, that I simply stopped pursuing it. I then heard later on that Selina had been relocated elsewhere, again.

At some point shortly after she had gone, I came to the realisation that she lied to me to get money, and that I should have known she was lying from the start. Of course, Magic wasn't real! Magic was nothing but stories of fantasy and out of this world imagination. The irony was that although I felt stupid for being gullible, I did not feel sorry for having a brief fling with fantasy and Magic. It was fun just being able to allow myself, even for a brief moment, to actively dream about nice things. And while I would have been inclined to fantasize some more, there was a pragmatic part of me that felt a bizarre sense of relief, knowing that Magic wasn't real; because I would never have known that for sure, if I hadn't tried to get it for myself.

Chapter 10
Once upon a time, a shithouse

They say that young children fully and easily adapt to their physical environment, unless they were born with allergies. I wish that were completely true.

As a kid, I have always found toilets and anything to do with the act of doing a pooh, to be a terrifying event. The first toilet I can remember was back in my mother's house in Cagampang Street. Her house was one of half a dozen houses, in a compound that shared only four outhouses. Two households were lucky enough to have their own, and the rest had to share two outhouses between themselves. We had our own, and my mother locked it with a key so that no other household would use it.

These poop chambers were made of concrete, save for their wooden doors that only went halfway up to provide for ventilation. They were untiled and unlit. If you needed to do a number two at night, you would need to bring a lamp, or just wait until the morning. For number ones during the middle of the night, people just kept a round, tin bowl, called *arinola*, under their bed. The outhouses were built on an elevated slab, literally sitting on its septic tank, where all the pooh would have been flushed and stacked. Plumbing and sewerage system back then was pretty basic. People built septic tanks in the '60s and '70s without any futuristic plan for what happens when they are filled. By the time I was old enough to remember, these septic tanks were full to the brim. The outhouses were always damp and dark inside, and they reeked of urine and feces from meters away. I would walk into our outhouse with my toes curled, and careful not to splash any stagnant water on me, holding my breath as much as I can for as long as I was in there.

Fast forward to the outhouse at my grandmother's, my experience was a little better but also a lot worse.

For the worse part, there were two toilets at my grandmother's house, one of them being an outhouse, and the other was inside, right next to the kitchen and dining room. A concrete wall separated the indoor toilet from the sink, but just like most toilets back in the day, the dividing wall didn't reach the ceiling, to allow for ventilation. Aside from the stench and proximity of the toilet to the kitchen and dining area, the biggest issue was once again, the septic tank. The toilet itself would not flush, and if one was hasty enough to go for a number two, it would take days for the poop to disappear from the toilet bowl; a mistake that I myself have made a couple of desperate times. It was stressful spending days trying to figure out how to make the pooh disappear.

Fortunately, through the financial help of my generous aunt, my grandmother was able to build an outhouse in the far corner of the backyard, next to an old, unused pigsty. It was a twenty-meter walk to get to the outhouse, which was a good thing. This outhouse being newly built, should've been in great working condition, but the problem was, they built the chamber but did not modify the sewerage and septic system to suit. Eventually the toilet bowl also became blocked, just like every other toilet in the world, or so it seemed. For a short period of time, the toilet would work well and then it would play up again; and every time I did a pooh, I would pray that the toilet would flush on me, so that I didn't have to face the problem of how to make the pooh disappear.

One day, two of my uncles, the eldest Ben and the youngest Cris, were working on the blocked toilet issue by trying to figure out the cause of the blockage. Uncle Ben and uncle Cris called me over, and the three of us had a toilet blockage convention, where they explained to me, like as if I cared, that they thought there was something inside the toilet bowl that's stuck; and they reckoned that the way to unstuck it was to pull out whatever it was that blocked the toilet bowl. They then told me that because I have small hands, they wanted me to stick my hand inside the toilet bowl and *feel around* for anything that could be stuck, and then pull it right out. I swallowed hard and looked up to these two towering men in front of me, feeling powerless to even try to protest. To say that the toilets back then were unsanitary, is a colossal understatement. We used recycled, stagnated and murky water with unidentified floating objects, to manually flush the toilet.

It crossed my mind to say no, but something told me that if I couldn't be asked nicely, I would be forced to do so. The only choice I had was if I wanted to keep some dignity, by agreeing to their request, or if I chose to play hard ball, then they would show me who's the boss. There was a pathetic voice in my head, consoling me that if I did what they said, they would then leave me alone and maybe they would be nicer to me. In hindsight, I wasn't sure that I ever really had a choice.

They gave me a plastic bag to *protect* and wrap my hand with, and I stuck my right hand deep into the toilet hole as they both cheered me on saying *"feel around, keep feeling for something, feel the other side, go deeper…"* The plastic bag did nothing to protect my hand, instead, it filled with the dirty toilet water, and by this time my hand was not only deep into the toilet hole, it was also swimming in filthy liquid inside the bag.

After a while, I finally said to them that I couldn't find any blockage. They finally got tired of the sick joke and told me I could go. I ran to the sink and scrubbed my hands with *Ajax*, as tears began to sting my eyes, threatening to cascade into an avalanche of loathing and self-pity. I swallowed the stinging lump in my throat, and held back my tears, as I finished obsessing with the Ajax on my hand; and then with my head held high, I went on with my day.

While most kids my age were developing a paradigm of self-love through love and worthiness; I was busy developing a paradigm of self-love through grit and fear. The child in me was dying a slow death, as Pandora was empowering itself to emerge in unspoken volume of hatred and anger.

Chapter 11
Slave, deprived

When I was in fourth grade, my aunt Ellie introduced my mother to her husband's friend, Mr. Hirsch, through air mail correspondence. I heard that Mr. Hirsch was quite smitten, and very keen to meet my mother and her two children. He invited my mother to Europe so that they can get to know each other more, with a view to forming a relationship as life partners. He sent monies to enable my mother to travel to the capital city of Manila, and begin the application for her passport and tourist visa.

A few months went by, and then one day my mother appeared at my grandmother's house. She had just come back from Manila and seemed really happy. It would've been safe to assume that her trip went well. That her future was set, to travel to Europe and then marry Mr. Hirsch. Or so I thought.

But then, there was a hub of activity over at my mother's house, and even I was asked to get involved. My mother's sari-sari store seemed to be doing great, because now she was moving a few doors down to a two-storey house, with a bigger shopfront, plus its own private backyard, outhouse and bathroom. Work was also underway in the new place, such as erecting a dividing wall to create two bedrooms upstairs, and a partition between the private parlour and the shopfront, downstairs. My mother hired a couple of helpers and her new shop was going to be a dressmaking business, as well as an eatery, serving sandwiches, soft drinks, alcohol, and a juke box for entertainment.

On the opening day of her new business, my mother's old sari-sari store was still operating, so that she was running two shops simultaneously. She and her helpers frantically shuffled and hustled in between the two shops, and I found myself minding a lot of the cash flow in the new shop. At one stage, I was holding so much cash in the little wooden till that it was overflowing with crumpled notes. I tried to count them and got close to five hundred pesos, when I got overwhelmed by the Math. I felt unsafe with the cash while minding the shop alone, surrounded by adult customers. So, I scooped most of the notes as well as some coins into my skirt and ran down a few doors to give it to my mother. I went right back to the new shop after I'd cleaned up the till, and from there the afternoon sped by until it was late at night. Business was strong, and I liked being part of it.

I got up early the next morning while the sun was just peeping into the sky. I marveled at the privacy of my mother's new place. It was still in the heart of a slummy, industrial area, just like her old place a few doors down, but this new place was fenced in; and being in the same house with my mother gave me a sense of belonging, which filled my heart with joy.

For lunch that day, the smell of home-made hamburger patties invaded my senses and I saw that my mother and her helpers were busy cooking on a flat, metal plate; a cooking tool that I've never seen before. I thought, *"Wow, even the cooking and the food had improved!"*

I was beginning to hope that life was finally returning back to normal, and that I would be living with my mother again. But after a couple of days, my hopes and hiatus were aborted when the hype of the new shop died down, and I was told that it was time to go back to my grandmother's. No other explanations served, and no objections were acceptable at any level. It was quite obvious that I was not a good enough child for a mother to keep. By this time, I had well and truly believed that this, must be what I deserved. I learned to become indifferent to being handballed like a handball.

I found out shortly afterwards that the progression of my mother's business was a partnership with her new husband, Sandro. From what I heard, Sandro was a nephew of the neighbour of my mother's landlord, while she was in Manila. A seaman who happened to be "at dock" while my mother was in the neighbourhood, waiting for the approval of her visa to Europe, Sandro swept my mother off her feet, and then they got married. As a seaman, my mother's new husband would sail for months at a time, and when he wasn't at sea he would be stationed in the city of Manila, which was over one thousand miles from our little town Dadiangas. As a child, it sounded to me like a logistically difficult, long distance kind of marriage arrangement. Which made me wonder, *why were relationships so hard to do?*

In no time, my mother became pregnant. She closed her new shop and moved to my great grandmother's rental place, at a peripheral side of town called *Lagao*. She simply went back to running a small sari-sari store, plus the occasional dressmaking job. She was focused on her pregnancy, and also decided to take my big brother back in with her, sending him to the most expensive, private school in town, which was located near *their home*.

In spite of my mother's nonchalant favouritism, Larry and I remained close to each other. I had completely accepted my status as the reject child, and I was happy for my big brother. Besides, he was pretty cool. In the short time that he lived at my grandmother's house, he protected me from bullies at *North Elementary Public School*, as much as he could, which I was very grateful for.

One day my mother came to my grandmother's house to fetch me. She was heavily pregnant, and my brother had just gone through circumcision, at the age of thirteen, so she needed an extra hand to help her around.

My great grandmother's rental place was only a quarter of the size of my mother's previous place. It had one small bedroom, a separate room that served as the kitchen, dining and living room, plus a shopfront where she put the ancient, wooden countertop that she'd had from her very first sari-sari store. She also had a slanted dressmaker's cutting table that resembled an architect's drawing board, and a glass display cabinet for the clothes she made. This was a far cry from the big, two-storey shop with a jukebox that she had, not long ago.

She took me home with her so I could help her out a little, like cutting the nails on her pinky toe that she couldn't see because of her huge belly; or wash clothes; or hand over the salve to my brother as he changed the dressing on his circumcision; or mind the sari-sari store while they both rested from their individual conditions.

I slept on the floor in the small dining/living/kitchen room, and during this entire time, I saw my mother struggle. She looked tired and waddled slowly. The baby was almost due, but I have never known her husband to have been to see her during her entire pregnancy. Then, like a borrowed maid that she no longer required, I was sent back to my grandmother's house as soon as my brother healed from his circumcision, and my services were no longer required.

Chapter 12
Touch us no more

I was in grade five when I started to feel increasingly wary of my battles at my grandmother's, where the only females in the house were myself and Mommy. We were both constantly surrounded by male energy, which was very oppressive. My uncles, my cousins, my grandfather, and even my uncles' customers, were all males. Their tyranny and sexism antagonized the living daylights out of my evil half, Pandora. My grandmother was constantly criticized for her bad cooking, and insulted for her lack of education, by her very own sons. When she tried to fuss over them, they dismissed her motherly concerns with blatant sarcasm and ridicule.

Although Mommy never praised me and made me do difficult chores, I was grateful that she provided shelter above my head and didn't give me away to other people. She took me in, when my own mother did not want me, and for that, I loved my grandmother. It hurt me to see when my uncles disrespected her. I felt very sad that she had resigned herself to the hostility and heartlessness of her kids and her husband.

Nevertheless, I had my own battles to fight. So, I never said anything. Not to my grandmother for her weakness, not to my uncles for their atrocity, and especially not to myself, for the anger and loathing that silently brewed under the surface of Pandora's indifferent façade.

The living room upstairs was my sanctuary, and I would only ever go downstairs when I had to do chores around the house, or to watch TV late at night, when the shop was empty. One evening, my Uncle Cris came upstairs and asked me to iron his trousers. When asked if I knew how to iron trousers properly, I said no, so he showed me how. Fold the trousers around the waist with the button and the buttonhole facing each other, then align the inner and outer leg stitching by the hem down the bottom, place the trousers sideways and flat on the table, and make sure to go over the corners and the creases. It was a thorough lesson, and I was an eager student.

He was about to leave me with the ironing, when he saw my notebooks on the desk, and in an afterthought, he casually asked if I had already done my school assignments. No one had ever asked me that question before. I was stoked. I felt like he cared. I said yes and showed him a piece of paper that I had carefully written for my science experiment. With this, he was once again pleased and said that I did a great job, and then he left. I felt light and joyful for the kind attention that I had just received, and as soon as I finished ironing the trousers, I couldn't wait to go downstairs and check out what else I could do to help.

With a spring in my step, I walked toward the main living room where a big TV sat in the middle, surrounded by a scattering of another hundred TVs, odd furniture and two cane chairs. As I entered, the song 'Eye of The Tiger' was playing in full blast, while four of my uncles had their eyes glued to the TV. Curious, I looked at the TV and then I was fixated. There were six voluptuous women dressed scantily in tiger costumes, with tiger tails and tiger ears. The bulge of their breasts and buttocks were shaking as they danced both slowly and fast into the tune of Eye of The Tiger. They walked up and down what looked like a makeshift stage and crouched and bent over and smiled to the camera.

I wasn't sure what kind of movie I was looking at, and no one seemed to care that I was standing there. So, I kept watching. There was a void in my memory where I don't remember how the dancing women finished their dance. The next thing that I was looking at were a pair of naked man and woman, writhing and moaning together as the man straddled the woman from behind, who was on her knees and hands. The volume was so loud that the neighbours would have heard the slow and fast moaning.

I realised what I was looking at, and ran away as fast as I could. I was in shock. I went back upstairs, scared that the sounds would haunt me, and the image of the naked people would stay with me. I sat in the corner of the bed against the wall and hugged my knees to my chest. I didn't know what to do and I hated myself for seeing what I saw, I hated my uncles for showing me what they were watching, I hated how open and unsafe I felt, I hated this place, I hated how I had nowhere to go. I rocked back and forth to the mantra of *"I hate this. I hate this. I hate this. I hate this."* Until my mind was numb and my heart shut down, that I couldn't hate anymore. I fell asleep.

I woke up the next day feeling like a different person. Once again, the child had been hidden away for protection, and Pandora was out in full force, feeling ever more invincible, ever stronger, ever more wretched.

In the beginning, I lived in constant transition between darkness and light, releasing my soul in the open fields that caressed me with promise and hope; and then coming home to the dungeon of persecution inside my grandmother's house. But over the course of time, the fine line between darkness and light had unknowingly dissolved, so that in a state of extreme emotional vacancy and mental torment, I had completely identified, and believed myself to be part of where I was. I had slowly but definitively, stigmatized my body, my mind and my spirit, as a part of, and nothing different from, the environment that I was in.

I was lost in the dark.

A few years had passed since the *whack-in-head-runaway* incident between me and my cousin Mark. I had since gone on to my own world of survival, as he had to his own world of teenage limbo. Just like myself, Mark's role models were the people at my grandmother's house, except that he was treated like the Prince, because his mother was the major financier of the household. While I spent my spare time exploring nature and daydreaming in the open fields, he had a completely different distraction. As a young teen, my Uncle Cris introduced Mark to a *beerhouse* experience. A beerhouse was a bar and a brothel in one. Mark did not spend his hours geeking out on science experiments, or playing sport with kids his age, instead he became sexually curious too much, too early.

One day I was upstairs as usual, when my cousins came up to say hello, including Mark, James and Carlo. I knew that they were looking for ways to terrorize me just for fun, but I've long since learned how not to get intimidated, by ignoring them. Mark was being particularly friendly, while James and Carlo got bored pretty soon and went downstairs.

I was left alone with Mark, who held me by the arm and ushered me to my grandfather's big bed, and then he laid me down. I was wearing a loose-fitting tracksuit pant that used to be my big brother's, which I've folded up to my knees because of the hot weather. Mark moved so fast that before I could say anything, he spread my legs apart, smiled and pleasantly told me not to worry because he just wanted to look at something very quickly. Somewhere in the back of my mind there was a voice that told me exactly what he was looking for, and then another voice said not to cause any issue, as he was only going to look at it, like he said.

Befuddled, I listened to the second voice while I froze in my position, and watched Mark shove the loose tracksuit pants, all the way up until he can see between my legs. He parted them wider and started to touch me. His eyes were shining, and his face resembled like that of a crazy clown. I pushed his hand away using my hands, and pushed his body away using my feet against his shoulders. I said, *"That's enough. Go away."* He went away with a wicked, satisfied look on his face; and again, I was left to ponder how much I hated myself for everything that was happening.

A week later, I was eating lunch alone on the six-seater, round dining table in the kitchen, when Mark came and sat right next to me. I was wearing an oversized, spaghetti straps blue dress, which was a hand-me-down from Mark's very own mother, my aunt Ellie. A surge of intense heat shot through my spine and this time, there was only one voice. It was clear, *"Be ready."* After a moment, I felt his hand on my knee, then just as quickly, he travelled his hands upwards through my inner thigh.

The heat on my spine bolted to the top of my head, causing my brain to explode like lava. I screamed a terrifying holler, and in one fluid motion, I stood up and swiped everything in front of me using my left forearm as it flew to his direction, smashing against the back of an old, retro style TV-turned kitchen bench. Food, cutlery, glass and ceramic plates flying everywhere, landing on the floor in smithereens. *"AAAaaaarrrgghhhhhh!!!! NNNnnnnoooooooooo!!!!!! AAAaaaaarrrrgghhhhh!!!!!!"*

The guttural sound of a wild animal was unleashed from the depths of somewhere I didn't even know existed. To say that I was angry wouldn't cut it. The young Pandora had been liberated for the first time, and she was ready for anything. Mark froze in shock. My grandmother heard the commotion and ran into the kitchen to see what happened. She looked at the broken plates, then she looked at the entire mess, then she looked at my cousin, who was still sitting there speechless, and finally she looked at me. I turned my head to her direction, with pure violence reeking out of my skin, making her flinch and step away. She didn't need my words. She didn't ask for my words. She told my cousin to leave and began to clean up the mess.

There is a moment in a girl's life when her innocence fades. For many, it is a sweet memory. For others, it is a tragedy. But for some of us, it is the purgatorial mark between heaven and hell, when you don't quite know who you've become except that you were no longer the child that you once were. As I stared down at my grandmother cleaning up the mess on the floor, her head bowed down in bewilderment, the child in me had inescapably disengaged to an enduring confine, while my demon, Pandora, remained seething for the bloodshed that she was hungry for.

Chapter 13
Ain't no communion for broken people

When I heard that my mother gave birth to a baby boy, I didn't give much thought to the fact that I had become a big sister, because I didn't live with *them*. But then three weeks after my baby brother was born, he became infected with meningitis. During all of this time and including the day of my baby brother's birth, my mother's husband had not come to see her, and I felt sorry for her aloneness. I could sense that it wasn't an easy feat giving birth without her husband and having to deal with the baby's illness all alone. So, I quietly hoped that her husband would come and make things easier for her.

Having wished my mother well, I was quick to then eject her out of my thoughts, as I had my own life to deal with. A life that I thought I would never share with her, ever again. But I was in for a big surprise.

One rainy afternoon, my mother, my big brother and the baby, came unannounced at my grandmother's doorstep with a few bags of clothes and belongings. I sensed an air of desperation in their arrival.

My mother was not visiting my grandmother's house; she was moving into my grandmother's house.

I was old enough to understand that no matter how many chances my mother had in the last five years to take me back, she never did. I was always *excess baggage*. So instead of rejoicing that my mother would be living with me in the same house, I felt a deep sadness that drained my energy. In my heart, I knew I would rather have my mother hate me from a distance, than live with her constant rejection each, and every day.

My mother coming to live at my grandmother's house caused so much suspicion and jealousy from my uncles. They questioned why she moved in with the new baby, and where was her husband in all this? They questioned what happened with her well to do business only twelve months ago. They questioned what contribution she would be making into the household expenses. The most bizarre thing of all was, they never asked these questions directly to my mother. It was as if they were afraid to confront their sister, but they never batted an eye in backstabbing her. It was fascinating as it was extremely stressful. In all of their bitching behind each other's backs, no one noticed that I was always in earshot of the conversations. So far, I've had five years of practise and had become very good at making myself inconspicuous.

The contrast between my uncles' growing wealth and my mother's poverty was stark. By now she had no business, no job, a new baby and an absent husband. Yet it seemed that she was too proud to acknowledge the uncertainty of her situation, and never offered much explanation about it. Her haughtiness, for me, felt like I was in the middle of two wrecking balls. Where I used to only have to answer to my uncles and grandma, I now have to answer to her also. The only thing worse than being a slave, was being a slave to your own family who didn't love you.

I was fourteen years old when three of my big brother's friends came over. They were gathered together out the back talking and eating. I went outside to say hello, and my big brother's friends warmly greeted me, like I was their own little sister, calling me by my nickname *Ging-ging*. I could tell by their friendliness that my brother must speak fondly of his little sister, to his friends. I felt loved. Loved by my big brother and cared for by his friends. I felt the muscles in my face relax, my voice softened a little, and my body moved fluidly rather than jerkily. It was a really good feeling to be acknowledged as a good human being.

Then I left my brother and his friends and went back to the kitchen where my mother was eating her dinner. Without warning she said, *"You are a flirt. You were practically throwing yourself to your brother's friends."* Her voice was scathing and hostile. Without flinching I retorted, slowly and succinctly, like every word was deliciously sliding out of my tongue *"I'm not a flirt. Those are my brother's friends. But don't you worry, I will never become like you, you have no idea how to choose your partners, you've already failed twice."* While I was taken aback by the eloquence of my opinion, I was more impressed by my mother's self-control. I half-expected her to slap me for my full-frontal disrespect, instead she did nothing and said nothing. *"Perhaps she was a coward after all."* The voice in my head said. Somewhere in my gut, I could feel my anger rising, and somehow, I knew that one day nothing could stop it, not even my mother.

I've never been an early riser, but one day something was pulling me to get up at the break of dawn, while everyone else was still sleeping. It was five o'clock in the morning, and I awoke to the roosters crowing; I gingerly walked to the top of the stairs and began climbing down in a lazy, sitting fashion, pausing for a few seconds between each step, with my eyes barely open. I stopped halfway down as I noticed something odd at the bottom of the stairs, where a cane lounge was nestled against the wall, facing away from the staircase. I opened my eyes wider as I tried to make sense of what I was staring at. Standing next to the cane lounge was a brown suitcase that my uncle Cris used when he travelled to Europe with my aunt and her husband. The suitcase looked worse for wear and there were splashes of what looked like blood on it. Cradled in the cane lounge were someone's bare feet poking out from the hem of denim jeans. The jeans and the feet were blood soaked. I ran the rest of the way down to see what happened, and there was my uncle Cris, blood stained and passed out.

I ran back upstairs to wake my grandmother and alerted her of what I've just seen. We both knew something was wrong and she immediately got out of bed to investigate.

It turned out that the bloodstained suitcase contained my uncle Cris' personal belongings. He had left his wife in the wee hours of the morning after he had shot her hand with a 9mm pistol, during a heated argument. According to his version of the story, he came home from having a couple of drinks with his mates, when she engaged in an argument with him, which had led to a gun wrestle between the two of them, and then the gun went off, and the bullet went through her hand. Of course, he didn't mean to shoot her.

A couple of weeks passed when my uncle Cris' wife, Lorna, came to my grandmother's house, visiting and making peace with my uncle, while her hand was still in a bandage. Shortly after that, they were back living together as a couple. My aunt Lorna was one of the sweetest women I have ever known. Albeit she hadn't had a lot of education, she was emotionally sound in that she was gentle, caring and sensitive. But on the day that she came to make peace with her husband after he had shot her with a gun, and then nobody intervened to counsel her for the decision that she was about to make, I felt profoundly disheartened. It was profound because I felt my aunt's loving light, and it was disheartening because I could also sense how much her light flickered with self-doubt and martyrdom; the martyrdom of *for better or for worse, in sickness and in health, till death, do we part*. It was hard to watch a woman waste herself wilfully, simply because she had been conditioned to do so. Conditioned by her family, by her community, by her religion, and ultimately, she had conditioned herself to believe all of her conditioning, with her heart and soul. Even after she had been shot with a gun.

"Is that what love is about?" I asked myself. And the strangest thing of all was, I didn't get an answer. Not from any one of the voices in my head.

I didn't know love. I didn't understand love. I didn't feel, love.

But I wanted it. So bad.

Chapter 14
Indifference breeds the darkest evil

For a period of time, my grandmother tried to keep a maid to help her out with all-around house chores. One of the maids, Minda, was a cool, calm and collected chick. She was short and dark skinned with curly black hair. And although her voice was small and purry, her eyes evoked a confidence that she was not someone you wanted to mess with. She walked with a graceful strength and her sense of power inspired me. She worked hard during the days, and at nights, she attended college using the salary she received from my grandmother. However, she abruptly left after three months, and none of the maids lasted longer than she did.

Another girl, Jasmine, was a different kettle of fish. Jasmine and I didn't talk much to each other, she was highly strung, as she was beautiful. She had short, brown hair, deep set eyes, high cheekbones and well-defined lips. She was about five feet four inches and had nice, voluptuous body shape, her breasts were pronounced as well as her bottom; and unlike Minda, she wore skirts instead of pants.

One afternoon Jasmine said that she was going upstairs to take a nap. But then a moment later, I saw her come back downstairs to the kitchen. Just when I thought she'd decided against her nap, she emerged from the kitchen and went back upstairs, carrying a kitchen knife. What a curious sight, I thought. She awoke one hour later, came downstairs and put the knife back in the kitchen. Jasmine had a witchlike quality which made me second guess what to say to her, nevertheless, I mustered up my guts and asked why she took a knife upstairs. Her response was *"I sleep with a knife all the time. I don't trust your cousin Mark, and if he ever tried to touch me, I will kill him."* She said in no uncertain terms.

The maid would always share a *banig* (wide mat made of straw) with me to sleep on, in the living room upstairs. We used a mosquito net the same size to keep the mosquitoes out. In the next couple of nights, I watched Jasmine place the kitchen knife under her pillow, right next to me. I was scared for my life. I told my grandmother that I couldn't sleep with Jasmine anymore and when asked why, I told her the truth, that I was scared of the knife that Jasmine slept with. I felt the urge to also tell my grandmother that I knew why Jasmine slept with it, but then I wasn't sure if Jasmine might prefer to say that for herself. The one thing I didn't want to do was make Jasmine angry.

The next day, the maid had left. I asked my grandmother what happened, and she told me that she let Jasmine go because of her dangerous behaviour. I tried to ask, *"What about Mark? Jasmine slept with the knife because of him!"* But my grandmother wouldn't hear any of it and dismissed me.

The next maid that we had wasn't really a maid. She was the daughter of my grandmother's brother. Rosie was ten years older than me and was technically my auntie to the second degree. I had known her years before, and while back then she was just a kid, now as a young woman she was more aloof. Like I did with the other maids, Rosie and I slept together on the same banig, but we didn't have the typical banter and friendship that I've had with the others. Rosie saw me as a much younger relative, and in turn, I saw her as a much older relative. Being relatives was like a barrier to being friends. Strange but true.

One night I was fast asleep when I woke to the sound of whispering and shuffling. It was dark but I could slightly see shadows. I looked to my right where Rosie was sleeping and I heard her whisper *"Mark, no, not tonight, I'm sleeping."* In the darkness I could see the form of two people on top of each other. When I realised what was happening, inches next to me, I froze, and my mind swirled in all different directions of panic, fear and abomination. I wanted to move but even breathing was a big risk. *"What am I supposed to do?"* My mind screamed. I heard Mark whisper *"Ssshh.. Paghilom lang. Ayaw saba."* (Be quiet. Don't make a noise.) to Rosie. And as he said the words, my mind blacked out, as if the 'erase' button was pressed on the VCR, and wiped out a section of a movie.

Maybe something happened, maybe not. How could I know. The next thing that I remember was Mark getting up and leaving, ever so stealthily. After he left, Rosie just lied there, motionless and soundless. I tried not to breathe, and even wished that I didn't exist. I counted the hours and when morning finally came, I stumbled in a state of fatigue and dishevel, feeling like I've been through a war. I found my mother and I never felt so relieved to be able to talk to her. I tried to tell her what happened as coherently as I could, and she listened to me until I couldn't say anything else. She saw that I was extremely upset, and felt some kind of pity for me, then she told me to take a walk to the fields in Bulaong Subdivision, which I gratefully did.

I came back hours later and found Rosie packing her bags. I stood a few feet from her just staring. She knew I was there, but she never lifted her eyes to meet mine. I wanted to say something to her and ask a question, but I had no words. How could she allow it to happen? She was older than Mark and should have stopped him instead of giving in to him. My young, idealistic mind was adamant. I felt that by allowing Mark to touch her, she had fed the demon a strength that will destroy more people. I waited to see if she had something to say, but she avoided me. After she left, I went and asked my grandmother if she could tell me why Rosie left. My grandmother said, *"She's not allowed to behave that way around here."* And as for Mark? Nothing. He wasn't punished, it was as if he didn't even do anything. I even doubt that it was ever discussed with him.

I've learned that when people are desperate enough, they are willing to become indifferent to abuse, abandonment, incest, violence, drug use and loneliness; if it means that they could beat poverty by even just one meal ahead. The indifference was palpable and contagious. It wasn't just my grandmother who was guilty, but everybody in that house, including myself, had become indifferent and culpable; in that, we were all in conspiracy and connivance to the inevitable destruction of my cousin's future.

Chapter 15
Just another high school weirdo

First day of high school was chaotic and confusing. Six hundred and fifty first-year high school students, including myself, huddled under the scorching sun waiting to be assigned a section. I was almost passed out from the heat when they called my name, and then after all of that, I didn't catch my section assignment. So, I ended up wandering around the campus, reading off of the lists posted on classroom doors, looking for where I belonged. When I finally I found my name, I was thirty minutes late for my first subject.

I was in section two, out of thirteen, which held the top seven to fifteen percentile smartest kids in the freshman block. Fifty-two smart bums to be exact, in a classroom with only fifty allocated seats. I made quite an entrance when the teacher put me on the spot by telling me to stand at the back and introduce myself. Everybody turned and looked at me from head to toe, as they whispered and giggled with one another. I was missing two front teeth, and my hand me down espadrilles were two sizes too big on my feet, so that they dangled by the heel. I wore white, knee-high socks, and I looked like a two-year-old playing dress-up with my grandmother's shoes, except that I was a skinny, curly-haired, brown, toothless teenager. In hindsight, I was indeed, a sight to behold.

I turned to the person standing next to me, who also missed out on the seats. Although she had milky white skin and smooth brown hair, she was overweight, awkward, and just as embarrassed as I was. Nevertheless, I held my ground and introduced myself, as I stared right back at my new classmates with just as much audacity as they did toward me. In doing so, I had immediately put them in their places as they stopped giggling and turned away. The teacher, on the other hand, had taken an entire week to provide two more seats for me and my friend. I was beginning to think that I would be standing for the entire ten months of freshman, when one day, two extra chairs appeared in the room, and the teacher sent two rowdy boys to sit at the back, and asked me and Nerissa, my chubby and sweet friend, to take the front row seats.

Halfway through freshman year, my aunt Ellie came home from Europe for a quick visit and gave some money for my mother to buy me some teeth. After seven years of missing my two front teeth, I was finally able to wear dentures. By then, my classmates had gotten used to me being toothless so that when I rocked up to school with my new teeth, they had mixed reactions. Some of them liked it, and some of them didn't. Nevertheless, I was relieved to feel a little less weird and more normal.

Then I discovered that I could wear hand me down socks that were too big for my feet, and then I could stuff the extra bit of the oversized socks, toward the front of my oversized shoes, to make the shoes look like they fit my feet. With this trick, I looked even more normal and a little less silly. Life was slowly starting to improve.

In sophomore, I was academically ranked down from section two, to section three. Our class adviser, Sir Barbero, was a Physical Education teacher who preferred to hold his classes in an improvised pig pen, near the vegetable gardens.

Sir Barbero's unconventional classroom had a hollow block wall as high as my knees, and the rest of the wall was made with barbed wire, just like a pigpen. Inside were four, long columns of wooden tables with wooden benches, arranged horizontally against the barbed wired wall. In hindsight, it was probably the most learning-conducive classroom experience I have ever had because of its organic vibe, and its alfresco atmosphere was refreshing rather than stifling. Listening to the teachers was literally a breeze. Consequently, it was the only time in my high school life that I enjoyed learning about Math and Sciences, like Algebra and Biology; subjects that I normally disliked.

It was in junior year when I discovered my passion for writing poems and sentimental content. My English teacher gave out an assignment for us to write a mock thesis on any subject that we wanted to tackle, with a vague premise that we should be able to present *quantifiable ideas*. My brain understood the instructions, but my heart screamed to write something rather out of the box. So I wrote a thesis on *"How To Fall Out Of Love"*. My main theory was that *by learning how to fall out of love, one can avoid disappointment and heartache*.

The summary of my thesis was, "When someone you love rejects you for not being good enough. Or when you feel like you're not good enough, as a result of a relationship breakdown. And then if you could simply accept that you are not good enough, whether that might be true or not, then the pragmatic act of acceptance for not being good enough, will pave the way to a more peaceful, albeit resigned, life." Further I explained, "When love is not to be expected, disappointment will never come."

I waited two weeks for some kind of feedback from my teacher. Nothing. So I approached her and asked if she had the chance to read my thesis. She looked at me matter-of-factly and said, *"Yes I have. Unfortunately, I cannot give you any feedback on your thesis because it wasn't a thesis. Your topic was unmeasurable and lacked substantiated evidence."* Maybe it was just me, but there was something about her swag when she walked away, and the way her eyes averted mine, that I felt she really had a lot more to say about it but held herself back. I then realized that my teacher was simply trying to do her job, and that if I wanted my expression to be heard, I had to find a different avenue.

Identity crisis and anxiety plagued me in the last two years of high school. By the end of it, I had derailed every ounce of my academic focus. Unlike my big brother who bagged thirteen medals on his high school graduation day, I took no honours home. And as much as I tried to tell myself that it didn't matter because nobody cares, a voice inside me said that it mattered to *us*. That *I* needed to do better so that *we* can out survive our current situation.

I was disappointed with myself and burned all my notebooks on the last day of school, to delete the symbols of my personal failings. This ritual seemed to have quietened the voices in my head, at least for a little while.

PART TWO

Chapter 16
Truth Seeker

I will forever be indebted to my aunt Ellie for paying for my college education. Four years in Notre Dame College brought me the best years of my life in the Philippines. I've made some really good friends and got to know so much more about the good side of myself.

In my freshman year, my Typing Professor, Ms. Gallente, blindfolded us on our speed and accuracy typing exams. The acceptable score was seventy words per minute, with no margin for errors. She walked around and dictated the sentences, holding a plastic ruler in her hand as we punched away on our mechanical typewriters. Every so often, she would slap someone's hand when they made a typographical error, and we would hear a loud whack when her plastic ruler landed on her victim's hand.

Many times, after her infamous classes of blindfolding, ruler whacking, typing marathons, a few loyal students would gather around her desk to discuss their test results, and also confess that although the whack of her ruler sounded razor-sharp, it hardly ever landed on the hand. She had mastered the art of whacking for terror, without landing the pain. It became a trade secret that she shared with half a dozen of her industrious students, including myself.

One afternoon, Ms. Gallente's post class conversations drifted towards personal excellence. She had a way of allowing us to be open and candid about our new experiences on the campus, and we felt safe sharing our awkward thoughts and personal stories. She offered one simple advise about personal excellence: *"Own the school."* It took me a long five seconds to digest and understand what she meant, while others didn't understand at all.

She believed that if we *owned* the school, we would do everything we can to uphold its mission and values, become fastidious with our research and study, and value our teachers and friends as part of our family. If each one of us owned the school, she promised, we would be able to form a movement strong enough that we can uproot the entire city out of its corrupt government and poverty-stricken streets.

The boldness of her statement was jaw dropping, and we asked that she elaborate on her "own the school" advise.

She began by explaining the difference between the paradigm of a mere student versus the paradigm of a school ambassador. If we were to behave like mere students, always relying on our teachers' and friends' points of view, we would end up brainwashed and plain academic at the end of our four-year college stint. But if we embodied the qualities of an ambassador for the school, championing our values and vision by applying our learnings inside and outside of the school campus, then we can be great, rather than just settle for good.

Ms. Gallente offered *"The key to excellence is a Paradigm Shift from your mere student mindset,to a school ambassador mindset."*

"Paradigm Shift? What is a Paradigm Shift?" I asked.

"A Paradigm is a model of the way that you think. To change that model, shift the way that you think. From Student to Ambassador." She said with her signature, wide-eyed, no-nonsense stare.

I'm not sure which one stunned me the most: Her profound advice, or her belief in our capacity to do great. "Own the school" was a silent mantra that I used not just throughout college, but for all of my life.

I wanted to become a linguist, but there was no school that offered such a degree in Gensan, and the next best thing that I could do was to study accountancy, despite knowing that numbers were my Achilles' heel. I could've have studied something more prestigious like Nursing, however given the choice of botching a medical operation or botching someone's profit and loss statements, I would rather do the latter. With this kind of student paradigm, I knew I had very little chance of excelling and achieving the greatness that Ms. Gallente had graciously implied. I had to think of other ways to own the school.

Notre Dame was a Catholic school, and one day I heard a nun talk about the biblical verse *"Seek, and you shall find"*. I decided to test the theory. I paid attention to the extra-curricular activities available in the campus and submitted my interest in becoming a writer for the student publication, THE VOICE. I was immediately welcomed to the team, which meant I could write anything I desired, a news article, a feature article, short story, or a poem. A huge breakthrough in my personal belief! Writing has always made feel happy and elevated; but back in high school, I was always in the student mindset, waiting for other people to urge me to get involved. Now in college, as I begin to own the school, I've landed myself a writing position, and found like-minded students who also loved to write.

The following year, I was appointed to step into the Feature Editor position, which magnified my passion for unadulterated ideas and strong opinions. Every fiction story, poem and feature article went through my editing eyes, an experience that inflamed my burning desire to create a wave of expression in and amongst the Notre Dameans. Having noticed that the school publication was seen more like an informative newsletter, instead of a highly engaging communication instrument, I made a promise to myself that I would overhaul the content and presentation of THE VOICE as soon as I became Editor in Chief.

On my third year, I was handed the Editor in Chief position, which I took gratefully and seriously. Most E-I-C's before me simply kept the old wheels running, while I wanted to revamp the entire vehicle and put a brand-new engine in it. First, I discharged the old publisher, and then I travelled three hours by bus, to negotiate with a new one. A company that had the technology to produce glossy and matte pages in one edition, plus the ability to print multi-toned art impressions. I was very fortunate that I had a team of writers and editors who had cardinal ideas like myself and were only too eager to champion the change that I envisioned.

I disseminated radical content involving world issues, with thought-provoking photographs that sometimes left too much, or too little, to the imagination, such as Nastassja Kinski wrapped only in a boa constrictor. Closer to home, I opened a 'comment section' where students could fully unleash, express, and have their thoughts published, unedited, bar none. The school paper became controversial, some said it was scandalous, while others thought it was timely. I was stoked to see that the students were not asleep. They read!

After my first round of publication, I was approached by two student-writers from the University of the Philippines, to join the freedom of expression movement of the College Editors Guild of the Philippines (CEGP). I worked with Teddy Casiño and Randy Malayao for a few months, with them travelling to Gensan a few times, supporting me in getting the CEGP Gensan chapter created. Together we rallied dozens of student editors from The Holy Trinity College, Mindanao Polytechnic College, Ramon Magsaysay Memorial College, Mindanao State University, and influenced them to think like activists.

Teddy and Randy's lives, as student-activists, were unpredictable and highly dependent on other people's generosity and willingness to help. They had no official funding from anybody and relied only on donations, as well as their own personal allowances. But they always got by. They hopped from cities to islands, up and down the entire country. They had the propensity to follow through in their tantalizing political passion. They thought outside of themselves and carried a clear mental model of a unified and peaceful country - the paradigm of common good.

Teddy would lead a fruitful career as a writer and became one of the most outstanding congressmen in Philippine politics, consistently championing the cause of the masses.

Randy was a man of solid principles. The last I personally heard from him was in 2016, when he wished me a *"Maligayang Kaarawan, Kapatid."* (Happy Birthday, Sister) through Facebook. He became a consultant for an indigenous rights movement, and in January of 2019, he was murdered with a gunshot to his chest. Even though Randy's life has passed, his legacy burns bright and he is distinctly remembered for his fearlessness and unshakeable morals.

In hindsight, activism was not something that I aspired for. Activism came to me, and I embraced it because it was the closest I had ever been to expressing truth. I was so hungry for emotional justice and I had so much suppressed energy calling to be unchained; so that CEGP was my perfect playground for expression. And even though I never got to tell my very own truth, I felt somewhat validated that at least I tried to harness the skill of uprising.

My favorite subject in college was Philosophy. One day the teacher asked us to write an essay about freedom. At first, I thought of writing about my ancestors who fought with their lives, so that I am a free citizen today. But then as I began to scribe on my yellow paper and penned down the required essay, I found myself longing for a deeper kind of freedom, the kind that was invisible but all consuming. Emotional freedom. In some parts of this epistle, I wrote:

"Freedom is a sad thing. It comes to you when you least need it and it is most elusive when you want it. True freedom comes from within a person. Most of the time we take it for granted and talk about superficial freedom – democracy and all. My family is the only entity that can really hurt me, so far. I don't like pain, but when it involves my family, the 'me' beneath my façade comes out and then the weakness shows up. I don't like it, in fact I almost hate it because it hurts, but I can't help it. I am not free, because my emotions are prisoners of my family."

A couple of days later the teacher had marked our essays and handed them back. My paper was riddled with red writing and a big A+ mark on the top. The teacher underlined a few sentences and at the bottom of the paper he asked me a question: *"How old are you?"*

Further he wrote, *"You feel there are a lot of things you are capable of doing but some people belittle your capacity. Within you there is a tremendous surge of power and such power, you believe would propel you to achieve your goal. You are indifferent about feelings, especially weakness; and showing of emotions make you uncomfortable. Mind you! You are vulnerable inside. You are loving, you are soft hearted. Your question is, you want to know more about yourself and meet people who can understand..."*

After reading the teacher's comments, I really wanted to have a deeper conversation with him. But I was apprehensive because other than his written feedback, he didn't show any signs of real, face to face empathy, and I was too frightened to initiate real vulnerability.

I look back now and it was clearly the time of my life when I needed to talk my baggage out with a professional. My essay was a cry for help, and had I been an ordinary student in the campus, the teacher would've probably recommended me to talk with the school counsellor. But because I was part of the school editorial board and had the ability to write stuff, my essay was considered nothing more than a literary piece. It was as if the ability to express oneself through the written word was a sign of sanity, rather than a sign of inner turmoil.

Writing was always a monologue experience; and at the fiery age of seventeen, those monologues were unhealthy self-internalizations that needed to be re-designed into healthy dialogues. Regrettably in my case, the dialogue about my longing for emotional freedom began with an essay and ended with an A+ mark, and then that was the end of it.

Nevertheless, I wanted to preserve my teacher's kindness, and use it as a source of strength in desperate times, so I neatly folded and tucked my essay inside the pages of my diary. Every few years or so,

I would open that old diary and unfold the yellow paper with the teacher's red writing on it, marveling at his kind words, and wishing I could remember his name.

Chapter 17
Queens have hearts, not crowns

The highlight of my college life came in the middle of my final year, when I had the opportunity to address an unresolved personal aspiration - to win a beauty pageant.

Every little girl wants to feel a deep sense of beauty that can only be manifested through the language of love, affection, and words of affirmation. Gestures that are usually shared inside of a loving family home. Without this kind of love experience, I learned to manage my powerful insecurities through daydreaming that I could be a ballerina, graceful, elegant and strong. I created a mental world of physical beauty, where I was in the centre stage of it all, with kind strangers giving me admiration and applause. And eventhough I couldn't conjure love and affection in it, because I didn't really know how love and affection felt or looked like, it was a delightful enough experience that sometimes I would switch my imagination from a ballerina to a concert pianist, a gymnast, or a beauty queen.

The Philippines is a fertile ground for beauty pageants, and girls could begin to participate as young as the age of two. Back in high school, my second-degree cousin Rita, learned to catwalk and do her own hair and makeup through joining a beauty pageant.

One day she came by my grandmother's house to regale everyone with her recent beauty pageant experience. Rita told me that beauty contests were scored based on physical beauty, wit, and intelligence. And with the right hair, makeup, and outfit, almost anyone can manufacture beauty, but no one can manufacture wit and intellect during the interview.

She suggested that she could make me look beauty pageant worthy, but it would be up to me to strut my stuff on the runway and outwit the others. I felt encouraged by the possibility of becoming a beauty pageant candidate, where perhaps I might win and be crowned as a beauty queen. A chance to feel that I am beautiful, a feeling that I have always daydreamed of.

My first chance was the Miss Young Mindanao State University Beauty Contest, at the tender age of fourteen. With Rita's full support, I placed second runner up, and also won a few minor awards such as "Best in *Malong* Gown", "Best in Casual Attire", and "Best in Interview".

I was very happy and grateful to my cousin for mentoring me, doing my hair and makeup, and lending me her clothes for my outfits. But did I feel beautiful? Not really. I felt confident and thoroughly enjoyed walking and twirling on the stage, and I especially liked the interview portion. But whilst it was a great experience, I don't know that I felt *a deep sense of beauty.*

After that pageant, I met a few organisers who were affiliated with the larger beauty pageant industry, who then encouraged me to continue to pursue my *dream* of becoming a crowned beauty queen. Their expert psychological perpetration had got me thinking, could

I really take a beauty queen's crown home? And would that then be a truly *"beautiful"* experience?

Curious and desperate for more validation, I signed up to compete for Miss General Santos City, alongside my classmate Jane, who took home the Miss Young MSU crown, and my big brother's classmate, Louise.

My friend Jane had milky white skin and blond, wavy bob that framed her beautiful, aristocratic face. She looked like she could be a cousin of Kate Winslet from the Titanic. Louise had long, shiny straight hair that fell down to her bottom, she was boyish but sexy, with lips that curled into a wicked smile, and razor-sharp eyes that were perfectly framed by her bushy eyebrows. I, on the other hand was the ugly duckling that turned into a goose. At the age of fifteen and during the most awkward time of my life, Miss Gensan pageant was a shockingly bold ambition for me.

But even though I knew people made fun of me for even thinking that I could be in a league of beauty queens, I had developed a numbness to criticism. The irony of growing up in a household of indifferent people was that I learned to mimic that indifference and use it, especially for ignoring critics. It didn't make me totally numb to criticism, but it did a temporary job of getting me through the day.

For this contest, I needed written parental consent, because it would cost time and money to get involved. The upside was, we could invite a business to sponsor our costumes, makeup and all other expenses, and in return we would promote their business on media. This was how I got my mother to give consent. After signing me up, she wasted no time in using her Chinese connections and asked the Chinese owner of the biggest shopping centre in town, Kimball Plaza, to sponsor the grandchild of *Kim Tong Tan*. Sure enough, the owner knew my grandfather and uncles, and immediately agreed to sponsor me.

For once, I felt like I was part of an inner circle, perhaps a very small part, like a pawn in a chess game, but a party, nonetheless. I had no idea how much money my mother had collected from them, but it would be more than safe to assume that she wouldn't have gone through all that trouble for me, if there was nothing in it for her. At the end of the day, it was a business transaction where I was the goods, and she made profit.

Altogether there were twelve candidates vying for the crown of *"Mutya ng Heneral Santos"* (Miss Gensan). In a pageant as big as this, there were several committees involved, and I felt that we, the twelve candidates, were not the most important thing in the pageant itself. There was a political inertia that pulled everything that we did towards the goal of making the event as favourable to the organizers as possible.

More than half of the judges were people who came from the 'old money' of Gensan. Understandably, they were biased towards the candidate who belonged to their social echelon, a girl named Lauren, well-bred, personable, bright, and pretty. Lauren's genealogy traced back to the founding politicians of Gensan, and her X Factor came with the quiet confidence of knowing that she, was going to win the crown. A couple of the women in the pageant committee and panel of judges, were people whom she referred to as "Auntie".

At the conclusion of the pageant night, Lauren won the crown, as well as the coveted, stand-alone Miss Rejoice award, from Rejoice

Shampoo. There was a general anticipation that the winner of Miss Rejoice had to be the girl with the most beautiful hair, which was no other than my friend Louise. If there was one thing that Louise was known for, it was her long, healthy, sexy hair. There was no one else in the city who had the same quality of hair as she did and there was no question in everyone's mind that she would take Miss Rejoice home. But the judges gave it to their favourite girl. Like many other beauty pageants in the Philippines, this was a highly controversial event.

Altogether, it was an educational experience. Did I feel beautiful? No. On the contrary, I felt invisible. It was like trying so hard to feel beautiful, only to be swallowed up by the rigmarole and politics of it all, so that more than anything, I felt like a used ragdoll.

I was rather tired and ready to put it behind me. But then a couple of days after the pageant, I found myself in a rare, round table family meeting. There was me, my big brother, mother and grandmother, in a heightened discussion about my recent beauty pageant experience, with my mother insinuating that it was rigged. Not that she thought I had a chance of winning, but at least she thought Louise should have won Miss Rejoice, and my friend Jane should have been the crown winner.

As I listened to her rant about me while she raved about other people, I considered getting up and walking away, when my brother summed up the discussion and said, *"What I can say to you little sister is this. Don't let this experience get you down, because you didn't win. Make this experience as a learning ground for you, think about how the people in it behaved, and the actions they chose to take to get what they want. This is an experience and a lesson in integrity and self-belief."* My mother then finally stopped ranting, and the conversation halted in a good note, much to my relief. They were really wise words, what my big brother said.

Five years later on, in my final year in college, the memory of that experience faded and the lessons from it moot, until one day, when I was approached by a student-organizer for the upcoming Miss Sportspower beauty contest.

Miss Sportspower was the finale of our campus sports intramurals. Intrams, as we called it, was a points system, cross-division competition, in areas of sports, essay writing, public speaking, debate, chess, and beauty contest. Every course division would call upon their best and most talented students to compete, with the aim of taking the "overall champion" prize, at the end of the annual, weeklong event.

What piqued my interest, beyond the fact that I was being invited to compete once more in a beauty pageant, was the little-known truth that my course division (Accountancy) had always come second to the Nursing division, year after year after year. The sports players from the Nursing division always seemed taller, faster, stronger, and better; hence they always won. It had become a running joke on the campus that nurses, not accountants, always came first.

I wondered then, if we could not beat Nursing at sports, then perhaps we should beat them at other areas, like the beauty contest? I had never been one to have a competitive spirit, but I remembered Ms. Gallente's advise when I was in freshman, "Own the school." I felt in my heart that if I was to do this pageant, it wouldn't just be for me. This time around, it wasn't just about feeling beautiful, but also about teamwork.

I had been in that campus for almost four years by then and had nothing but a beautiful time coming out of my own shell. I realised that in the years that I'd embraced college life and 'owned the school', I had inadvertently felt beautiful from the inside. Beauty in the presence of my friends, beauty in the form of my writing, beauty in the sounds of laughter and bantering around me, beauty in the way that I felt each and every day, when I stepped inside the campus.

There were five divisions in the campus, and each division had two candidates for the Miss Sportspower. My co-candidate from the accountancy division was a petite, fiery and exotic freshman, named Alma. She oozed with youthful self-esteem and big, bold, beautiful smile. I imagined that it would be a grand slam if Alma and I would win the first two titles, the Miss Sportspower, and the first runner-up, which will then bring our division to become the overall champion.

Now the question was, how do I win a legitimate beauty contest? One that was not rigged, and against nine beautiful, and crown-worthy girls? I asked myself.

During the rehearsals, I observed my fellow candidates closely, and paid attention to their feelings and thoughts. I also spoke in depth with the emcee, choreographer and event committees. By understanding their way of thinking, I gained an insight of what opportunities and threats we were all working with. *"This is an experience and a lesson in integrity and self-belief."* The words that my brother said to me five years ago came reverberating back in my head, and I made a vow to myself that never again will I be a puppet in anyone's show. This one, will be *our* show, all ten of us in the pageant, fair and square.

On the night of the pageant, we were backstage two hours before the show, and the waiting was a fidgety, boring ordeal. We didn't have smartphones then, so I could not simply kill time by posting selfies and *#waitingtostrutmystuff* on Instagram.

I had a moment of envy when I saw that all the other candidates had their mother, father, siblings, fish and stuffed toy, there with them for support. I had no family with me. My mother had no interest in attending the event, and there was no sponsorship to be had. While my friends had chosen to support me by getting themselves the best seats in the house and lead the cheering squad for me. Backstage, I had one support person, a student named Sherrie, whose duty was to see that I was okay. She fed me a small bottle of Lipovitan for dinner, the Asian equivalent of Red Bull, which I slurped gratefully with gusto, as I hadn't eaten since seven o'clock that morning.

Finally, the show began, and as we all came out for an opening dance number to Kylie Minogue's 'I should be so lucky', I saw thousands of students sitting by the bleachers go wildly excited, cheering, whistling and rooting for their favourites. The music and the noise were overwhelming and welcoming at the same time. We were on a triangular stage with a ten-metre, inverted V runway, at an elevation of two and a half meters off the ground. The backdrop moved and changed as we transitioned into different outfits throughout the night, wearing the same cut, colour and shape for everything, except our evening gowns, which we were allowed to pick and choose, as we wished.

My strategy was to stand out as THE one out of ten. Easy said, impossible to do. But I intentionally did subtle tricks that perhaps made me just a little bit more memorable than the others. I was candidate number six, and every single time candidate number five disappeared from the stage after strutting her stuff, I would count a painfully slow one, two, three, four and five… which gave the judges enough time to finish scoring and thinking about candidate number five, take a breath, then a little moment to wait just long enough for them to wonder "Who's next?" *Anticipation.*

By the time I came out to the stage, I had their full attention. As I stood by the stand-up microphone to introduce myself, I counted another painfully slow one, two, three and four… to give the audience time to finish hollering and clapping, as they all held their breath wondering if I had forgotten my words. And then I declared a short, punchy intro line, delivered in a tone full of conviction. *"My name is Grace. Representing the Accountancy Division."* With that, the audience erupted in a frenzied state and the impact was three times more powerful than the intros delivered before me, causing the judges' hearts to beat a little faster and their adrenalines rise a little higher. *Strategy.*

Stage presence was also very important. I realised that I needed to move fluidly, and yet have the grace to look around like I was eyeballing the audience, even if I couldn't see a thing with the glaring lights. What I could easily see from the stage though were the judges, smack bang in the front and centre, looking at me. So I looked at them back, one by one, in counts of approximately one and a half seconds each. Long enough to make them think I was having a silent conversation with them, but short enough to snap them right back into reality. *Seduction.*

Closer to the end of the show, they announced the top three in no particular order, and when they called both my name and Alma's, my heart beat faster, because the possibility of us taking the top two winning spots was high.

And then when they rolled the drums for the second runner-up, I held Alma's hand and prepared for the possibility that one of us could be leaving the stage, but then… the second runner-up went to a girl from the Nursing division… and then there were two. Alma and me. That's when I knew we won. I was filled with great joy knowing that we both delivered. At that point, it didn't matter to me who would take the crown. What mattered was we have made our division the proud, overall champion for that year's Intramurals.

The emcee's voice came on the PA system to announce the first runner-up, explaining that the last person standing was the winner of Miss Sportspower 1994. As they called the first runner up, Alma released my hand and stepped away, leaving me on the stage as the crown winner. And then I was alone, staring at the wild crowd. People whistling, hollering, clapping, and there was someone with an aluminium basin, banging on it in a fast, tribal rhythm. As I stood there, people came to the stage and began putting stuff on me, crown, sash, sceptre, flowers. My eyes adjusted to the darkness and I could see real people in the crowd. Shapes of boys, girls, different coloured shirts, some dancing and gyrating here and there, an atmosphere of high energy and vivacity. And then I thought, *"So. This, is what it's like to be crowned as a beauty queen"*

The truth was, everyone in that group of ten girls deserved to win, simply because each of us embodied the spirit of participation, cooperation, and value giving, for the benefit of a greater good.

The distinction that I had was that I empathized with the lens from which the judges were looking. I imagined the pressure that they were under, looking, admiring, scoring, and making notes in a flurry of ten beautiful contestants, while surrounded by thousands of people making thunderous noise, in a colourful show with a moving backdrop. The judges, who were teachers, professionals and business owners from different industries in the city, would have had their senses overloaded, and I simply made it easier for them to see me. And that's how I won their highest votes.

It took an hour for the pictorials to finish, then afterwards my friends took me home. Before calling it a day, I wiped my makeup off using some expensive, divine smelling, Clinique make up remover pads that my aunt Ellie left behind on her last visit. It worked wonders, so that the following morning, there was absolutely no trace of the pageant on my face, and that was how I wanted it to be. Like a mirage, a very special experience that I know I will no longer pursue.

When I woke up, I spent a moment cradling my crown in my lap and traced my fingers through its intricacies. And then I knew, that no amount of beauty contests, win or lose, will ever be able to give me what I truly longed for – *love*. Whatever love was.

Chapter 18
Who invented the treadmill

I never once asked my mother for anything. She was the steward of my academic scholarship from my aunt Ellie, but she also made it clear that there was nothing that she could do for me beyond that. In order to support myself, and by the time I stepped into my senior year in college, I've already held four different jobs and been fired from one.

My first job was in the summer of 1992, as a typist at General Santos Doctors Hospital. I sat in a cubicle and fed the typewriter with small, tri carbonated pieces of paper, and typed the words *macroset* or *vasocan* next to a patient's name, for a total of one hundred and twenty hours, and got paid six hundred and forty-two pesos for it.

The second job was a one-off contract as a field researcher for a juice company, where I randomly interviewed grocery shoppers at various grocery stores, about their juice and beverage preferences. I was paid five pesos per interview, and there was this one time when I interviewed ten people within a short span of sixty minutes, earning an easy fifty pesos. It was a neat gig.

My third job was for Phela Grande Hotel. Someone from my school recommended me as an ad copy writer for their new campaign, and I wrote a couple of brief pieces in their brochure for two-hundred and fifty pesos.

On my final year in college, the country's biggest fast food chain, Jollibee, was set to launch its first store in Gensan. One of my big brother's former classmate, Jenny was the marketing manager, and she needed to create a team of mascots and Smart Officers. When Jenny heard that I was applying for a job with Jollibee, she nabbed me to become one of her Smart Officers, which was a more sought-after role than being a crew.

As a Smart Officer, I wore a dress uniform instead of a crew uniform, and I got to meet and hobnob with politicians and celebrities like Congressman Antonino, Mayor Nunez, Rica Peralejo and Jeffrey Santos, on special events. It was an especially hyped period of time and through this unspoken sense of being separate, and seemingly above the operations crew, I subconsciously began acting like I was separate, and above the operations crew. An attitude of arrogance that I shared with one other Smart Officer, Jim. Soon enough everything Jim and I did during our shifts were quietly scrutinized by other crew members.

One day Jim and I decided to take our break together. As staff, we were entitled to a small meal for free during our break. Jim offered to assemble, and also upsize, my meal for me. "Are we allowed to do that?" I asked. He shrugged his shoulders and said, "Why not." I felt a momentary inner battle and thought. *"That can't be right, we can't just upsize our meal simply because we want to."* But my ignorance and poor judgement prevailed, and I shrugged my shoulders back at him and said, "Okay, why not then." Somehow, I knew I was doing something wrong, but a part of me thought that maybe I can get away with it.

Two days later, my boss and friend, Jenny came by my grandmother's house, unannounced. We talked for a long time as she gently broke the news that Jim and I had been let go. She shared that through all the negative feedback, plus the meal upsizing incident, she had grounds to let me go, even though she didn't want to. I cried in front of her in silent sobs, feeling sorry for myself, yet feeling safe to break down in her presence.

I would never have bothered to tell anyone that I got fired, but when Jenny left, my mother was curious to see what the visit was for, and why I was crying. I told her that I had been fired from my job, to which she responded with a nonchalant, *"Oh."* End of discussion.

My biggest saving grace all throughout college life, was becoming proactive and keeping myself busy. Between my academics, extracurricular activities, and trying to hold down a job, I found almost no time to pay attention to the voices in my head.

But when all was said and done in my four years of blissful college life, I graduated in an anticlimactic fashion. There were no celebrations or fuss made over by anyone for my benefit, only a gaping, unspoken question of "What now?" Having just completed a degree that I didn't know what to do with, I felt like my life was flatlining to a nomadic plight.

Being a broke graduate with an undefined future, I was totally open to any and all possibilities, no-holds-barred. The kind of open faith that I've always carried in my heart since I was a child. With this ingrained self-belief, a divine coincidence fell through my lap, two weeks after my college graduation.

I was standing outside the gate of my alma mater, having just collected my transcript of records and other credentials, when one of my former professors approached me. *"We've had an unexpectedly high influx of brand-new enrolees, and we are short for teachers. Would you be available to teach English to some freshman students this coming semester?"* I silently squealed, *"Well, I have absolutely no formal qualifications to teach, but hell yeah I'll give it my best shot!"* Aloud I said, *"Yes ma'am, I can do that."*

And so it became that my first professional job was teaching. I taught five days a week from eight o'clock to twelve noon, and during the evenings, I attended Law school, studying Family Law, Criminal Law, Political Law and Shariah (Islamic) Law.

Although teaching was fun, my biggest technical concern was how to grade my students. I did not have a clue on how to make a lesson plan, let alone a grading system. I once overheard my mother say that my job was shady and *colorum* by nature. I was twenty years old and almost completely numb to her consistent insinuations and snide comments. Almost.

I held three different classes and my students ranged from nerds to rebels. I taught them the quickest way that I learned to appreciate the English language – through *thinking and writing* in English. I equipped them with the four basic sentence patterns, sent them to the library for book review assignments, and had each of them stand up in front of the class, to verbally share their written book reviews.

By teaching and then assessing their English communication skills, through the combination of reading, writing and speaking the language, I gained the self-confidence to grade them, because I saw their progress over time. By the end of the semester, almost every one of my students passed, and only three failed.

Part of me felt like I was in no position to fail anyone's grades, but the truth was, those who failed did so not because of their lack of knowledge. They failed because they didn't show up, when required to show up. Due to the evidence-based grading system, I could not justify someone's ability without their tangible efforts, no matter how much I believed in them.

Such was the irony of my life as an academic teacher. I was constantly needing concrete evidence that my students were learning; and as a result of such need, I was perpetually sacrificing the very essence of my students' purpose of learning, the purpose of unmeasurable evolution.

My brain was a little rattled at law school. For the most part we had to read hundreds of pages of case studies on our own time, and be prepared to discuss any random case, at the whim of our professors. My classmates were a mix of doctors, teachers, businessmen, and housewives, and most nights after class, we would go somewhere to eat, drink and make fun of our self-important professors behind their backs. None of us had enough balls to challenge their intimidation and cross-examination type tactics during class. These lawyer-professors were some of the best attorneys in the city, and we were deeply privileged to be their students, but also secretly infuriated by them treating us like criminals in a real trial. Law school was full of egomaniacs. Both professors and students alike, and yours truly was no exception.

While teaching and attending law school seemed like a productive way of spending my life, my deepest longing was to get out of the city and live in Manila, away from everything and everyone. I have never been to Manila before, but I imagined that I could get blissfully lost in its chaos, and begin to search for who I truly am.

Chapter 19
Goodbye, mother

During my time teaching English, I serendipitously met a boy named Leon through a mutual friend, Mary. Mary lived half the time in Manila as a student of University of Santo Tomas, and half the time in Gensan, when she came back to spend her semestral breaks with her family. She connected Leon and I through a pen pal style of introduction, which paved the way to long letters, that turned into long distance telephone calls, that turned into a strong, mutual infatuation.

Over the years, a few boys have asked to date me, but I'd never been interested, until I got to know Leon. He was a medical student, the eldest of six, and his Dad was an international banker, his mum a government executive, and two of his sisters were in a music band. His world seemed so much bigger, brighter and more exciting, plus he liked me. The only downside was, he lived a thousand kilometres away from me, and we have never actually seen each other in person.

So I focused on a specific hope, which was to travel to Manila and meet Leon. At the time I didn't know what else to do but pray. Every day after teaching my students, I would go to the main church and light up a wishing candle, and then pray for twenty minutes.

Although I didn't believe that wishes were fulfilled simply by praying, it was such a strong desire that I couldn't keep it all to myself. So I prayed my wishes out of my heart, because it made me feel better when I have told "someone" about it. I prayed the same prayer and wished the same one wish, every day in silence, for five days a week, and three consecutive months. I prayed for some way that I would end up living in Manila and be with Leon.

When my teaching contract was about to finish and law school was due for a semestral break, I had a phone call from my friend and ex Jollibee boss Jenny. She wanted to tell me that Jollibee was opening a second store in the next twelve months, and they were interviewing for store manager positions. Further, she mentioned that the successful applicants would be sent to Manila for six months of comprehensive training on a full salary. She said that she had highly recommended me and wanted to ask if I would be interested to take the aptitude tests and be interviewed for the position.

I thought about the time not so long ago when she fired me from my job. The pregnant pause on the phone explained my silent question, and Jenny said that what happened when I got fired was not entirely my fault, and she urged me to forget about it. After briefly considering what she said, I knew I had nothing to lose so I eagerly and gratefully submitted my resume. The next day, I went through a series of written tests and face to face interviews, and within thirty-six hours, I was hired.

I couldn't believe the timing, and my luck. My teaching job was just wrapping up, law school was on a semestral break, and I was about to train as a manager for six months, in the city of my dreams, on full salary. I was torn between excitement and suspicion. Excited for a great adventure ahead, and suspicious that it all seemed too good to be true. It was all I could do not to sabotage my good fortune, and I went and prayed at the church even more intensely, thanking God for granting me a miracle.

Manila was everything I imagined it was going to be, and more. Extremely crowded, polluted, busy, noisy, vibrant, aggressive, dirty, modern, sophisticated, electric, eclectic and nauseating. I became lost in its crescendo and for the first time in my life, there was only me and the shadow that lurked in the darkness of my soul, Pandora. She and I, on our own in the big city.

My body shrunk to a small forty-two kgs in the six months that I was in Manila. Working shift hours was exhausting and getting to know Leon consumed what was left of my personal time. I lived with him and his siblings, at their condo unit in Santa Mesa. At this time both their parents lived in Hong Kong, while Leon and his siblings ran their own household, helping and raising one another.

Leon's family was an upper-working class sort. They went to the biggest universities and they had a five-bedroom family home outside of the city. His parents were highly educated, kind, and understandably very protective of the well-being of their children. It was a wonder that they allowed someone like me to live with their kids in their own house.

Suffice to say that Leon and I have taken our friendship to the next level. I developed a friendship with most of Leon's siblings, while those who weren't so friendly were also respectful and cordial towards me.

Six months passed with lightning speed and then I was unceremoniously pulled out from training, and then sent back to General Santos.

As soon as I was back at my grandmother's house, my mother didn't waste time in telling me to remit a certain portion of my salary to her, every pay day. I felt obliged, and yet I hated it. In fact, I was repulsed by my obligation. It quickly dawned on me that the reason why children would be happily obliged to help their parents would be because their parents loved, nurtured, and made sacrifices for them. Based on that, I had no obligation to anyone, hence I hated being made to feel obliged.

Although I could feel a slow uprising from my gut against my mother's sustained attempts to oppress and abuse me, I tried to keep cool and simply gave her what she wanted. I paid her money because I was obliged. And as I did, my self-loathing bubbled to the surface of my throat, disabling my ability to express my true emotions. *"I hate this place."* Pandora's voice reverberated through my spine.

After two months of being back in Gensan, Leon flew over from Manila to be with me, while he was on semestral break from medical school. In that period of time my aunt Ellie had built a property on the outskirts of Gensan. And in what could only be divine timing, she happened to be in town and offered for Leon to stay at her place, which would be clean, comfortable, and away from the chaos at my grandmother's house. I was grateful for her hospitality and decided to join Leon at her place.

My aunt had built three townhouses in a two thousand square metre lot. She lived in the first townhouse and reserved the second for her guests, where Leon and I slept. Word got out fast and the very next day, an army of relatives came by my aunt's house, including my mother and my uncles, to check out this "boyfriend from Manila".

Within the first hour of the relatives arriving, my mother cornered me to herself, and ordered me to follow her into the second townhouse, where Leon and I had spent his very first night in town. Once in, my mother told me to sit, and then she closed the front door so that nobody could walk in. She said that she knew I slept with my boyfriend in the same bed last night, and I responded with a perplexed, "Yes." With that confirmation, she verbally lunged at me without preamble.

"How could you be so low? You are a slut and you shame me in front of your uncles. What are they going to say? Nakaka-lalaki ka! (You make a man want to hit you!) What is going on in your brain? You didn't even have the decency to hide anything! You think you can just flaunt your loose shenanigans around here! You have no shame! What face have you got to show to people now? Who do you think you are? You were a nobody, and now you're a slut!"

Her venom was palpable and paralysing. I couldn't move or breathe. I felt tears on my face, but it was my heart that had completely and utterly broken in big, solid, hard pieces. Like a blackened, toasted volcano stumped over by a galactical, ferocious giant.

Having seen and gone through a fair bit of emotional violence, I was no delicate princess at the age of twenty, and my heart was relatively hardened and shut down; but this final massacre was something else. It was like my mother had bottled up years of hatred inside of her that she couldn't wait to unleash. And now that she found her chance, which happened to be me being a so called "slut", she had finally released and allowed her monster to take over.

It felt like it went on for hours, but maybe it was only a few minutes, I was too shocked to notice the time. There was a moment when I looked at the open back door and my cousin Mark's girlfriend, Myra, was standing there witnessing everything in silence. Myra and I had grown close over time, and we always tried to help each other. She had the look of an aggravated cat on her eyes, who wanted to barge in and rescue me, so I looked back at her in the midst of my tears and shook my head. I didn't want this drama to be bigger than it was, and better that I only cop the beating and no one else. This too, will pass. Myra understood and walked away.

The saddest thing about this final storm was that my mother thought she knew me well enough to judge and slander me. The truth was I remained a virgin until I met the person that was to become my husband, years later. Leon was too scared of his parents' punishment if he did anything that could jeopardize his future ambition to become a neurosurgeon. As for me, I imagined sex as an experience to be enjoyed with a real man, not a young boy like Leon still was. So we just slept together because we enjoyed each other's company so much, but we also remained virgins together. I just never thought it would cause so much trouble.

Night fell and the relatives went home. I went up to my aunt's bedroom for some words of comfort. I found her with Myra who was talking about what she saw between me and my mother earlier that day. My aunt was livid, then she turned to me and said *"Is this true? Did your mother do this to you today?"* I nodded slowly and silently. I wished there was something more I could say, but once again I was rendered speechless by my mother's emotional violence. My aunt's heart went out to me and then she threw me a lifeline and said that should I ever want to move in with her, she would be more than happy to have me, if that would make my life easier.

That night I cried and then I prayed, grateful that from that day forward, I will never have to live with my mother, ever again.

The next day, I took a taxi and stopped by my grandmother's house to collect everything that I owned and leave the house of hell that I grew up in, once and for all. My mother was there with a look of regret on her face. She asked where I was going, and as I watched the wounded expression on her face, I wanted to feel sorry for what was happening.

I waited for the slightest urge to want to make it better with her, but much as I tried, I had none. I didn't feel sorry for what was happening, and I could not feel the slightest tug that I hoped would pull me toward her, mentally, emotionally, or physically. I simply continued to throw things into baskets and bags and said nothing to her. I said goodbye to my grandmother who did her best in spite of it all; and then just like that, I pivoted and walked out of the house that encapsulated my soul for fifteen years.

It should have been a liberating moment, but the truth was I've been suspended in limbo during the entire time that I was physically forced to live there. And now that I was walking away from it, I had a strange feeling that I was more haunted, rather than liberated.

Chapter 20
Sovereign beings above the mud

The most important thing I've learnt from Jollibee was the emphasis on creating a fun atmosphere, inside of a high performing team. I've learnt that the success of an organization lies not only on their external customers, but more so on their internal customers.

However, working shift hours led to a sedentary lifestyle that took its toll on my health, and after two years I called it a day and resigned. At the same time, my aunt Ellie went back to Europe and handed over the affairs of her property to me. Whilst I intended to use that time to rest and revive my health for a few months, I ended up watching too much TV, sleeping in till noon every day, and obsessing over Ronan Keating. I packed the weight on my tiny frame, and although I was very grateful for the space that my aunt gave me to rest, without having to worry about a thing, I was literally sleeping my life away and became way too comfortable, for my own health. I was alive but I was living a dead life at the same time.

I hated the feeling of being wasted, so I decided to go back and brave the concrete jungle of Manila and find my future there. I loved being back in the big city because it was a great distraction for a fragmented mind like mine. The traffic, the pollution, the million throng of people everywhere, the fight to get a jeepney or bus ride, the paranoia of getting pickpocketed, the city lights, the billboards, the promise of corporate bliss, the singsong sound of Tagalog language, the famous landmarks of Intramuros, Cultural Centre of the Philippines, Makati, Greenhills, Tagaytay; I loved it all.

Manila was a place to drown Pandora. Her voice was quiet amidst the chaos of looking for a future. It was like her and I were staring at a blank canvass together, pondering what colours, lines and shapes were going to shape a new life for both of us. And the best thing was we had absolutely nothing to prove, much less defend, to anything or anyone. Anonymity, was a powerful relief.

I found a room for rent along C. Arellano, a few streets from Leon's house in Santa Mesa, for three thousand pesos a month. A mighty steep cost of living compared to what you could get in Gensan at the time, where the going rate was one thousand five hundred pesos a month for a three-bedroom house with a fully fenced backyard.

The room was one of four rental rooms built at the back of some wealthy family's home. There were six other tenants; one room had a brother and sister who attended university together, another was a pair of temperamental teenage couple who constantly fought; and the last was a pregnant couple, the girl was around nineteen years old and the boy was a little older and worked every day to support his young wife. Rumour has it that the young wife ran away from her wealthy family to hide her pregnancy, afraid of the punishment that would befall her. We all used a common sink, toilet, dining, and a yard where we did our laundry.

The toilet triggered my old toilet phobia. It had a dilapidated door that you had to push hard to shut and yank vigorously to open. Inside the toilet was a rusty, life size mirror, and a broken water tap that dripped 24/7, making the toilet floor half flooded all of the time. The toilet itself was an imposing, old marble piece that looked like a shallow soup bowl with its standing water almost always up to its inner brim.

My room was three metres wide and six metres long. On two sides, the walls went from floor to ceiling while the other two sides were a makeshift plywood partition that left half a metre of opening at the top. For two months I was intermittently scared of either getting robbed or getting raped at any given night.

As soon as the young teenage couple moved out, I immediately moved into their room, which was slightly bigger at six and a half by three metres. It was more secure with all around floor to ceiling walls, a window with security steel bars, plus it was the closest room to the sink and washing area. I was thrilled.

I lost weight from the stress of adjusting to my new environment and gained muscles from lugging big pails of water from the outdoor tap for my bathing and clothes washing. I didn't eat much not because I was too poor, but because I didn't have cooking pots, cooking skills, or cooking desires. Domestic bliss was something that I wouldn't appreciate for a long time yet. I often bought *pan de sal* from the corner bakery and have it with a cup of instant coffee. I owned a tiny kettle which I also used to boil water for my usual dinner of two-minute noodles. For lunch, I would stop by wherever I happen to be, either at a fast food store or a *karenderya* (street eatery) and order the cheapest food going. Every now and then, I would go to Red Ribbon bakery at SM Centrepoint mall and treat myself with *Palabok*, iced tea and blueberry cheesecake. This meal would cost me forty-three pesos, while a cheap meal from a karenderya, of rice and *chicken adobo* would be no more than eighteen pesos.

At one stage my big brother flew over with his girlfriend Bella to attend a wedding in Paranaque, Metro Manila. Whilst in town, they came to see my living quarters, and when my brother laid eyes on my miniscule, sparse room, I saw the broken look on his face that he tried to hide. Worried about my safety and how faraway I was from Gensan all on my own, he disguised his brotherly concern by saying that our mother did not understand why I had to live this way. Technically it meant that my mother was curious, nothing more, nothing less. And if I have learned anything over the years, it was to be wary of my mother's interest, including her curiosity. I wasn't interested in any dramatic conversations involving our mother, so I deliberately ignored Larry's comment. It would take another twenty years before my big brother and I would openly discuss what happened during our childhood.

Armed with an average looking resume and copious amounts of courage, I scoured the classified ads religiously and went out dressed to impress every day, looking for a job. I once attended a job interview for a pharmaceutical company where there were four hundred and thirty-four applicants vying for five medical representative positions. This high level of uncertainty didn't really faze me, instead it made me try harder. I literally had no time to be discouraged as I was always exhausted every night after getting home from scouring this dog eat dog city. Yet at the back of my mind I knew that something will come along, as long as I didn't stop looking. The childlike, ever present sense of hope that I've always had since I was a kid, was proving to be a handy amulet.

The first job I landed on was for Ubix Corporation based in Makati, the direct competitor of Xerox. Before the internet came along, a document copier, sorter and printer all in one was an indispensable equipment for any business, and my job was to 'service' these equipment in person, not as a technician, but as a *customer service representative*, the cute code for upselling.

I was assigned around the areas of Malate, Quiapo, Binondo, and Roxas Boulevard, and travelled from business to business by trains, jeepneys and buses. I lasted about eight and a half weeks in the job before the extreme pollution had eroded my unacclimatised respiratory tract system, and then I got very sick. I ended up bedridden in my boyfriend Leon's bedroom for two weeks, until I was strong enough to walk a few blocks back to my own space.

A friend of mine who worked for the Video City chain of stores (the equivalent of Blockbuster Videos) knew that I was out of job and referred me to their hiring team. Video City was owned by the biggest film company in the Philippines, so I was curious to see if I could land an interview at their head office in E. Rodriguez Avenue, and get to see some celebrities. I thought of it as another unique adventure and sure enough, I saw the famous bad boy Robin Padilla on the day of my interview. He had legs that went forever. He wore tight jeans, long sleeved starched shirt, and shiny, pointy shoes. He walked with a confident but nonchalant swagger that oozed charisma from a million miles away. He wasn't typically my kind of celebrity idol, but boy was he so charming and generous with his attention. He waved hello and smiled to everyone in the office, exuding a *makalaglag panty* (knickers kicker) sex appeal.

This pre-interview perve experience put me in a happy state so that I was beside myself and landed a store management trainee job. The only thing that I remembered from the interview, was being asked if I would like to work at their biggest store, the Mega Mall outlet. The question brought me back to reality and in my mind, I squealed, *"Hell yeah Mega mall!"* Aloud I said, *"Yes sir, that would be fine."*

Life had a way of synchronizing itself. In the summer of 1999, my cousin Sherrie who lived five hundred miles away, came to Manila to visit some of her friends. We met up one day, and she mentioned that she knew someone who had a spare bedroom for rent, in a condo in Cubao. It was a fancy place, but the price of the rent was the same as what I've been paying for my tiny room. After accepting the new job and completely recovering from being ill, the thought of a nice, new place to live was like icing to the cupcake.

Martin, my new, landlord-to-be, was a Filipino American businessman who had decided to come back and live in the Philippines for good. And knowing my cousin Sherrie, she always had a good taste for people. Hence, I had no qualms about moving in with Martin and out of the dreary place that I'd been living in.

Martin and I got along very well. We lived on the second floor and my room had a window overlooking an urban river. In the living room, there was a fish tank, a bookshelf, a big, sand coloured couch, a large, glass coffee table, and a beige, floor lamp. The place was like heaven to me. Modern, clean, comfortable, and very private.

Martin only dated good looking men and micro celebrities, and when he entertained, I respectfully gave him the space to do so and kept to myself. When he wasn't entertaining, we would stay up till late at night just talking about life in general, often injecting silly imagination and humour into our ideas. As a businessman, Martin took his affairs seriously, but as a person he loved to have fun.

One day, my boyfriend Leon and I were driving back to the city after a day out of town, in his parents' brand-new Toyota Corolla. He was running late for his shift as an intern in the university hospital, so instead of dropping me off at my place first, I dropped him off to the hospital. He then asked if I could take his parents' car back to my place and then he would just collect it from me the next day, when his shift was over. I had driven his parents' car once before, but it was during the middle of the night in downtown Makati, where there had been no traffic. Unlike this time, the university hospital was in the heart of an urban chaos. I felt rather tired and wasn't sure that it was such a good idea, but I was also too tired to make a better judgement.

Leon pulled over by the side of the road in front of the hospital. A few yards behind us were the traffic lights on the intersection of Dapitan St. and Lacson Avenue. Leon jumped out and I slid over to the driver's seat. It was just after six o'clock in the evening and the glare of streetlights and high beams were shining at me from every direction. I veered away from the shoulder of the road to start driving forward, when suddenly the entire world seemed to have been covered with darkness, and I heard the loudest sounds of crushing steel and tyres, skidding and braking violently on the concrete. I was aghast as I watched the wall of a giant truck pass me by on a slow motion, like an eel next to a little goldfish. The truck kept moving as it dragged pieces of metal off of Leon's parents' car, and then it stopped in the middle of the road, causing severe traffic jam.

I sat in silence, frozen. The truck driver came over to me and yelled, *"What were you thinking? I could've got you killed, girl! Look at this mess? Who's going to pay for my truck?!"* I was in shock, and all I could do was lift my butt a little from the driver's seat and peep to the side to see what happened. The entire front of the car was completely detached and strewn around some ten metres away on the road. The bumper, fender, grilles and headlights were completely gone, and the driver's side had one massive dent. It was my fault for not looking. I had been sideswiped by a sixteen-wheeler truck. The driver was right, he could've killed me. I apologised to him and asked if he could forgive me for not looking. He glanced at me through the darkness of the evening sky and sensed how grief stricken I was. With compassion, he told me to figure out what to do, and then he sat on the sidewalk and lit a cigarette.

When I finally mustered the courage to get on my feet, I ran inside the hospital to find Leon, I wanted to tell him that I was almost killed in a car accident, but that I was okay. As soon as he saw my face, he knew something had happened, and the first thing he said to me was, *"Ang kotse, anong nangyari?!"* (What happened to the car?!) I was stunned by his reaction, and even more precisely, I was stunned by his lack of empathy. But in fairness to the medical student that he was, he could see that I was okay because I was standing, walking and breathing, hence why he didn't feel the need to ask if I was okay or not. It was a logical thing. But the thing was there was nothing logical about a car accident. I was shaking, scared and alone. Leon proceeded to call his parents to report what happened, while I tried to think of one person who may want to know if I was okay or not.

Martin didn't ask many questions. He simply showed up with his driver twenty minutes after I called him, to see that I was okay. He kept me company at the police station where we met with the truck driver and Leon's parents, who were surprisingly cool, calm and collected. They acknowledged me, and they were neither friendly nor unfriendly, which I was very grateful for. The one thing I neglected to do though, was apologize to them. That was the least I could've done after what happened to their brand-new car, but I was too hung up on their son's lack of empathy; and now I wish that I hadn't forgotten to apologize.

On the way home, Martin and I didn't talk much about the accident, but he made a joke about how close I was to getting injured and then hospitalized, which he said, would've been easy because I was literally right next to the hospital. Funny but not so funny, his way of saying that everything was going to be fine.

Leon's internship was about to conclude, and his entire family was excited for him to progress to medical residency. I have seen how hard he worked and studied to become a great doctor. But after the car accident, I finally realized that his priority was always going to be medicine, and then I would come second, if we ever got married. And while we weren't married, I would never come before his family, because he was still under the financial support of his parents.

As a fully independent, working class girl, I could not wait six more years for him to complete his medical residency before becoming a full pledged medical practitioner, while I lived my life on the sideline, waiting to possibly become a doctor's wife. So I waited for a couple of months to see him finish his internship. His parents threw a dinner celebration for his graduation at *Kalde-Kaldero*, with thirty friends and family members. I knew that it was going to be the last time that I would join them. I felt sad but I was sure of my decision. A couple of days later, I broke it off with Leon, and even though it hurt to hurt him, it was the right thing for both of us.

Leon would eventually marry a woman who complemented and amplified his medical vocation and mothered their beautiful children.

Chapter 21
Impostor breeding transitions

My all-time favourite cousin Skye, who lived and worked in Macau, China, as lead singer for a band, came and stayed with me while she renewed her overseas working visa. She had been singing since we were thirteen and always loved to party. One Saturday night, we went nightclubbing and stumbled into a bar called Verve Room in the Malate area.

The music in Verve Room was so loud that you had to shout into someone's ear to have a conversation. There was a sea of people standing shoulder to shoulder, hip to hip and I had to jostle and push my way into a stool just to get a little space for myself, while Skye was having a great time dancing.

From my precious stool by the bar, I noticed a young man from the corner of my eye pushing his way towards my direction and beaming as if we knew each other. Within a flash he was by my side and introduced himself as Myrick. We started chatting and the night sped by into early morning. At first, I wondered why he was talking to me, but then after buying me a couple of drinks, I figured that he was trying to pick me up and *take me home*. I was silently suspicious why, out of hundreds of sexy and fully made up girls in that bar, young

Myrick was eyeing me to be his conquest for the night. I was hardly dressed up in a pair of faded jeans, a black, crew shirt, and my trusty, office boots. If anything, I looked like the *nerd in the verve.*

He was four years younger than me, unwaveringly enthusiastic and trying hard to be smooth. Nevertheless, I was flattered by his attention. At four o'clock in the morning, my cousin finally got tired and wanted to call it a night. It was raining when we got out of the bar and Myrick put his sports jacket on me and suggested that we share a taxi. Sharing didn't make sense because we lived in totally opposite ends of the city, but he was adamant that he wanted to make sure we got home safely. Skye sat next to the taxi driver while Myrick and I held hands at the backseat. The emotional attention that he had paid me in the last few hours were more than I ever had from my ex-boyfriend at any one given time, and I was starting to feel a little special in myself.

By the time we reached home, he had managed to get my number and insisted that I keep his jacket on to keep me dry during my two-minute trek from the taxi to my doorstep. Just before going to bed, I put his rain jacket on the back of a chair and went to sleep tickled pink by the night's shenanigan.

He was a street-smart boy whose family lived in Tondo, a well-known area in Manila for its resident gangsters and hoodlums. There was this one time when Myrick asked me if I would like to learn how to shoot a gun.

I asked, *"What kind of gun?"*

He said *"We can go to a shooting range in Tondo and do two magazines of 9mm, that should get you going. I will also show you how to disassemble and reassemble the gun."*

So we went on a gun shooting date together. In a period of ninety minutes I aimed and shot at a dummy with a 9mm pistol and learned to dismantle and reload a magazine. I had to pay for the hire of two guns, the use of the shooting range and two magazines of 9mm bullets. I could tell from the look on Myrick's eyes that he loved what we were doing. For me it was simply like learning an essential skill, I felt neither excited nor bored.

Afterwards we proceeded to the movies to watch "Eyes Wide Shut" with Nicole Kidman and Tom Cruise and then to Kenny Rogers restaurant for dinner. The entire day cost me thousands of pesos, equivalent to someone else's monthly salary. Myrick never once offered to pay. At the back of my mind it was a huge turnoff.

But while I felt like I was being used by Myrick, I found that I did not know what to do with it. Being emotionally manipulated was my norm when I was a child, and it was then when I've lost the ability to assert myself.

But this time I was no longer a child, and I was a thousand miles away from the people who used to control and abuse me. Left to my own devices, I discovered that I didn't know how to express my feelings of disappointment, without turning it into an out of control rage. I felt that if I said something to Myrick about sharing the bill on our dates, he would abandon me and not want to go out with me anymore. Besides, I told myself that I should be more responsible because I was older than him and I was the one with a job. Myrick was just a poor, out of school youth who was trying hard to save money so he could go back to study

Criminology in Uni and become a police officer, just like one of his uncles. Or at least that's what he told me.

The curious thing was, if Myrick was really trying to save money so he could go back to Uni, why wasn't he working in any jobs? It slowly occurred to me that he was literally a handsome bum scouring the clubs at night, looking for a working class, vulnerable and lonely girl just like me. Nowadays they call those types of people, a gold digger.

The straw that broke the camel's back was when one day, I scrolled through my phone and saw a number that I didn't recognize. According to my Nokia, I had called it two days ago. I dialled to see who would pick it up, and it was a young girl, around seventeen or so. She said she was Myrick's girlfriend and that she's had a couple of conversations with Myrick on my number. Albeit I was a little heartbroken, I was not at all surprised. Somehow, I've always known that Myrick was just a diversion, although I never expected for such diversion to cost me a precious few thousand pesos.

When I thought I was going to have fun and play around; I, was played around. It was an ironic lesson that I knew I could not afford to dishonour. So I bade Myrick farewell in a friendly tone and sent him away with good vibes. After all, we had a great time even though I was broke.

Speaking of broke, I started looking for a better job than the one I had at Video City. Although it was a lot of fun having free access to movie premiers, it did not pay nor challenge me enough.

As if I'd plugged into The Universe's direct frequency, one of my former colleagues from Ubix Corporation, walked into my Video

City outlet on a Friday afternoon. Jennifer was my trainer back at Ubix and together we have shared a few bus rides, lunch hours, and one very long dinner conversation, talking exclusively about the issues of her romantic life.

We were stoked to run into each other, and she shared that she now worked with a New Zealand-based company called Berkeley International. As a sales consultant, Jennifer earned dazzling sales commissions, and then she encouraged me to join her at Berkeley.

Without a second thought, I went to an interview with two hundred other people vying for twenty-five sales consultant positions. I made it clear on my resume that I was referred by Jen. During my interview, Stephen, the Filipino-Chinese boss, wrote the words "SOFT" in big, capital letters across the top of my resume. He would later admit that his impression of me was too soft spoken and with not enough self-confidence.

I felt so dismayed, but just when he was about to dismiss me, he took one last look at my resume, and then my friend Jennifer's name, caught his attention. He asked how I knew Jen, so I said that we used to work together. He then crossed out the words "SOFT" and asked me to come back the next day for the second round of interviews. It was the first time that the direction of my life was largely influenced not by what I knew, but by who I knew, which felt surprisingly empowering.

In the next round, it was down to eighty people vying for the same twenty-five sales consultant positions. This time we had to speak in front of a panel and deliver a pitch. Knowing that they didn't like soft spoken people, I practised acting and looking more aloof and self-assured, over and over again, in the ladies' room. It was nerve wracking.

I was competing with people who graduated from top academes like De La Salle University, Miriam College, University of the Philippines, University of Santo Tomas, Ateneo de Manila, etc... And when I looked at these contenders, I saw certainty and conviction oozing out of their upper-class personalities, while I looked at me, and I was just some province girl trying her luck out in the big city. Part of me said that I didn't belong there, but Pandora's familiar bravado bled through my awareness, and screamed *"You are just as good as any of them!"*

So I seized the day and stumbled my way into the interview room. Once in, I took a deep breath and looked the panel in the eyes as I delivered my pitch and controlled the emotions in my voice, so that I could produce a steady smile. They were fixated at me, they nodded, they listened, and then they said nothing, except *"Thank you." "It was my pleasure."* I responded with a genuine, happy smile. I walked away feeling almost certain that I've got the job, and even if I didn't, I thought to myself, I was proud of how I showed up. I did my best and expected nothing in return. And in return, The Universe granted what I wished for, a better paying, more challenging, job.

Working with Berkeley International was great fun. The salary was very low, but the commissions were exorbitant. I was a consistent team player and earned tens of thousands of pesos in commissions, within a couple of weeks of getting started. For the first time in my life, I shopped in boutique places and had a healthy bank balance. At Berkeley, we worked hard and earned well, some liked to party lavishly, others shopped like there was no tomorrow, while I chose to moderate my spending, and save for the rainy days.

I never told any of my friends or colleagues about my childhood because there was nothing presentable about it, compared to everyone else's stories of dollhouses, bedtime stories, and family reunions. When they asked me about my family, and where I was from, I would simply say "I'm from Gensan." No one had ever been curious enough to ask for any more details, so I offered none.

One day, the CEO came to visit all the way from New Zealand, to deliver a pep talk and give due recognition to high achievers. At the time, I happened to be the week's top consultant, and he encouraged my efforts by shaking my hand and complimenting me in front of the entire sales team, like I was some kind of a respectable person. Not that I thought I wasn't respectable, but there was a strange, nagging sensation somewhere inside of me that didn't feel like I deserved to be recognised. Outwardly, I looked like I was in control and loving my success, but inwardly, I secretly felt like an impostor.

Chapter 22
Blue-eyed monster

Within eighteen months in Manila, I had been in three jobs, two addresses, a car accident and two boyfriends. Although life seemed fast-paced, the irony was it also seemed like I was going nowhere.

It is no secret that the Philippine economy is crippled by corruption. In most cases, the poor get even poorer, and the rich get even richer, while the working class spend the majority of their lives on the hamster wheel, perpetually working but never getting anywhere. Hence, the Philippines is the 9th country with the highest number of emigrants in the world, people leaving to work and settle for good overseas in pursuit of greener pastures, away from the hamster wheel.

I started a plan that I would work and live overseas. Canada was a popular destination for hardworking, talented *Pinoys*, so I delved my research into their immigration laws and working policies.

The flaw in my plan was lack of financial back-up. I had some money in the bank that sat aimlessly at a cash rate of 5.75% per annum, which would never grow quickly enough to afford myself the required overseas working bond of at least one hundred thousand pesos. Most Filipinos who emigrate, borrow their bond money from family and friends, and then they would work tirelessly to pay that debt as quickly as possible.

In a moment of desperation, I thought of my family and wished that I could ask them to support my dream of working abroad and lend me money for bond. But then again, I remembered what it was like to be caught in the middle of the mud-slinging whirlpool that my mother and her siblings loved to engage in, when it came to their obsession with money, and the never-ending lack of it.

The words from my essay back in college haunted me, *"I am not free, because my emotions are prisoners of my family"*

It dawned on me that freedom won, was freedom fought for. It wouldn't be real freedom unless I have bled, sweated and cried for it. So I made a pact with me and the other voice in my head, that I would rather bleed, sweat and cry to be free, even if it kills me, before I would ever consider asking my family for any help.

Little did I know that by making that pact with Pandora, I had spoken my own curse into reality. The bleeding, sweating and crying to be free, became a self-fulfilling prophecy.

It began with my cousin Sherrie who was back again in Manila, but this time she wasn't gallivanting, instead she was on a mission. She had met a handsome South African architect who lived in Cape Town, through a website called Heart of Asia. His name was Shane, and my cousin was in Manila to apply for a South African travel visa. To date, Sherrie and Shane have now been married for over twenty years.

My cousin was happy and excited, and I was happy and excited for her. With the happiness and excitement between the two of us, I let Sherrie talk me into creating a profile for myself on Heart of Asia also. She was genuinely ecstatic, and it was contagious. I uploaded a photo of me wearing a toga and the blurb underneath the picture said, *"Looking for an honest, reliable and kind man."*

In the following months, I was inundated with letters and messages by men from different countries, ranging from twenty-nine to sixty-four-year-olds. Most of them emailed me, while a couple were old fashioned and wrote real, handwritten, air mails with pictures of themselves, their dogs, kids, boats and what have you. The teacher in me was diligent in reading all their letters and responding to them, but that's where it ended, being diligent. None of them really struck any chords in my heart, and I wasn't sure why, until I received an email from Pedro.

Unlike all the others who talked a lot about their profession, their houses and cars, Pedro talked about a way of life. His emails took me to another world, beyond anything that money can pay for, like his passion for surfing big waves and the long history of his surfboard shaping craft. There was a sense of hope and promise of an idyllic life near the ocean. I was hooked to his emails right from the very beginning.

Born in the Northern beaches of Sydney, Pedro grew up with a love for riding the waves, and the surfing community that shaped the way he lived his life. He manufactured handmade surfboards for a living and loved to re-live and tell tales of his hey days as a professional surfer. Our emails revolved around his life, but hardly on mine. The only thing he wanted to know about me was if there was surf, where

I came from. At the time, I thought that his lack of interest in my personal history was convenient because I never really liked discussing it either. It would take me a long time to realize that my self-avoidance was a classic sign of a lack of self-worth.

I asked how old he was, and I balked when he said he was forty-four, because I was only twenty-four. Then I remembered that my aunt Ellie and her husband also had a twenty-year age gap, and for them it didn't matter because her husband was very lean, active and youthful. So I thought to myself, if Pedro was the same, then it would be okay too. He then sent me a black and white professional headshot where he looked like Harrison Ford. I asked if he looked the same as he did in the Harrison Ford photo, and his response was, *"I'm the youngest forty-four-year-old you would ever meet."*

Our online courtship was snappy. After two months of writing to each other, Pedro didn't waste time in making plans to come and see me. I felt uneasy about how fast things were happening, and I would've been quite happy to just write letters for a while.

Sensing my apprehension, he volunteered a way to make me feel a little more comfortable before we met in person. He said that his brother happened to be in Manila spending some time with his Filipino fiancée. A piece of seemingly big information which he never told me before. I thought it was remarkable that his brother just happened to be in my country, and that he too, had a Filipino girlfriend. It was too much to be happenstance.

Pedro offered to arrange a meeting between me, his brother, and soon to be sister in law. Curious, I agreed to meet them and made the arrangement for our rendezvous at a hip restaurant in the heart of

Ortigas Centre. I came straight from the office in my skirt suit and high heels. Little did I know that his brother hated fancy places and fancy people. To this day, his brother Remy refers to me as *"Makati arty farty"*, his own coined version of *"Makati girl"* (an overindulged yuppie who works in Makati and acts in a certain Makati-ish fashion).

Meanwhile, I was oblivious to the silent judgement that Remy has formed about me. I myself thought that he was friendly and even resembled Robin Williams. As for his fiancée, I liked her too. Melinda was a shy woman. Kindness emanated from her as we sat next to each other.

In the course of our conversation, Remy bluntly said, *"My brother is looking for a wife."* I felt the challenge in his voice, the silent question of *"Are you good enough to be my brother's wife?"* I looked him in the eye and did not flinch. In my mind, I asked the silent question of, *"Are you good enough to be my brother in law?"* But I was thoroughly enjoying the funky crowd and elite atmosphere, that I wasn't in the mood for a challenging conversation, so I simply said *"Cool."* Then I turned my attention to the music and the food.

In spite of my misgivings, I felt slightly more open to taking the next step of meeting Pedro in person. In my mind, he was no longer a serial killer in disguise, now that I've met his brother who was going to be married to a Filipino like myself.

On the day of Pedro's arrival, Martin offered to drive me to the airport. I was so nervous and said to Martin *"Why am I so scared to meet this person?"* To which he said, *"It's because there's so much at stake. I think you're scared to see him in case you get disappointed, and then your dream of a life by the ocean would be shattered. But then if you turn back now and don't see him, how would you know, and how many chances will you get?"* With such logic, I decided that I didn't want to miss any chances of a great future with a potential life partner, even when my gut instinct was telling me otherwise.

Pedro arrived on time. I recognized him from a distance as he pushed his suitcase trolley down the ramp and exchanged a friendly banter with airport security. He moved with the ease of a sports athlete, albeit he had a slightly hunched posture. He was charming, but he reeked of cigarettes, which repulsed me.

I should've just walked away then. But I was totally lost in the dark. I knew I was looking for a relationship, yet I had no idea of the kind of relationship I was supposed to be looking for.

If I was an older, wiser, and more confident woman, I would have given Pedro a hug, hailed him a taxi and wished him well in life, gracefully explaining that it wasn't going to work. This kind of confident woman would have put Pedro off right from the start, and he would have jumped in that taxi so quick and started looking for the next girl. But I wasn't that kind of confident woman. I was naïve and desperate. I was the perfect kind of woman for him. So instead, I opened the door for Pedro into Martin's car, and effectively taken the biggest course alteration of my life.

Chapter 23
Moral prostitution

Just like our online courtship, our real-life courtship was quick and snappy. We spent a few days together in a coastal town called Puerto Galera, Pedro trying to woo me into bed as quickly as he can, and me hoping to unveil a much-needed soulmate out of a blue-eyed stranger.

On the first night, I found myself staggering drunk on the beach, on the way back to our hotel. Even though I wasn't a big fan of the taste of alcohol, I sculled three shots of tequila over Bob Dylan's "Knockin' on heaven's door", trying to settle my nerves about what I knew was about to happen. I thought I was mentally ready for sex, yet I wondered why I was such a nervous wreck. In hindsight being mentally ready for sex simply meant that I wasn't ready at all, because there was no heart connection.

I was too scared. Not so much of Pedro, but of sex in general. It had never been a sanctioned subject in all of my life, notwithstanding the fact that I had been acquainted more to the dark side of sex, rather than its intimate and loving potential. For girls like me, the first time was never going to be a good time. The tequila was my friend.

I bled so much that I thought I was haemorrhaging. I stood in the bathroom, not knowing what to do, when he came in to shower me like a child and settle me down, and then we noticed some blood smeared on the tiles, which upset me even more. I was in tears. But Pedro had a way of making me look towards the future, and he had always acknowledged my love of writing ever since we met. So to make light of what was happening, he made a declaration, *"One day you will write about this in your book and you will call it 'Blood On The Wall'".* I felt cheered up by what he said and forgot about my own real, bloody situation.

After Puerto Galera, Pedro wanted to take me to Bali and party with him. I had never been overseas before and Bali sounded like such an exotic place to see. He promised that the world was my oyster, so I said yes. But as soon as we landed at Ngurah Rai airport, Pedro had somehow forgotten that I was a living, breathing, walking and talking human being with a living, breathing, walking and talking need to interact with people. Pedro instantaneously stopped interacting with me, which left an eerily familiar feeling of being alone and lost, and ignited an eerily familiar sensation of angst and internal rage.

Like a kid in a playground, he went straight to talking and drinking with his friends, which there were so many of them. While I would later learn that Pedro had been coming to Bali in the last twenty years, all for the surfing, the drinking, the drugs, and the women; I had absolutely no idea, let alone a preview, of the kind of world that I was about to experience for myself.

Having Pedro as a life teacher was treacherous. I was so curious and liberated that I did everything he suggested to me, including drugs. At the time, ecstasy was the cheapest and most popular drug in the world.

I've read of ecstasy through the Sydney Sheldon mystery books that I used to love, and I knew that it was a dangerous, lethal, recreational drug. Pedro told me that he took them almost every time he went out to the night clubs, which was almost every second weekend in Australia, and almost every second night in Bali. He illustrated a kaleidoscope of fun and high experience, and he promised that he would look after me if I chose to take it.

The first time was at the famous Double-Six nightclub in Seminyak. The interiors of Double- Six was designed like a giant *Nipa Hut* (traditional Filipino house made from bamboo and straw) with extremely high ceilings, a high stage, and a long V shaped runway, that encapsulated the big, open dance floor. The lights and dry ice were insanely mesmerising, and the techno music reverberated up to two hundred yards away.

At the back of the nightclub was an Olympic-size swimming pool. On one side of the pool stood what looked like a hundred feet high, set of metal poles that held up a bungee jumping ledge. Patrons of Double-Six would pay money to climb to the top of the ledge, so they can jump to the pool with ropes tied around their ankles, just for fun. After the initial drop, their heads and bodies smashed and splashed into the water and they would yoyo up and down until the bungee momentum ceased, and then someone would catch them from the side of the pool, untie the bungee rope from their ankles, and off they went for a quick swim – drunk and high on ecstasy, and basking on the cheers of hundreds of spectators who were either just as drunk and high as everyone else, or there to do business through sex and drugs. It was all crazy and it was all real. Having had a relatively sheltered life so far, I was fascinated just by simply being part of it.

Pedro gave me half a pill which I happily swallowed. Then I couldn't stop dancing. I felt like if I stopped the world wouldn't mean a thing – so I danced, and danced, and danced. Pedro watched me and pushed bottles of water to my mouth to drink every now and then. I danced with everyone, men, women, tourists, locals, pimps and prostitutes. I remember being in the present moment of every move I made, no thinking required, just movement and feeling. I was high.

I was hardly dressed for a nightclub scene, in my singlet and a pair of Hawaiian boardshorts. Somewhere during the course of the evening, I had lost my thongs, which apparently, was more of a concern for Pedro than the fact that I had taken a drug that could potentially stop my heart from beating. Halfway through the night, he found my thongs and gave them to me on the dancefloor. I screamed through the music and told him I wanted the other half of my pill. He said, *"Okay but you have to wear your thongs because there's some broken glass on the floor."*

After swallowing the second half of the pill, I went outside to watch more bungee jumping. The sight of a semi limp body, tied on both ankles, yo-yoing fifty to one hundred feet in the air, eventually made me queasy, and then I asked to go home. The drive back to our hotel was refreshing as the balmy air fanned my face and gave me some relief from the smoke and sweat in the nightclub. But while Pedro was happy to go to sleep, I was still high on my second half of ecstasy.

We were staying at a hotel located halfway in between Jimbaran bay and Dreamland. It was one o'clock in the morning and as we lay in bed together, the night was sullen and dark, except for a lone streetlamp that pierced through the French windows. My eyes were wide open and through the darkness I looked at Pedro and tried to see the familiar shape of his face. Just when I thought I could see the silhouette of his head, he moved, and the streetlamp created a dancing shadow on his face. As I looked closely through the dancing shadows, his face disintegrated into a thousand squiggly worms some four inches from my nose. It reminded me of Freddie Kuger's face, but with live worms eating away at its host.

Disturbed but not too perturbed, I pushed my body away from the bed and picked up a book that I've started reading earlier that week. I opened the door to the terrace and sat on a wooden chair with my feet on the coffee table. I flipped through the pages and found the words to be a little boring, so I stopped reading and looked up to the pitch-black sky, and then curiously down on the grounds of the hotel property. Some fifty yards in front of me was a four-foot high, brick fence that had a six-metre gateless opening, which guests used as a side entrance to the property. On the left side of this gap stood the lone streetlamp.

As my eyes settled on the foot of the streetlamp, I noticed an Indonesian looking man in his fifties, wearing an old, faded pair of trousers, a dark undershirt, and a jacquard aqua and white, long-sleeved shirt. The man walked from around the corner in quick steps, and just as I thought he looked like he was coming through to the footpath, he took flight and transformed into a one-foot size flying tornado. I never took my eyes off him, and as he swivelled through the air, he stopped dead centre two feet in front of my face. This time he took the form of a face that I have never seen before. It wasn't a human face. It was a creature with a geometric shaped face, and skin with grey, charcoal texture. Its jaw was square, where its eyes should be there were only two piercing black holes, where its hair should be there were only ridges that resembled the wall of China, its mouth was wide and impressive. It wore a cotton, black and white jacquard scarf around where its neck should be, and as it floated in front of me, it began to open its mouth in elaborate shapes. I felt that it was trying to say something. The creature kept floating with wide, open, moving mouth, and as if to make its point, it looked like it was beginning to scream, but I still couldn't hear a thing, so I spoke back and said, *"Who are you? What are you trying to say? I cannot hear you."*

As I spoke, I heard Pedro call my name from the bedroom, *"Gracey! Gracey! What are you doing? Come back in here."* I turned to look at Pedro and found that the worms on his face had gone, I told him I was just talking to someone and dismissed him. I turned back to the floating creature and as I tried to talk to it again, it left slowly and dissipated into the darkness.

I spent the rest of the night lying awake in bed.

Over breakfast, Pedro asked who I was talking to, last night at the terrace. I told him about the old man by the streetlamp, and how he floated like a tornado, and turned into a face, and tried to say something to me. After I described the face and the scarf, Pedro took me to the front gate of the hotel and pointed to two, identical statues that guarded both sides of the gate. They were the statues of the *Barong*, a Hindu mythical creature that's believed to be a symbol of health and good fortune.

The statues were wearing the black and white jacquard cotton cloth that I saw around the neck of the creature that tried to talk to me. I studied the statues, and then I realised that without any knowledge of the Hindu customs, culture, and belief systems, I had either been directly confronted by the spirit of a creature that's not so mythical after all, or that I had an ecstasy induced hallucination, or maybe it was both. Could it be possible that the drug gave me an incidental access to a part of my brain that could sense beyond physical being? A super consciousness that's capable of connecting to the spiritual realm? I shook the thought off of my head and decided that it was all a little too confronting to make sense of.

Twenty years after my ecstasy and ghost experience, I was in Bali on a *Kundalini Yoga* retreat at *Om Ham* in *Ubud*. I immersed in the holy practise at *Ashram Munivara*, spending hours in meditation, and gaining an understanding of the cyclical nature of the Gods, *Brahma, Vishnu and Shiva*.

On the day of my flight back to Australia, the driver asked about my Yoga retreat experience, on the way to the airport. I told him that I felt so lucky having received a personal blessing from the guru *Ketut Arsana* himself. Sensing my strong spiritual practise, the driver asked me, *"Do you actually believe in spirits and have you ever seen one?"* To which I replied, *"Yes of course I do. I have a soul, you have a soul, we are all spirits and energies. Have I actually seen one? Perhaps I have!"* remembering my ghost encounter at the other side of the very same island, twenty years ago.

Then for the first time, I told my Bali ghost experience to a Balinese, something that I probably should have done two decades ago. As I was telling the story, he rubbed his neck and arms smoothing over his goose bumps. When I finished the story, he gently and cautiously said that it was hard to tell *exactly whom* I've seen. But in his personal opinion, he believed that I had an encounter with a negative, harmful spirit called *Li-ak*, and that I was lucky nothing had happened to me. I asked him to spell the name out for me, and he said in his best English *"Spell like it sound, L.I.A.K"*

I looked up "Li-ak" as soon as I got home and found nothing. But my conversation with the Balinese driver sparked a real curiosity in me, so I went back to the story of the mythical Barong and followed the traces from there, and then I was blown away by what I found.

The Barong symbolizes health and good fortune. In Balinese customs and traditions, there is a dance that features a battle between the good and the evil. The good being the *Barong*, and the evil being the *Rangda*. Rangda was a widow witch, and the queen of demons in Bali. She has an army of three *"Leyaks"*. These three Leyaks were made up of two females and one male. Leyaks were humans that practise black magic and cannibalism. In daylight, they have the power to appear as an ordinary human, but at night, their head and entrails break loose from their body, and then they fly.

After learning about the Leyaks, I felt compelled to spend a little time reflecting on my discarnate experience twenty years ago. Granted I was on drugs. But of all the things that I could hallucinate on, how could it be of something that I have never seen before? And with such vivid appearance and intensity? Why did I see it? Why did it show itself to me? Was I in danger? Did I attract the negative energy? Had I been sober, would it have shown itself instead in its *human form*? Was I crazy? Or was I simply too open for weirdness?

But then again, perhaps it was the dark side of my own psyche, disguised in the form of a dark spirit, warning me of what was about to come. Forewarned, becomes forearmed.

Having survived that first night in Double-Six, Pedro and I went back for more collateral damage a few nights later. This time I was a little more dressed for the occasion and knew that Pedro had drugs with him again. I was like a ragdoll getting carried away on the current of a wicked river. Everything was new and dangerous, and I was curious as much as I was vulnerable. I invited Pedro's corruption just as much as he offered it to me.

I swallowed one whole pill and started to dance on the V shaped runway. There were triple the number of people there compared to the other night, the music seemed twice as loud, the lights lasered into my brain with lightning intensity, and the dry ice was thicker, denser, and relentless. My senses have never been so heightened, and everything seemed supersonically amplified, that I felt like I was going to choke.

I found myself pushing through a sea of people, weaving my small frame in between sweaty bodies, and went searching for the ladies' room, which thankfully, was outside of the nightclub, next to the swimming pool. It was a separate, wooden building with giant mirrors, and in it were women of different nationalities like Brazil, Germany, USA, Australia, Japan, England, speaking English in different accents but with the same tune of what I call, the *drug-love-language*.

When people were high on drugs, they all loved each other. Everyone wanted to hug one another, and everybody *"oohheeddd"* and *"aahhheeeddd"* at every inanimate object, and every living thing; admiring the divinity of all that there was, including the toilet paper and soap.

I was exactly the same huggy-kissy woman as everyone in that Double-Six washroom, but I knew that I had a different high on this night compared to my first time. It was a subdued kind of high, to the extent of being bored. The music wasn't enticing me to dance and the bungee jumping was getting rather silly to watch. To solve my boredom, I thought I would ask Pedro for a second pill so I could chase the high that I wanted. I would like to think that he hesitated and was a little protective of my life. But I'm not too sure, because I got hold of my second pill pretty much in a heartbeat.

Fifteen minutes after my second pill, the room began to spin, and the music blurred to a deafening lull. The colours of things became two shades of brown and a tinge of red, and the people looked like a suspended ocean of spasmodic movement. My sense of focus was leaving my body and I was not having a good time whatsoever. I found myself hanging on to Pedro for strength, and a distant voice in my head told me to get out of there, stat.

The rest of the night was a blur and I woke up the next day feeling like a half-resurrected zombie. The neurosis of coming down from ecstasy hit me hard, and I spent a quiet afternoon staring at the sea, withdrawn from the rest of the world. After that, I never bothered taking ecstasy again. Aside from it being the stupidest thing I have ever done, and I could've killed myself, there was nothing in it for me. Through such an imbecile and dangerous experiment, I realized that there was so much more fun to be had when my faculties were fully functional and my awareness intact. I didn't need drugs to feel good.

So alcohol was not my thing, and now drugs wasn't my thing either. The two major sources of Pedro's high. And when he wasn't on any of those, his demeanour was a spectrum of charming and funny on one extreme, and malevolent on the other. Every day was either a yo-yo, or a toss of a coin, when it came to Pedro's moods and behaviour.

I was treading such a dangerous path, and I was totally unaware of it. It was my first time being with a man who's a real man-of-the-world, and because I've never had a strong and loving male/father role model, I was just as enamoured by Pedro's dominance as I was with his desire for me. Disempowered and desperate, it was more than enough for me to turn a blind eye to his mental and emotional volatility.

Chapter 24
Crystal Tunnel

Shortly after Bali, Pedro proposed to take me back to Australia with him and promised that I could become whoever and whatever I wanted to be, with his full support. I was very receptive to this idea thinking that we had plenty of time to get comfortable with each other through our long-distance relationship. But as fate would have it, my fiancée visa was approved in a record-breaking immigration approval of five and a half weeks, compared to the average waiting period of two years. Suddenly, Pedro and I were catapulted into the deep end of being a real, full time couple.

I landed in Brisbane on a crisp, August morning. Driving down to the Gold Coast for the first time was unforgettable. The traffic free, six-lane highway felt so welcoming as I wound the window down and stared out the views of the hinterlands. The cautious voice in my head said, *"Welcome to your new life."*

"Our, new life." I corrected.

Armed with only my zest for adventure and with what I thought was love for the man who proposed to be my husband, I began the most tumultuous era of my adult life.

Living with Pedro became the most fertile breeding ground for my demon to fester; Pandora had finally been given an arena to unleash, and I had no idea what I was about to get into.

On the morning of our wedding that following summer, I felt extremely alone. For the first time in my whole life, I wished that I had my family with me, just for once. I longed for a familiar face, someone who had known me since I was a kid, whom I could ask, *"How do I know that I love this man enough to declare a life together through thick and thin, in sickness and in health, till death do we part?"* Of course, I was aware that such counsel would never materialize, so when Pedro, as if sensing my misgivings, asked me, *"I'm not marrying someone today who doesn't want to be married to me, am I?"* I responded by saying, *"No, I'm fine. I'm just a little nervous, I wish that I had some of my family here but it's okay."* With that, he was satisfied and proceeded with the business of getting ready for our afternoon wedding and dinner reception.

The mistake that people make when getting married is thinking they can afford to compromise their values in the name of marriage and that things would work out eventually. I thought that I was willing to compromise and tolerate Pedro's drinking and partying, even if they were totally against my personal values, because Pedro said that he wanted to take care of me and have children with me. As for Pedro, he thought that he was willing to compromise and tolerate my smart mouth and fearless personality, even if he hated women who stood up for themselves, because I said that I wanted to take care of him and start a family with him. We both assumed that things would work out eventually.

One night he came home in a particularly aggressive, drunken state and viciously complained about my awful body. He went on a rant regarding the fact that while he had the body of a twenty-year-old in his forties, I had a flabby stomach and flat boobs, in my twenties, and that I looked more like a boy rather than a woman. The look of disdain in his eyes was heartbreaking. The realization that the man I married saw me as nothing short of grotesque was a shocking moment.

I was torn between retaliation and self-preservation. Yet despite my shattered ego, I tried to reason with my husband about his drinking. But he dismissed me with a wave of his cigarette-clutching fingers, while his mouth curved askew to the left side, a sure-fire sign that he had had more than just alcohol. Pedro was a handsome man with proportionate facial features, but all of his good looks mutated into a spastic version of The Joker when he was high on drugs.

The sight of him so high and incomprehensibly belligerent set me off to a rage that I didn't know what to do with. I needed release, so I stood up from the chair and found one of his surfboards in the hallway. I kicked the board in anger, and then I was going to kick it some more when suddenly I felt Pedro's hand wrap around my neck as he maneuvered me to face him and then pinned me against the wall. The hallway was dimly lit, and all I could see was the slight flicker of murder in his eyes.

His brute strength was just enough to put me in my place of fear and submission, and I could sense that his actions were well calculated and very much controlled. Bewildered, it dawned on me that this was something he had done before, somewhere else, to someone else. My rage immediately coiled back into a ball of superficial calm. A voice in my head said that fear could get us killed, and we must survive by masking fear with surrender.

I tried to relax my shaking body and breathe in any air I could, two inches from Pedro's face and still dangling by the neck with his hand tightly choking me. I took my eyes off him and stared into the dark space, indicating that I will not fight back, that I surrendered. Pedro released my neck and walked off saying "You deserved it, you f**n C**t"

The next day, he went to work, and I went to the hospital to talk to someone. I told the nurse that I had a fight with my husband and she nodded her head. She simply examined my neck for deep tissue injuries and when she found none, she gave me an all clear. No other questions, no comments.

On the same day, Pedro went for a quick surf after work, came back home, and then we ate dinner and talked about the stuff that was on TV. After two hours of watching TV, I finally realised that my husband did not have plans of drinking that night. I felt my whole body shift and then relax. Like a freshly fluffed up pillow carefully and lovingly placed back on its dedicated spot on the bed, looking nice and feeling nice.

While the thought of Pedro being sober all night excited me, I knew it was an effort for him. And because he was making an effort, I'd forgiven him for everything he said and did to me the night before. I was still sore in my heart, and my neck still stung from the finger marks, but wasn't that what love and marriage was about, I said to myself, having faith that things will work out eventually?

A couple of months after our wedding, we travelled to the Philippines so that he could meet my family. But Pedro was only ever interested in one thing: surfing. Every conversation revolved around his surfboards, the places he's surfed before, where the waves could be in the Philippines, and how to get there. My family, just like myself when I first met Pedro, knew nothing about surfing. And by the end of our visit, Pedro had made almost a non-impression. My original world could not be more separate than my new one.

Back in Australia, we lived in a two-bedroom unit on a hill called Duranbah, on one of the best surfing points in the country. And even though my emotions and psyche were on shaky grounds, I felt that my soul was in the right place. I was surrounded by hundred-and-eighty-degree views of the Pacific Ocean, and I could see a stretch of the south-eastern Australian coastline through our bedroom window.

The ocean became my talisman, and through it, I discovered the potential powers of self-therapy. There were times when I've taken myself to the beach in the middle of the pitch-black night to recover my sanity. The merciless crashing of the waves onto the rocks became my thunder of hope, giving me a sense of knowing that something beautiful was meant to be, no matter how lost I often felt. While the howling winds teased me to be brave and challenged me to face the karma that I had bestowed upon myself. The elements had their own way of telling me to have faith.

And then in the fall of that year, something wonderful happened to me. I became pregnant and I was so ecstatic that there was a life that pulsated in my belly. To know that I have been granted the gift of creating and giving life was like an infusion of white magic in my veins, making me feel worthy, excited, and alive. For the first time in my life, I felt True Love. It was the kind of feeling that no one would ever be capable of taking away from me.

I was in such a state of gratitude that hardly anything could faze me. Our baby would not be Pedro's first child, and even though his reaction was lukewarm when he found out that he was having another daughter instead of a son, he was stoked and proud of his own virility. And as I breezed through my pregnancy, I reminded myself that marrying Pedro was my decision, and I was determined to honour that decision and do the best I can, whatever that may be.

Chapter 25
No Deal

During this time, Pedro sealed a forty-year lease on a two-bedroom apartment in Bali. I initially thought that he was making a real estate business decision, but then I quickly realized that he intended to use it as our residence half the time of the year.

Pedro knew how much I hated our trips to Bali because of his drinking, drugs and womanizing. I've never actually caught him physically cheating on me, but he might as well have, with the number of times that he had insulted me for being so prude. Often, he would quote Mick Jagger, *"A good woman is a maid in the kitchen and a slut in the bedroom."* To insinuate that I was nowhere near the standard of a woman that he would ideally like to have.

Hence, he never spoke directly to me about his intention of living in Bali for six months each year. Instead, he invited a friend over one night and started a long-winded conversation about the new apartment in Bali and his excitement in living there, half of the time. Somehow, I knew it was an entrapment. Pedro wanted me to say yes to the plan and completely disregarded any opinions I may have had as his wife. They talked as if I wasn't at the same dinner table, so I acted as if I wasn't there, and kept a powerful silence.

Pedro hated silence and non-response with a vengeance, to a point that it could drive him to the top of the Richter scale. Finally, he couldn't stand my stoicism and decided to put me on the spot in front of his friend, *"You haven't said much about this Grace, living in Bali for six months and six months here in Australia."* I was then in my second trimester and had created a small world with a small routine for me and my soon to be born baby. I touched my belly, looked Pedro and his friend in the eye and said, *"You can. But I won't be living in Bali, not for any length of time. I'm staying in Australia. With. Or without you."*

Many of Pedro's American and Australian friends in Bali were married to women from different parts of Asia, living the bi-cultural life that Pedro so badly wanted to live: half the time in Bali and then the other half back in their own Western countries. It was the dream life of a Western surfer: Big waves, insane parties and a yes-woman by their side to compliment the entire picture. It occurred to me that Pedro had invested a fortune in his new apartment in Bali, with this in mind. But had I known beforehand that this was his ultimate dream, we probably never would have gotten married. Because my dream was to live in a wholesome, family-friendly community, and while surfing communities in third world countries were great for surfers, I couldn't envisage myself and my child in it.

The moment I said no to Pedro, with such certainty and conviction, I effectively crushed his dreams. My punishment was not direct, but it was imminent.

The psychological battery that ensued afterwards was highly combustible. In the heights of his anger, Pedro used to say, *"Never get in the ring with me."* Meaning to never make the mistake of fighting back at him, which I did almost every time he got drunk and lashed out with his repertoire of expletives. It wasn't that I enjoyed fighting with him, I simply could not become the subservient wife that he needed.

Although there was hardly any physical violence that transpired, the cold hatred and racial insults I was subjected to, were like nuclear bombs consistently erupting underneath the surface. The constant hostility and psychological violence cooked my spirit into a million pieces of debris, breaking me down until I couldn't recognise my own wholeness.

Chapter 26
Tidal waves make me sink or swim

Twelve months and ten days after our wedding, I gave birth to my beautiful baby girl. She was so perfect when she came out, and I was so speechless. She had delicate fingers and eyes so big and bright they often reflected the moon's illumination. At night I would stand next to her crib with the lights off and the windows open, and I would look at her eyes; and as she smiled up at me, I understood that the purest lights were those you find in the midst of darkness. My daughter conveyed hope and strength, long before she uttered her first words.

Just before my daughter's first birthday, Pedro and I had been in a long, drawn out, ugly fight that finally reached a crunch. My self-hate and loathing for my marriage and my husband became too much to bear. I was exhausted, and my desperation for love and support made me feel physically sick. So I packed my bags and told Pedro that I was leaving him, and as I was stepping out of the door with my baby and my belongings, he told me to *"go and get f**k*d"*.

Within twenty minutes of driving on the highway and away from the house of hell that was my marital home, I started to feel so lost and bone-weary. I looked at my baby girl through the rear vision mirror, and in a moment of weakness, I decided to turn around and head back to my husband. I felt an all-consuming urge to *"rest"*. I was so mentally, emotionally and spiritually beat that I felt like, if I could just have *"one big rest and feel no pain"*.

I managed to stumble back into the house and unceremoniously put my baby in Pedro's arms, as I ran into the kitchen and rummaged the medicine Tupperware. The last thing I remember was crawling into bed whispering, *"please look after my baby, I am very tired and I'm going to sleep"*. I was in a semi deranged state, and had just swallowed an entire bottle, twenty-eight pills to be exact, of *Kalma 1*, a powerful drug for anxiety and panic attacks.

They were prescribed to me in September of 2002. When my baby was eight months old, I went to the emergency section of Tweed Hospital, demanding to speak to a doctor. I had become paranoid and wanted to find out if I was "crazy" and "lunatic", as my husband accused me of, every chance he had. I also confessed that I had nightmares, and woke up most nights violently screaming and convulsing. My husband would shake me even more violently to wake me up and tell me to *"Shut the f**k up you f**k*n' lunatic."*

The doctor listened to me patiently, then he disappeared to another room and left me with a dreadful feeling of suspense, while waiting for his verdict on my mental state. After one long hour of waiting, I started to wonder if I had hallucinated talking to the doctor, which would mean that I was indeed a lunatic. But then suddenly he reappeared and said that I was neither crazy nor lunatic. Rather, he suggested that I was *"under a fair bit of stress"*.

He handed me a prescription to ease my nightmares. I was very grateful for having deemed to be 'not crazy', and as I took the prescription from his hand, he tugged at it for a moment, looked me straight in the eye and said, *"Don't do anything stupid with it."* The gravity of his gaze was clear enough for me to know that he had just given me something that could potentially be fatal.

I used half of a pill that night which did not only give me one great night sleep, but it also numbed me. The numbness gave me a sense of relief in the midst of my chaotic life. And for the next few days, I would become invincible and non-reactive to Pedro's tirade of abuse, as a result of one half of a pill that I had taken a few days ago. I was detached from everything, including myself and all of the voices that drove me insane in my own head, all but except for my baby girl. The numbness gave me a breathing space to enjoy playtime and *thoughtlessness* with my child.

I was proud of myself for not getting in the ring with Pedro, no matter what he said or how drunk he got, but then again it also made me realise the truth, that I wasn't only trying to escape emotional brutality from my husband, I was also desperate to escape from the mental pandemonium that I couldn't seem to stop, inside my own head. The pandemonium of guilt, fear and shame.

There were 30 pills in the bottle, and they were so strong that I only used half a pill every two weeks. Then after consuming a total of two, I figured I was drugged up and numbed up enough to stop taking them. *I then put the bottle of pills away, knowing that there were twenty-eight left.*

I woke up three days later after swallowing twenty-eight Kalma 1's, in a hospital room. Upon waking up, a nurse immediately began taking multiple tubes and needles off of my body and orifices and asked what I wanted to do. I said, *"I'd like to go home to my baby now."* I was allowed to brush my teeth and then, still in my blood-stained, white hospital gown, I was unceremoniously ushered to a waiting taxi and headed home.

If Pedro was happy to see me alive, he never showed it. Instead he was livid about the things that I told the nurses and doctors when he rushed me to the hospital. I was apparently in a state of hysteria and gave a thorough verbal vomit on how much my husband hated me and how often we fought, and how much he drank and drugged himself up at parties, etc.

I have no recollection of the entire seventy-two hours that I was *away,* but I wished that I was *there* to hear myself *courageously* say all of it. Because that was my *truth*. That person, under the influence of powerful drugs that removed all of my walls and eroded all of the voices in my head, was the real, core person inside of me. Vulnerable, afraid, weak and desperate, yes; but nonetheless honest and raw.

In the following days, I reflected on how lucky I was to still be alive. I didn't want to die, and I felt guilty for the utter stupidity and selfishness of what I tried to do. As I thought about what could have happened to my baby girl had I not woken up, it finally dawned on me that I must pay close attention to *my own mind*. That the only person who could rescue me, was myself.

I could talk to doctors and nurses who would give me things to numb me from my own work of hell; but at the end of the day, it was still up to me to operate this fragile thing called my mind, which, if left to its own weak devices, could kill the mother of my baby.

I was dumbfounded by this realization of separation between me, and the mind that controlled my actions. I started to contemplate the possibility that maybe *I* can control my mind. That maybe I can get it to choose not to believe Pedro, whenever he put me down. It was an exciting new prospect that gave me a sense of curiosity and took me away from feeling guilty.

A nurse called two weeks later to check on me. She was on duty when I was 'asleep' at the hospital, and she was calling me to see how I was feeling. I told her that I was fine, meaning that I was alive, but there wasn't much more I could say. There was a lump in my throat from the compassion that she showed me, and I felt like asking for help on the phone, but I didn't know what kind of help to ask for, and I was afraid she wouldn't understand.

I worried of being ungrateful. Most of the people whom I called friends at the time, seemed to think that because my husband provided well for me and my baby, that I should be fine; and because I was not fine in spite of Pedro's provisions, I felt guilty for my unhappiness.

I felt so confused, unworthy and desperately lonely. I was at a loss for words with the nurse, but despite the awkward silence, her voice remained warm, and she gave me the phone number of a not for profit community called *The Family Centre*. "Try them" she said, "*They have programs that may be useful for you and your family.*"

Nervous, I wasted no time and called the Family Centre. Within the next thirty minutes, I had completed a welcoming conversation with a lady named Elaine, who invited me to come along and join their weekly Mother's group program every Thursday mornings. I felt a threadbare spark of electricity ignite inside of me. People, women, mothers, togetherness, conversations, two hours, morning tea, creche, safe, neutral, no judgement… These were the words that I ran through my head as I waited the next forty-eight hours to attend my first mother's group session.

There were ten women in the group including myself. The kids ranged between the ages of two months to sixteen years. Some of the mums were single parents while the rest were in a marriage or domestic partnership in varying degrees of misery or joy. We all had different challenges that we faced as women, like post-natal depression, domestic violence, financial abuse, mental abuse, emotional abuse, cultural isolation, chronic fatigue and even loss of intimate relations due to childbirth. These women ranged from primary school educated, master's degree holders through to businesswomen. We were so diverse, yet so similar. We all came to the same place every Thursday morning because it was our safe haven.

Then there was Merri O'Donoghue, my friend and life mentor. A counsellor by profession, Merri facilitated our mother's group in a very inclusive and nurturing way, and we hung on to her quiet strength and tireless love.

The very first thing I learned from Merri was the concept of "me time" as a form of self-care. I realised that although I was already spending most of my time alone, I always viewed it as being lonely. Once I learned how to turn these times of aloneness into times of reflection, rest and rejuvenation, I gained a little more energy and zest in the way that I tackled things on a daily basis.

I became more self-assured and I didn't buy into Pedro's B.S. as often as I used to. I found that he was less able to throw me an invitation to "get in the ring" with him. I became more in control of my thoughts, and more aware of where my conversations with Pedro were heading. For a change, I was one step ahead of Pedro, in Pedro's own game.

We also learned practical skills like learning how to read the nutrition information on food labels, we quenched our social thirst by organizing a girl's night out in the city, and created memories by inviting one another to our kids' birthday parties, as well as picnics at the park. When I think of the ladies from my mother's group now, my heart is filled with a sense of enchantment. In the midst of a treacherous time of my life, I found a solace that protected me from complete breakdown, strength that held me together as a young mother, and playfulness that kept my spirits high amidst the impending doom of depression.

Inevitably though, trying not to fight with Pedro became a losing battle, and my situation escalated to what was considered a medium to high level mental health danger, as far as the Family Centre was concerned. Fortunately, they were able to assign Merri as my personal counsellor on a fortnightly home visit program. Merri's home visits lasted six months and she became part of my lifeline. She was fastidious in supporting me, and through her intensive counselling, I worked hard to achieve the resilience that I needed to keep myself safe.

For the first time in my life, I opened up about my upbringing, or lack thereof, during my life growing up at my grandmother's house. Merri slowly tried to uncover my emotional wounds by asking difficult questions like, *"How did you feel when you came back to your grandmother's house after running away that night?"* Or *"Do you remember your mother giving you a kiss and a hug?"* (To which the answer was no) And *"Have you told your mother how you really feel about her leaving you at your grandmother's house?"* (Again, the answer was no)

Merri allowed me to see how much unfinished business I had left behind in the Philippines, how far I've come in spite of it all, and that I have so much to live for. But through reliving and retelling the story of my abandonment, I had inadvertently awakened my half-sleeping demon, Pandora. It was like she had gotten anointed to paint the town red. I became fixated by the realization that my anger stemmed from such deep-seated sorrows, so that instead of feeling better, I mostly drifted between nostalgia and deep resentment. A type of anger that had a concrete quality to it. Cold, hard and impenetrable.

Fighting with Pedro became a sport. It was like an addiction. One could ask, why didn't I just leave right away? But the journey to making that final decision was not straightforward. It's like swimming for your life without a life vest, after surviving a shipwreck in the middle of the Atlantic Ocean. More often than not, drowning seems like a much simpler and easier option, than anything else.

Other than trying to kill myself, I also tried to leave through a shelter for victims of domestic violence program, where I could've begun a brand-new life. All I needed to do was get in my car and drive to an undisclosed location. I could've disappeared from the grid and be surrounded by mental health professionals who would've resuscitated some sense back into my brain. Merri pulled her contacts together and made this escape available for me one day, but on the very last minute, I chickened out and changed my mind. The thought of completely severing contact from my husband was painful. I was afraid of separating my child away from her father, just as I was separated from my own, and consequently growing up with no capacity to understand and love men.

Chapter 27
Sober comeuppance

Unable to muster the courage to leave my husband, I tried a different strategy to make my marriage work, by working on myself some more. One day I walked into a Yoga class without really knowing what it was about, except for a hunch that it was going to be a beautiful experience. It was in a big, beautiful ballet studio with bars and mirrors all around the room. The class had up to thirty students, and we laid out in a beautiful U formation, making everyone feel like they are a small part of the big picture.

When the student is ready, the teacher will appear. Robyn Hansen was in her fifties, had been a Yogi for decades and a real guru in my opinion. She had an ethereal face that emanated both softness and strength. She moved with a lightness akin to an earth angel. A very wise earth angel. Her classes went for one hour and forty-five minutes, in a beautiful sequence starting with Ujayi breath work, sun salutations, Hatha Yoga, Shavasana, meditation, and ending with kirtan sound healing. Unlike the commercialized and frantic yoga classes they offer in gyms, Robyn spent meticulous time teaching and correcting our alignment and showing us variations of the asanas to suit our body types and pre-existing conditions.

On my days coming out of a Yoga class, I would be in a deep state of calm, and even Pedro was affected by it. Robyn's classes were helping to lull my otherwise permanently stormy marriage. I never wanted to stop my yoga practice and went to Robyn's weekly classes for two straight years, until I was seven months pregnant with my second baby, and it became too awkward to hold a downward facing dog.

The first trimester of my second pregnancy was physically challenging, and through this, I knew it was a baby boy because the experience was a total opposite of my first. I was extremely fatigued and developed multiple lymph nodes around my neck area. I preserved all of my strength for my baby girl, who was just over two years old at the time. Luckily, she slept as much as I did, while Pedro was always busy at his surfboard shaping bay six days a week, shaping surfboards half of the time.

On my sixteenth week of pregnancy, the fatigue and exhaustion suddenly stopped; but just when I thought everything was going back to normal, a lump the size of a mini golf ball had been detected in my thyroid. It grew out of nowhere at an alarming speed that the doctors were keen to remove it as soon as possible. They assured me that the operation would not hurt my baby; and for the first time in a long time, I thought about Leon. He would've been an intern by now and well on his way to becoming a surgeon. I missed him and wished that I could talk to him about the medical issues that I was going through. But I was on my own, Pedro didn't really care about what's going to happen, so for lack of better options, I decided to just trust the specialists.

During the weeks leading up to my operation, Pedro was drinking at an out-of-control level. On the first Friday of December 2004 at around eleven o'clock at night, I called his cell phone to ask him what time he would be home. He was at his surfboard shaping bay with his friend Brad and judging by the slur of his speech, he had been drinking for hours. His response was, *"I'll be home when I'm lookin' at ya"* As fate would have it, Pedro was too drunk to press the hang up button on his dial-padded cell phone properly, and I was still on the other end of the line listening to him and his friend, loudly and clearly.

Up until that point, the worst I've seen of Pedro's inebriated state was when he once crawled on the grass, picked up some dog poop, and tried to eat it. There were also times in his drunken stupor when he would reach a rare tipping point and talk about his father with forlorn eyes, and reminisce the only time his old man came to watch him surf when he was nineteen. He would say that he had then felt deeply connected to his father, who was otherwise emotionally unavailable and always out partying and drinking.

On this particular December Friday night at Pedro's surfboard shaping bay, he was in one of these tipping points, except he wasn't talking about his father. He was talking about me. Thinking he had hung up the phone and ended our conversation, he placed it somewhere where I could hear every word they were saying. I listened on the phone for the next forty-five minutes as my heart slowly sealed itself shut to protect me from extreme heartbreak. I heard Pedro tell his friend Brad of how disappointed he had been when he first laid eyes on me in Manila, hoping that I would look like one of those chicks on the sexy calendar above his desk, with big tits and flat stomach, not some straight rod, flat-chested girl who looked like a boy.

And speaking of boys, he said to his friend, that *"Grace's brother is a joshy boy."* I wasn't quite sure what that meant but I knew it was a highly derogatory language. He carried on to say many more things and I stayed on the line until I was numb. Heavily pregnant and waiting for my thyroid operation in a few days, I laid in bed wide awake until the sun came up. Pedro came home after midnight without a clue of what just happened.

First the shock of what I heard kept me awake, then the transcendence followed rather quickly afterwards, which I was grateful for. By seven o'clock the following morning, I felt a sense of deep sadness, but also a sense of white relief. This was what I had been waiting for, to understand why my husband hated me so much; and now I finally get it, he had never liked me as much as he hoped he would. The irony was, although I was determined to make our marriage work, I had never liked him as much as I hoped I would either. It was the absolution that needed to be laid out on the table. We were both as guilty as each other.

I came out to the kitchen where I found him clumsily trying to cut a watermelon. His energy was still angry and the resentment in his eyes palpable. I felt sorry for him and for the situation that he felt trapped in, being a husband to a woman he didn't like and father of one and a half small kids. Whereas he could be living it up in Bali, drinking Bintangs, surfing waves with the locals, and having the women of his current liking. His life so far, was not the life that he preferred. I, on the other hand, was living the life that I preferred, as a mother. And even though my soul was beat by Pedro's lack of kindness, my heart was grateful for what he had given me, a baby girl and a baby boy on the way. For this, I forgave Pedro. Nothing he ever said or did to me would ever cloud the magic of the children that we have together.

I waved the imaginary white flag as I approached him, and calmly spoke about what I heard him say to his friend last night. At first, he projected anger and accused me that I was making things up. But when I repeated his words verbatim, we both knew that I couldn't have made up those words on my own, and he realised that I had indeed, become privy to his deepest resentments and true feelings toward me and some members of my family.

To his credit, Pedro immediately felt remorse. He knew that I was in a fragile state of pregnancy plus pending major operation. But I assured him that I was okay. I felt hurt, but I didn't hold enmity for his true feelings. I suggested that we both try and get through the next couple of months for my operation and the birth of our son, and then we can figure things out later. My calm demeanour threw him completely off guard. Fighting would have been so much easier, but the boxing ring, so to speak, had now collapsed. The parameters of our usual contentions had been dismantled by the burning truth from last night's revelation. I no longer felt the need to prove or defend anything. I was free.

As a form of apology, Pedro said that I deserved to have some peace and distance away from him, so he decided to stay away at a nearby hotel for a few days. I was grateful for this move and as he left that day, I sat on the couch counting the hours that I had been awake – thirty-seven and still going. The adrenaline of self-preservation was still pumping through my veins.

That night I tucked my baby girl in bed as we both touched my belly, and then I promised her and her baby brother to be, that the three of us were going to be just fine. Her angelic face softened into a dreamy state as she closed her eyes and fell asleep.

Once alone, I fished out my high school graduation book from a storage box. It had glossy photos and memories of my final year in high school. Each graduate had a professional head shot with their name, and then below the name was their life motto. I flipped the pages and there I saw myself, a young girl smiling with such exuberance and innocence. The motto said: *"It is better to have loved and lost, than never to have loved at all."* I touched the photo with my fingers and said, *"Promise me you won't ever give up loving."* Then I let my tears fall freely as I mourned the loss of my dream to have a happy family.

I closed the book and took a big breath, trying not to freak out from a sudden familiar sensation of fear. My oldest fear. The fear of being alone. The fear of abandonment.

It took almost three days until my body finally gave in, and I fell into a deep slumber.

Pedro came back in time for my thyroidectomy operation. It went smoothly as planned and the lump was found to be benign.

A month later, I gave birth to a handsome, nine-pound baby boy. His fingers were so long, and his head was huge. He had a cute crease in between his eyebrows, his gaze so noticeably intense even at zero days old, and he pooped non-stop that I couldn't figure out where it was all coming from. But then a nurse assured me that it was a healthy sign for a newborn to release meconium, a.k.a. black jelly baby poop. Well in that case, I thought to myself, what a legend my newborn was.

I was a happy mommy of two beautiful babies, and not even Pedro could diffuse the sunshine that burst through my heart just from looking at my kids, sniffing, kissing, and nursing them. Pedro himself was a proud man, having sired a gorgeous little boy. His family was good to me and especially my mother in law who always had thoughtful little gifts for my kids. Pedro's eldest daughter came to see us regularly to spend time with her siblings.

I focused on making me strong. And because I couldn't attend Robyn's yoga classes for lack of a babysitter, I opted to enroll myself in a gym that provided a good creche service, and I went rain or shine, sometimes twice a day, to channel my mental and emotional energy. During this time, my mother's group was on a hiatus, and my good friend Merri had been in an out of the hospital relapsing into breast cancer.

Pedro didn't drink any less, but then again, I needed a lot less from him. I stopped expecting him to show up as a husband and I consciously quit needing him to love me. It was such a counterintuitive decision to make, but there was no way I could have continued to show vulnerability to Pedro. He was too hard to love. Besides, I was getting a lot of love from my kids and I was beginning to like myself more and more as I got stronger and fitter.

In spite of the bad blood lurking in the shadows within my marriage, it seemed like my life was on the upswing. Like a wounded soldier walking away from the battlefield, somehow it felt like I had already survived the darkest days of my life with Pedro.

Chapter 28
Walking away with an army of angels

In the winter of the following year we moved out of the beach apartment so that Pedro can renovate and sell it for a profit. We rented a house in the burbs with a spacious yard, which was great for the kids, but it had no ocean views to appease Pedro's style. I loved the feeling of being grounded on the dirt after living in a three-storey walk up all these years. But my husband found it almost nightmarish being tethered to suburbia, and to be living amongst people who were not part of the surfing community.

We began to struggle financially as I still wasn't working, and Pedro had to pay the mortgage, the renovations, the rental, plus support his vices as well as me and the kids. It was a big financial cross on his shoulder, and I felt like such an imposition on his life. I wanted nothing more than for both of us to just be free. Whether that's free being together, or free being separated. Co-dependency without mutual love was the most depressing part of my reality at the time.

Despite the work I've done for my physical fitness and emotional resilience, I couldn't deny the hollowness of my soul. But I never stopped praying for strength and I never ran out of hope for a better tomorrow. Somewhere deep inside of me was still that little girl playing in the open fields with the wind blowing her hair and the breeze caressing her face; free to live, free to love, free to be.

One day I got invited to sign up for an internet social platform called *"Friendster"*, which was a lot like the *facebook* of today. I created a profile and immediately got connected with some friends back in the Philippines. After uploading my profile photo, a friend made a comment and said, *"Wow, you still look the same as you always did, you are such a beautiful person inside and out."* I was astounded by their unexpected, generous and loving words. I stared at the screen of the computer as my brain struggled to process the information I just received.

And then the bickering of the voices in my head:

First voice: *"I'm a beautiful person.... I'm a beautiful person? I'm a beautiful person! I am a good person!"*

Second voice: *"So?"*

First voice: *"No, you don't understand. I'm a beautiful person. I'm a good person. But I forgot. And now I remember. I AM A GOOD PERSON."*

Second voice: *"So?"*

First voice: *"So it means I am a good person. I don't deserve to be sad."*

Feeling paranoid, I shunned the voices, walked away from the computer and turned my attention to reading the newspaper. I turned the page to the daily horoscope and mindlessly scanned the little paragraphs, more so out of habit than intention. I have been reading horoscopes since time immemorial, and none of it ever made any sense. Except on that day, it read in no uncertain terms, *"If things aren't working out for you, what are you still doing here?"* The words screamed at me, and I shut the paper so quickly then looked around to make sure that I was alone in the room, that it wasn't some kind of a prank.

That night when Pedro came home, his eyes were blazing from a certain high. Cocaine. I was sitting by the computer desk when he grabbed some mail from the kitchen bench and started waving them on my face. Bills. He yelled at me saying that I was a hoax, and that I couldn't pay a f**n bill if my life depended on it. I swivelled the chair to face him and I watched as his face moved in some kind of a slow motion movie: I tried to pay attention to what exactly he was saying to me but all I could hear was: *"You're such a beautiful person."* And *"If things aren't working out for you, what are you still doing here?"* My body was physically in the same room with Pedro, but my soul was floating so high that even his verbal assault could not match my vibrational frequency. It was a most unexpected, transcendent moment.

As I sipped my coffee the following morning, the fear of being alone as a single mother was gone, and it was replaced by excitement about the possibility of living a good life on my own. I felt a definite shift, and I knew that my angels were in full force when I saw an email telling me that unexpected government assistance of over fifteen hundred dollars had been paid into my bank account. Instantly I knew I was going to use that money to get a place for me and the kids, and I thanked the universe for explicitly pushing me out into a new life.

I kept putting one foot in front of the other. I found a three-bedroom villa in a gated complex and I was quite surprised by how easy it was to secure the lease. Then I told Pedro that I was leaving him within a couple of weeks. His reaction was half sarcasm and half amusement. He had heard this before and didn't believe a word I said. *"Whatever, Grace."* Was his comment.

Every night within those two weeks of waiting to move out, I prayed that I won't wake up the next day and change my mind. I summoned every ounce of courage that I can muster from my bones, and as a result, I woke up every morning feeling more and more determined to do what I wanted to do.

Seven days before the day of moving, Pedro approached me quietly and said, *"I screwed up didn't I?"* I nodded my head and said nothing. He then proposed that he was willing to try and work things out between us for the sake of the kids; and although he made a valid point of trying to work things out for the sake of the kids, I still said nothing, indicating that I wasn't willing to work it out. This time I knew I wasn't leaving because I hated Pedro. I was leaving because I loved me.

In the light of my upcoming separation from my husband, I thought that I could tie a neat bow on my entire past by speaking to my mother. After all these years, a part of me still longed for someone that I could call and just get that one good advice from; someone like a parent.

I thought that in spite of everything, it was worth the phone call to see what great insight my mother could partake with me. She was my mother, after all. But I realised my mistake as soon as she gave me her piece of wisdom. *"Why don't you split the kids, one for him and one for you so that it's easier?"* I was so horrified by her suggestion that I had to sleep in a foetal position with the blanket over my head that night. She had single-handedly re-lived my worst experience, and blatantly told me to do to my children, exactly what she had done to me. Abandon a child for your own personal convenience. I lied awake under my blanket, seething and blaming myself for reaching out to her. *"What a fucked-up piece of advice that was."* Me and my voices huddled together in unison.

In hindsight I realised that the thing I was really looking for, was a form of validation, a blessing of some kind, and maybe even closure. Closure for my marriage, and closure for the broken relationship between my mother and myself. Like two birds in one shot. I wanted a clean slate and to call everything good. But of course, it wasn't to be. How ambitious and naïve was I to think that I had no karma to face, after all the transgressions I have induced to myself, my husband, my kids and many other people along the way. As a matter of fact, my karma was just beginning, rather than ending.

Chapter 29
The last Tango

Becoming a single parent was bittersweet. I thoroughly enjoyed having a peaceful home, but I was also very lonely, and sometimes scared. In a classic form of escapism, I jumped straight into work instead of taking time out to heal and reflect on the lessons I've learned from my broken marriage.

One week into my new life, I went to an employment agency called Mission Australia and told the manager, Janet, that I was available for work even if I didn't get paid. I explained to her that I was a newly single mother and that I would like to spend my time doing something productive during the days that my kids attended day care, with or without pay. This was really my code for *"I don't want to be alone in my house."* She looked a little surprised but nevertheless promised to help. Twenty-four hours later, she called to see if I would be interested in working for them as an admin volunteer for four hours a day, three days a week. In my mind, I screamed, "Hell yeah!" aloud, I said, "I would love to."

Meanwhile, Pedro's first stop straight after I walked out was Bali. While over there on Valentine's day, he sent me a short email saying that on a day like this, there were no other people he would prefer to spend it with, than his family. His way of saying *"I miss you and the kids."* I was touched. That was so Pedro. Trying his best to communicate. It was like we were back to our very first time emailing each other many, many years ago. Full of dreams, expectations and hope. Rosy eyed and delusional.

After six months of volunteering with Mission Australia I've built enough confidence to think that I was ready for a paying job, so I started looking. As it happens, the local Commonwealth Bank of Australia was hiring, and they were located only two minutes from my house. It was the perfect nine-to-five for a new single mother like me.

Getting the job itself was like going through an obstacle course. After a series of online aptitude tests and phone interviews, I was invited to a one-to-three interview with the managers of the local branch. They interrogated me for over an hour which left me very thirsty, with questions like:

"What was the one biggest thing that you had to do above and beyond your duty of responsibility?"
"What would you do if you had been working on a specific sales and service technique and you're not getting any results?"
"What is good service?"
"What makes you a good customer service provider?"
"Who are your customers?"
"Why do you choose to work for the CBA?"
"What is your view of money?"
"What was the largest cash you've ever handled before?"

I felt like I was in a firing squad. There was no water to be had anywhere and by the time they finished with me, my throat was dry as a bone. One of the managers said, *"We usually don't contact you if you're not successful at this stage of the application."* I smiled and eagerly extended my hand to each of them, quietly thinking *"You really should have some water in here."* aloud I said, *"Well it has been a great pleasure meeting you all."*

Thirst aside, I felt empowered by their questions, and for the first time in a long time, a part of me that had been dormant for so long, felt alive again.

Working for the CBA was not just a job but a symbol of worthiness. On a deeper personal level, it was my proof to Pedro, who's opinion still mattered to me at the time, that I wasn't stupid or crazy.

For a closet abuse victim and self-sabotage addict like myself, working in an emotionally sterile environment such as the bank was the perfect hideout. Right from day one, I knew I was going to stay in there for a long, long time, maybe even forever, if it meant that I could escape from facing my demons. Never mind the random racist customer and the odd racist colleague, or even the bully manager and the perverse male patrons; the bank itself was a faceless, publicly owned, well-oiled machine that was on the cusp of shifting its values from being process-centred to being people-centred.

After several corporate jobs in the Philippines, I've seen enough to understand that there was no such thing as a perfect company. And in the years to come I witnessed scores of great colleagues come on board, only to leave the bank shortly after, in search for better working conditions, better pay, better colleagues, better culture, better technology, better values, quicker career progression, etc.… But I stayed for the simple and unshakeable purpose of providing stability and security for my kids. I wanted so badly, so desperately, to become the total opposite of who my mother was to me, and I was extremely overcompensating for my own lost dreams.

Shortly after getting started at the bank, Pedro and I began talking to each other again. I allowed him to see the kids as often as he wished and even to stay at my place whenever he liked. Eventually I let him back into my life again, thinking that maybe this time we can really make it work. Now that I had a job, he could no longer call me stupid and useless.

In my heart, I wanted to try one last time for the sake of my beautiful kids. I felt that I owed it to them to make sure that I left no stones unturned, and to try my absolute best to give them an unbroken, happy family.

With that in mind, Pedro and I began making plans to buy a house in the suburbs together, and started to pick up the pieces of our shattered relationship. But then one Friday afternoon on the eighth of February 2008, came the inevitable coup de grace.

I came home from work to find him drunk and ranting in front of the computer, while the kids were watching TV. I proceeded to cook four pieces of T-Bone steak for dinner and made a comment to no one in particular, *"Hhhmmm, I'm starving, I think I'm gonna have the biggest piece if that's okay by everybody."* Pedro stood up from the computer desk, looking rather tall and menacing with a belligerent face, as he yelled *"Who the f**k do you think you are to think you should have the biggest steak?"*

Then he accused the Commonwealth Bank of stealing money from his redraw account saying that our mortgage officers were all a bunch of incompetent hoots. As I watched and listened to his litany, my heart sank like a pancake. He had finally beaten the last straw.

My job was my newfound source of wellbeing and self-worth, and the moment he attacked my employer and my colleagues, it became clear as day that Pedro simply hated everything that I represented. Everything that I would do, he would find a way to destroy, for as long as we were together. It was a sensible, sobering realisation, and I was grateful that it happened sooner rather than later.

I went about the business of cleaning the kitchen. I saw him retire to the bedroom and never heard from him again for the rest of the night. He was sloshed and out to it. I snuggled up with the kids in my daughter's bedroom and slept like a baby. When morning came he was nowhere to be found, and at two o'clock in the afternoon he sent me a casual text saying he had been for a surf, and suggested that we arrange a time to look at a house for sale, together; like as if nothing had happened the night before. I texted back *"What makes you think that we can successfully buy a house together? No thanks. Goodbye Pedro."* After eight years of trying, I finally ran out of steam. It was time to move on, on my own terms.

He later tried to entice me to get back together by using the threat of poverty, saying that I would not be getting a cent off of him. But I simply didn't give a rat's arse. My currency was love, and in that department, Pedro was bankrupt.

When sober, Pedro was quite a smart man and he finally put his heightened emotions aside and split our affairs in an out of court settlement. At first, we agreed to share the custody of our children based on a rigid schedule. But it quickly became null and void, as we proceeded to simply play everything by ear and be flexible with each other for the benefit of the kids.

Pedro and I almost always disagreed on everything under the sun, but when it came to the kids' welfare and wellbeing, we were always on the same page. Desperate not to duplicate each of our childhood trauma, we were determined to raise our kids as best we can, together or separately.

And so, the tale of almost-love between a high functioning alcoholic and a high functioning emotional zombie had ended in a not so happily ever after, but amicably enough so that nobody killed anyone, and everybody lived to tell their own versions.

There was no healing to be had and my cycle of self-sabotage lived on.

PART THREE

Chapter 30
My beloved, demonic self

Fourteen days after the stock market crashed in 2008, I signed a contract to sell my first home during a most economically vulnerable time. The property market was rapidly sliding and the whole world was weary of what could become a global financial crisis.

To market the property, the agent had to open my house for buyers' inspection every weekend, making my home available to anyone who owned a heartbeat, regardless if they were genuinely interested in property buying, plain stickybeaks, or a single mother's worst nightmare: stalkers.

The first inkling I had of a stalker was from the agent's open house report on week two of advertising. Four prospects inspected my property that weekend, and according to the agent's rundown of their profiles, there was a man who wouldn't elaborate his purpose of inspection, except that he lived in the neighbourhood and that he was there to *'have a look'*. My intuition told me that this was suspect, but I ignored the feeling for lack of substantial information and evidence.

A few days later, a man knocked on my door. He was in his early thirties like me, with blue eyes, curly blond hair, and a hook nose similar to a witch's. He was wearing a work uniform from one of the big entertainment clubs in the area and looked harmless enough through the screen door.

I said, *"Hello?"*

His very first sentence was *"Have you sold the house yet?"*

A red flag instantly came up in my brain and a voice that said, *"Beware, how does he know you're selling your house."*

Then another voice said, *"He's soft spoken and young"*

One of my ex-husband's worst traits was his loud voice and how he constantly yelled at me. I became obsessed in making sure I spoke only to people who never yelled, and were preferably soft spoken.

So I listened to the second voice and entertained the stranger's question. *"Not yet, are you interested in buying?"*

He laughed a nervous, somewhat stupid laugh and smirked, *"Maybe when I win the lotto."*

Second red flag. *"This guy's is a loser."* The voice said.

But a part of me seemed hell bent toward the dangerous path of lonely desperation. At this point, I had been a single mother for almost ten months and deeply craving for company and affirmation. Something that none of my friends seemed to be able to fulfil. I had somehow quietly developed a belief that I needed a man to do life alongside and help me raise my little kids. I was in an exhausted, empty space, and witlessly looking at the wrong things and wrong people for the answers.

In the course of my short conversation with the stranger, he mentioned that he lived only four doors down from me, and that's when I deduced that he was the stalker in question, but I didn't confront him about it. Instead, I allowed him to suggest that one day we should have a drink together.

And just like that, out of loneliness and desperation, I dove headfirst into the hands of my next abuser, by this stranger, stalker-neighbour, Luke.

During this time, I had begun looking for my next home and immediately found the ideal one in a peaceful suburb. A cozy, three-bedroom house that backed on to a beautiful retaining rock wall with dainty ferns, shaded by a couple of young Lilly Pilly trees. It had an old rose feature wall in the living room, a Fuschia feature wall in the main bedroom, and an organic green feature wall in the dining room. The moment I stepped into the house, I was enveloped by a feeling of warmth and comfort, and immediately fell in love with it. But it was fifty thousand dollars above my affordability scale. So I made an outrageous offer for fifty thousand dollars less than the sale price, because I loved it too much to not give it a try.

Naturally, the vendor said no. In fact, I was told that they said *"Hell no."* But because they had already been trying to sell this house for a couple of months, and there's been hardly any interest in it, I offered a sunset clause, which meant that if they had a buyer who offered them their desired sale price, I would get the first dibs to outbid that prospective buyer. The only problem with this clause was, I had to have the money if I ever had to outbid anyone, which brought me back to the challenge of selling my current property for a neat profit, to make up for the difference.

By this time, the GFC was still in the upswing. Thousands of people have lost millions of dollars on their high-risk investments in Australia, and the property market was predicted to follow suit. It was arguably the worst time to sell a property; but I had a hunch that my buyer was just around the corner.

As you believe, so it will be. A buyer surfaced from out of the blue and offered to pay thirty thousand dollars more than what I paid for the property, a short five months ago. Suddenly I was poised to buy the cute little home with the Lilly Pilly trees and feature walls.

I found that the logistical side of life was like a walk in the park. Buying, selling, re furbishing property, working, cooking, paying bills, mentoring my kids, doing homework, dealing with teachers, handling my clients, handling difficult clients, managing difficult colleagues; you name it, I got it covered. One would think that I was on top of this game called life.

The strangest thing of all was, it was the other way around. Life was toppling me over. Deep inside, I felt so dry and barren. I had a yearning for something without a name.

That year on Christmas holidays, Pedro took my kids for an entire week. It was the longest I'd ever been separated from my kids, and it rocked me to the core.

I was fine for the first two days of them being away, but on the third day, I started to feel strangely ill at ease and on edge. To make use of my time and restless energy, I decided to run a couple of errands including going to the doctor to get an overdue Pap Smear. Once there, the medical receptionist asked if my contact details were still the same. Having moved house and all, I was obliged to give her new and correct information. After going through my new address, phone number and allergies, she asked, *"Your next of kin?"* I was baffled. *"Next of kin is the contact person in case of emergency."* She insisted. I was still baffled. *"Like a relative? Family member?"* She badgered me. *"Yes, yes, I understand you. Just give me a minute."* I mumbled. My brain was like scrambled eggs as I tried to think of someone. Finally, I gave up thinking and told her the name of the one and only 'next of kin' I had in Australia. My ex-husband.

The depressing realization that I had no one in case of emergency, but my ex-husband, numbed the indignity of cold steel probing and poking my womanhood during the pap smear. Afterwards, I walked briskly away from the doctor's office, and once in my car, I began to weep. I wept silently at first, then I started to sob. On the road, I couldn't stop sobbing for the entire eight-minute drive on the way home. And as I stepped inside my house, I was greeted by an emptiness and silence that haunted the deepest crevice of my broken soul.

I tried to breathe deep to diffuse the build-up of my emotions. But instead of pacifying what was building up inside of me, the deeper I breathed the more I lost control, and then I began to hyperventilate. I remember hearing a deafening roar coming out of my mind, it was so powerful that I couldn't hear it in my ears, but I felt it shatter all of my superficial defences.

Every inch of bravado and every ounce of courage in my gut crumbled into a blinding dust of fury. I screamed. *Aaaaaaaarrrrrr-ggggghhhhhhhhh!!!!!!!* I screamed and roared repeatedly until I couldn't hold my body and dropped to the floor. Then I wailed. I wailed like a banshee and cried for the mother that I never had. All of a sudden, I was a little girl again. Hopeless, afraid and exposed.

There was a voice I could hear from somewhere, a voice so weak and so far away, telling me that I will be okay, but I couldn't see where the voice was coming from, I couldn't feel the presence of the voice, and ultimately I felt betrayed by its whisper. *"How dare you!"* I said to the weak voice. *"How dare you say I will be okay! You have no f***c**ng clue what it's like to live in here! Aaaaarrrrgggghhhhh!!!!"* I screamed again, the anger transforming into wild energy, so volatile that my body was levitating and retracting, seemingly at once.

Then I opened my eyes, and I looked towards the window, and it was dark. I was lying on the kitchen floor with my left cheek on the tiles, half of my torso was flat on the floor while the rest of my body was in some kind of a letter S knot. I didn't know how long I've been lying there for. I listened to the silence, and then after what seemed like eternity, I focused my attention on my fingers and willed each of them to move the way I wanted them to. *Forefinger, up, down. Thumb, left, right. Pinky finger, flex, curl. Rude finger, fuck you.* Finally, I moved my legs and squared my hips.

Miraculously, I had somehow regained my grip on the monsters spewing out of my body. I slowly crawled my way upstairs, praying. I prayed that I would refrain from hurting myself, and I prayed for salvation from whatever it was that was taking over me. I began to notice my tears for the first time during the entire ordeal, and I touched my face, grateful that I still have my life in the palm of my hands.

I found a small window of strength and half walked to the bathroom, like an injured gorilla hanging on to the railing. I stepped in the shower and turned the cold water on, and sat there for a long, long time, crying. The anger had abated, by my sorrow was unfathomable. I began calling the name that I never, ever call. *"Mama."* I gathered my knees together and hugged myself as I whispered her name again, *"Ma."*

Since the day when I was a small child, and my mother threatened to take me to the police should I fight and hurt other kids again, I made a silent pact with myself that I would never look to my mother for help, ever again. From that day forward, every wall that I built was designed to barricade myself from calling upon her, ever again. But on this night, I could no longer contain the toxicity of my suppressed loss and hatred. I was broken. I had to utter the name of the one that broke me.

Later that night I turned the shower off. I was cold. Hungry. Tired. With every pain that my human body could articulate, meant that the face of my collective self, the one for the show, was back on. So I dried myself, stared at the mirror, and relieved to see that I haven't dismembered my body or tried to hospitalize myself. I gave out a big sigh of relief and walked around the house aimlessly, before I finally fell asleep with all the lights on, a tell-tale sign that I was scared shitless of my other self. Because I never, ever sleep with the lights on.

Chapter 31
The shadows are full of piranhas

One thing I hated when I was a bank teller was having to deal with creepy male customers who tried to pick me up, or made some snide, sexually disparaging comment toward me. They would greet me with a sleazy, *"Hey baby girl how are you today?"* or *"Where are you from?"* or *"You don't look like you're old enough to have kids, sweetheart."* And it wasn't so much what they said, as much as how they said it, like the emphasis in their words or the lewd quality of their facial expressions.

The one thing that these men had in common were their age bracket of forty-five and upwards, while men my age were always polite and normal. It was a vexation that I faced almost every day for the first four years of working in the bank, and I never complained to my colleagues because somehow, I blamed myself for being susceptible to it. I thought that because no one else seemed to have the same problem, then maybe it was just me.

After a few months of this near-daily experience, I learned to identify the typical *profile* of these pervert customers, and I developed a radar that I could spot them from ten metres away, which is probably otherwise known as paranoia. I learned how to block their energy and made them feel that I had absolute zero interest in conversing with them, no matter that they were the bank's customers. I would only make a half a second eye contact with them, and I would keep the conversations to a bare minimum, focusing on the transaction at hand, so that when they asked invasive questions like *"How's your kids?"* or *"What's been happenin?"* or *"How was your weekend?"* I would deliberately dismiss them by saying *"It's allright."* Then I would look behind them and yell out *"Next please?"* Which forced them to literally move away and leave.

I knew that I risked getting customer complaints for being rude to bank patrons, but the fact that none of these sleazy customers ever complained to the manager about my unprofessionalism, was a clear sign that they were indeed predators looking for prey, or so I believed.

The thought that some people would take me for being vulnerable and victimizable, gave me a feeling of quiet rage. I hated being made to feel weak, and the more I was exposed to those creepy voyeurs, the more diabolical I felt.

Without being consciously aware that I had become paranoid, not to mention bone weary over this cat and mouse game of self-protection from perverse men, I went on with life oblivious to the build-up of my anger, resentment and emotional isolation. One thing that I failed to recognize, was how the behaviours of these opportunistic, rather vulgar men were very similar to someone whom I used to be married to. Little did I know that I wasn't really trying to run away from strangers, as much as I was trying to run away from my past.

Upon waking up the next morning after that spine-chilling nervous breakdown, I began to feel the familiar clutch of heightened uncertainty. A trepidation that being all alone as a single mother was a burden, instead of freedom. From a haunting loneliness in the pit of my soul, I conjured an image of a man beside me to help me raise my kids. I became attached to the idea that if only there was a soft spoken, kind man who did not present as a sugar daddy material would come into my world, then I will be happy.

Again, as you believe, so it will be. A couple of weeks before moving to my new house, I bumped into the neighbour Luke again. I was driving slowly down an alleyway to take my kids to the park on a Saturday morning, when I saw a shirtless man in a pair of shorts and runners. He was young and fit, and as my car got closer to him, I drove even slower, curious to see his face. When he turned, it was the stalker Luke, and he flashed a smile at me and I smiled back. I braced myself for any red flag raising voices in my head, but they didn't come. I could instead hear the chatter of my kids at the back, like little birds singing, so I drove away with an impetuous verdict that Luke seemed nice after all.

As if he read my thoughts, he knocked on my door again later that week and offered to have a drink with me. I accepted without a second thought, even though I couldn't remember the last time I tasted alcohol. *"What are you doing?"* The voice in my head said. *"I'm willing to 'learn' what we may have in common. If this guy likes a to have a casual drink, then perhaps that is fine."* Was what I told the voice, signalling it to shut up and leave me alone.

It didn't take long for me to allow Luke to take space in my life. One drink turned into a couple, a couple turned into a night out, a night out turned into a sleepover and a sleepover turned into a toxic relationship between a desperate single mother and her stalker turned boyfriend.

Right from the start, it was obvious what kind of a person Luke was, but I wasn't willing to see him for who he really was. Always forgetting his wallet when we were out together, always having his petrol gauge on near empty, and consistently insinuating the stress of having to borrow money from his mother to pay his rent arrears, he was a chronic gambler.

Luke was soft spoken, and he worked a full-time retail job during the day and a casual job as a bar man during the nights, and most weekends. I have never seen anyone work such long hours for such cheap labour. He told me that he worked hard so he can pay off all the debts that his ex-wife had left him. He said he got really depressed when his father suddenly died and then his wife left him shortly after, which was why he got started with the drinking.

What he failed to explain was why he was always broke, even though he technically earned more than I did, due to the sheer amount of overtime he was doing. What I failed to see was the stark difference between my natural tendency to create abundance, and his natural tendency to wallow in poverty.

Instead, I chose to see him as an injured bird that I can rescue from its state of brokenness and become the heroine that the bird deserved to have. The biggest problem with my intention was not that I was trying to be a hero, but that Luke was never in the market for rescuing. You can lead the horse to the water, but you can never make the horse drink the water.

After settling into my new house, Luke came over to see me more and more often. One night I questioned why he never contributed into anything we ate, drank or did together, hoping that he would stop freeloading on me. He was enraged by my audacity to call him out. He called me names and yelled at me for all the neighbours to hear as he drove away in his car under the influence of several beers.

By mid-morning the next day, I received thirty-two missed calls from him while I was at work, none of which I returned. But then on my lunch break, I tried to go for a brief walk to get some fresh air, when Luke ambushed me from around the corner. We ended up making a scene in public where I told him to go away and leave me alone, using swear words and screaming from the top of my lungs. The sickest part of it was, the angrier I became, the meeker he turned. He steadily said *"I'm so sorry I love you I promise I didn't know what came over me. Forgive me, I love you, I'm sorry."* Over and over again until I became so exhausted, I couldn't scream anymore. After the devil in me was spent, then the desperate, lonely, self-sabotaging single mother was left to pick up the shrapnel from my rage.

The biggest torture that a man can ever subject a weak woman to, is by beating the hell out of her spirit with vilification and shame, and then breaking her down some more by pleading with can't-live-without-you-apology, effectively placing her in an emotional dead end.

The most vicious self-sabotage that a woman can subject herself to, is a co-dependent, toxic relationship with an addict. Whether that addiction is on alcohol, drugs, gambling, sex, self-harm or all of the above, a woman will never win over any kind of addiction. This was the biggest lesson that I would later learn in a most painful way, but not before getting through a long four-year battle between hope and fear.

Hope that one day, through showing Luke good examples of how his life can change, then maybe we could have a future together. Fear that if I broke up with him, he would hurt me as much as he had threatened to do so, each time I've tried breaking up with him.

The battle between good and evil in my body, mind, and soul was ferocious. Every day, I lived for my kids and to do good in my career, and then there was my relationship with Luke. In this pecking order of priorities, none of them included me. In my mind, I believed that my job and my relationship status defined who I was. That if I had a decent job and a man who didn't resemble a sugar daddy, then I would be happy. I thought that in order to feel better inside, I had to make everything on the outside look "normal". But the truth was, there had never been anything normal about my life, ever.

One day I received a message from my dear friend and mentor Merri. It was a batch text that she sent to me and my friends from the mother's group: *"It appears that my battle with this cancer isn't over yet, and it has been four months now since I've been calling Pindara, my home. I look forward to one day soon when I will be sitting with you over coffee and catching up."*

I had a pressing feeling about her text, so I left work and immediately drove to Pindara hospital. During the fourty-five-minute drive, I reflected on how much Merri meant to me as a friend. I knew she had been on remission from cancer ever since we met seven years ago, but because her role in my life was a cross between friendship and professional counsellor, we hardly ever talked about the details of her breast cancer journey. Merri was always a quiet force to reckon with, especially for the women in my mother's group. I couldn't shake the gnawing sensation that her message had a finality to it, like she was reaching out before things could be too late. I was scared. But I willed myself to drive and just focus on being with her again.

Apart from a turban that covered the aftermaths of chemotherapy on her head, Merri looked rested and at peace, like she always did. Her voice was the same low toned, soothing sound that felt like Aloe Vera had been poured inside my chest. If she felt sick, she showed it only through a tinge of fleeting discomfort in her eyes.

Above her hospital bed hung small, colourful affirmation banners in English and Sanskrit, with beautiful words about happiness, life, and love written on them. The window was half open and a slight breeze swayed the banners ever so slightly, creating an energy of serenity.

She wanted to sit up on her bed, but she couldn't get her head comfortable and wished she had a neck pillow. Luckily, I've always kept a couple in my car, so I fetched one for Merri and as she cradled her neck inside the curve of the pillow, she closed her eyes and gave a slight sigh of relief. It was such a happy experience just being next to her again. I massaged her swollen feet, and she said that I was a natural healer and that maybe I have a gift for *Reiki*, and she urged me to look into it.

This woman knew the depths of my despair during my marriage with Pedro, and she understood me, more than I ever understood myself. In many ways, Merri had walked the path that I was treading on, having been through divorce and single motherhood herself.

Then I felt that she wanted to say something important. She took a deep, sharp breath and spoke carefully and deliberately,

"Grace, you have always found it hard to forgive. Forgiveness never came easy for you, forgiveness of yourself and forgiveness of others. Grace, there's something I want to say to you, and I hope that you will always remember this. I want you to know that everyone, every single person, every single soul - when they do something, they are always doing their best."

She took another breath while I held mine, and as we looked at each other's eyes, time seemed to hold very still. My mind was racing, trying to digest the depth of what she said, whilst also panicking about the urgency in her voice.

"When your mother abandoned you, she was doing her best. When Pedro did the things and said all the things he said to you, he was doing his best. The criminal who commits a crime, no matter how hideous.... you must one day know, that everyone, does their best, at the very moment that they were doing it. Every single one of us, we do our best, at the very moment that we do so. We do our best, at the very moment..."

She repeated herself a couple more times as the intensity of her voice subsided, and finally she said, *"Promise me that you will remember that."* I nodded as I quietly accepted that this was my final gift. Somehow, she knew that she may not have another chance to say it, and it tore me up to think that I may never see her again.

We sat in silence for the rest of the time as I quietly touched, and pressed, and patted the joints of her toes and the roundness of her ankle. It was a contemplative day spent in her company, and she let me be with no judgement, just love and acceptance.

I didn't ask my beloved friend about her prognosis, because I didn't want her to tell me that she was dying, I only wanted her to hear me say that we will see each other again. I gave her a big hug and told her that I will see her again.

She passed away six weeks after that day.

Chapter 32

Classic, elegant fear

Merri's death subdued my demons. For a little while I didn't hear any voices, and my life seemed to be in some kind of a lull. Despite the undercurrent of bad blood between Luke and I, we had some truly beautiful experiences during our time together. We went on a few road trips to see his family, some six hours away into the mountainous regions of western New South Wales.

This was the period of my life when I discovered how much I loved long-distance driving and the therapeutic effect of the forests, hills, and quiet country towns; the sobering pleasure of cold, winter nights away from the coastline, and the grounding presence of farms and country folks. The experience of such a simple kind of life, just like the way it was when I was a little girl, was calming for me.

One day Luke said it would really make him happy if he had his name on a piece of property and feel that his hard work was going into something tangible. I wanted to be proactive and find ways for my relationship with Luke to improve, so I tried to make bold actions to make him happy.

Being the banker that I was, I went to work on the maths and came up with a solution. We could buy an investment property together, using my house equity as collateral, and his disposable income combined with the rental income to pay off the investment. After a period of five to ten years, we can then look at reselling the investment for a neat profit.

To protect my interest, we drew up a "tenants in common only" investment contract, on a 60/40 profit share, in his favour. Aware of his gambling habit, the caveat was for me to manage the rental income and investment repayments, by becoming his "cashflow manager". The biggest advantage for him was I agreed to absorb his unsecured car loan and credit card debts into the secured investment loan and reduce the life of his residual debts from fifteen years down to two and a half.

I don't know that Luke cared to fully understand the ins and outs of our business agreement, but he jumped at the idea that his own personally accumulated debts would be cleared and absorbed into an investment loan. An investment that promised to make him tens of thousands of dollars in capital gains, without having to fork out any capital himself, and all he had to do was to limit his alcohol consumption and gambling shenanigans.

This was, hands down, the most reckless decision I have ever made in my entire life.

Irrespective of the "tenants in common only" protection clause, not only did I expose myself to potential financial ruin, I had also inadvertently given Luke more weapons to threaten me with, as far as our relationship was concerned.

Before the investment property, Luke could only threaten to beat up my future boyfriends if we ever broke up. After we took on the investment property, Luke threatened to clean me out for everything I've got, every time I wanted out of the relationship.

And of all the things that Luke threatened me with, there was one thing that I was truly afraid of. I was afraid to be alone. I would never have admitted it to myself at the time, but that was the bare truth of why it took me so long to finally, once and for all, bust the shackles of abusive relationships and wake up to myself.

Chapter 33
Fatal Resurrection

One day I was at home dusting a high cabinet when I felt a sharp pain shoot from my right arm through to my collarbone. The pain lingered for a few days until it became too painful for me to do my tasks at work. I decided to see my doctor who then immediately referred me to an orthopaedic surgeon. An x-ray showed that my right shoulder socket was semi dislodged. There was an abnormal cartilage growth in between the shoulder socket and the base that connected the collarbone and shoulder girdle. It was the size of a newborn's thumb, and it caused sharp, stinging pain, grinding my bones and muscles with each movement I made.

The surgeon's opinion was the injury was old and most likely caused by high impact from playing sports. I begged to differ, *"With all due respect Doc, but I have never played sport in my life."* He looked at me nonchalantly and said, *"Then perhaps it was from something else, nonetheless a sudden impact that's similar to sport-related injuries."*

I looked away as I mentally recalled an incident over ten years ago in Bali when I was pregnant with my daughter. Pedro was teaching me how to do boxing. *"So that you can fight and defend yourself if you need to."* Were his words. He also boasted that he was one of the best boxers he personally knew.

I watched him demonstrate a straight jab and carefully observed his calculated footing. Pedro maintained laser focus on the imaginary face of his opponent, while he explained the moves to me. His wrists were poised in front of him, with his dominant arm just a couple of inches higher than the other, barricading himself from his opponent. I was a spring chicken and I soaked up everything that my new husband taught me.

One night, Pedro was getting ready to go out partying till the wee hours of the morning. Being pregnant, I didn't want to go anywhere near clubs, but I also didn't want to be alone all night in a strange house, in a strange country, with nothing to do. We had no pay TV in the house, smart phones and social media weren't invented yet, all the TV channels were in Indonesian, and hardly anyone in the compound spoke proper English. I felt trapped and extremely weary being alone. But Pedro didn't care, by this time he had already popped a party pill and just wanted to get to the clubs.

I was sitting on the bed begging him to stay, but he just told me to shut up as he walked past me. I was so enraged that I jumped up, and in a quick stride I was standing on the edge of the bed, towering over him. Suddenly I took a stance where I was poised to jab, raised both my fists in front of my face, and with laser focus on my target, I gave the mightiest punch I could muster, and *wham!*

The entire three second transition took him by surprise, and as he turned to face me, my right fist landed on the space between his ear and jawline. The impact was so strong that Pedro temporarily lost balance and put his hand on his left ear. My right arm recoiled and went numb for a little while. When Pedro took his hand off his face, his left ear was split open and thick, crimson blood gushed down his neck. I was in so much shock that I fell back on my sitting position and didn't really move much for the next few hours. (Pedro rushed to stop at the emergency clinic and got stitched up before heading over to his nightclub parties.)

It was the only sudden impact involving my arm and shoulder that I can think about, and it happened such a long time ago that the growth in my shoulder socket made sense. Feeling smug, I smirked at the memory of it.

Puzzled by the strange expression on my face, the doctor asked me, "Are you okay?" Aloud I responded "Yes, I'm okay, thank you." Silently I thought *"Son of a bitch deserved it."*

The doctor suggested an arthroscopic surgery to fix my shoulder and liberate me from pain. He would use a probing device with a built-in camera to poke and re-adjust my human joints without the need to slice up my human body. It sounded simple and easy compared to the thyroidectomy I've had, where the doctors literally slit my throat open and stitched it back together like I was a ragdoll. I briefly weighed the options that I didn't really have and said yes to the arthroscopic operation.

On the day of the surgery, I was in a particularly vulnerable mood. Luke and I just had another fight and I was thinking about my kids. Knowing that there were risks to receiving general anaesthesia, fear came over me. And when the anaesthetist stood over my head on the operating table, I cried and said, *"Please take care of me. I have two small children and I would like to be here to look after them."* The anaesthetist looked at me compassionately and assured me that everything will be okay, then I closed my eyes and fell asleep.

Hours passed.

I listened closely and felt alarmed to hear new voices other than the usual residents in my head. High pitched and demanding, as opposed to Pandora's low tone and compelling, these new voices were switching from the right to the left. I tried to open my eyes and see where they were coming from, but it felt like there were metal plates weighing my eyes down.

Through the tiny slit that I could peep through my eyelids, I sensed shadows and shapes in white and blue moving around. *"Grace, Grace, can you hear me!"* A woman's voice yelled out. *"We're getting her back, she can hear!"* Another high-pitched voice yelled out. I felt so sleepy and so tired that I wished they would stop invading my peace and quiet. I just wanted to rest. *"Grace. Grace. Grace!"* It was relentless.

And then I sensed a man in white standing next to my bed, he didn't move or say much. Instead he just stood there like a rock, and his presence willed me to fight the sleepiness. I felt like I was being hypnotised to arise. *"Wake up."* Was the language I felt from this man, although I didn't hear him say anything.

I jerked my body to an upward position, not fully realising that I had been completely flat on my back and zonked out for hours. As I tried to move my neck, I doubled over and then a gush of heat shot from my stomach to my throat. My head hung on the edge of the bed as I puked hot slime out of my mouth, and as my eyes adjusted a little more, I realized I was coughing out blood. The tiled, bloodied hospital floor beaming at my efforts. "Aaarrrggghhh..." I sighed in half relief, half bewilderment. Questions started racing in my head, so fast that they made dizzy and weak.

I couldn't utter my words, I just lied there willing the voices to tell me more. By this time, I had figured that the voices weren't mine, they were of other, real people moving around me.

Then suddenly I remembered that I was in the hospital, and judging by the fact that I had just vomited, I knew I was alive. *"Oh, yay."* I flatly congratulated myself, feeling exhaustion and relief wash over me. While the sullen voice of Pandora declared, almost in sarcasm, *"You made it."*

Eventually the owner of the high-pitched voices took shape in the form of three female nurses. They were very efficient and strong. I looked around the room for the man who stood by my bed and hypnotised me out of my slumber; and although I couldn't see his presence, I felt like he guided me out of the darkness. I uttered a silent *"Thank you."*

After cleaning me up and checking my vitals, the nurses left, and the room became hushed with the occasional haunting sound of gale force winds. I looked out the window and it was a dismal, stormy summer day, as if nature commiserated to what was happening inside the hospital room.

Suddenly the surgeon appeared in front of me, soaking wet from rain and somewhat mollified. Taking in his appearance, I could tell that he didn't just come fresh out of the operating room. I, on the other hand, had clearly just come fresh out of the operating room.

I was confused, so I asked, "What happened Doctor?" A nurse came in behind him and explained that the doctor was already on his way home, but they asked him to turn around and come back. "Why?" I probed. The doctor gently and casually mentioned to me that they were having trouble waking me up. "Why?" I insisted. The surgeon looked at me and explained *"You were a little upset right before surgery, and the anaesthetist had given you just a little more than your dose because of it. We thought it would be no problem, but it took the nurses a little longer to wake you up. You're going to be okay now."* It was the compassionate code for "You almost died from an overdose of anaesthesia but you're good now."

That I almost died due to a slight error in judgement was a hard piece of information to take, and even harder to process. My mind shifted in different states of invincibility, vulnerability and gratitude. I realised that I had, once again, survived another near-death experience. Yet I shuddered at the thought of how fickle human life can be and felt so humbled that I have been given one more chance, one more time.

Unable to go back to work with my shoulder in a sling, I had time in my hands to contemplate some existential affirmations. The universe had given me a brush with death that made me appreciate my very own existence, my very own blood that circulated through my veins, my own muscles that protected my bones, the skin on my own body that allowed me to enjoy the sunshine.

It was as if, for the first time, *I became aware of me.* I became aware of a beautiful, strange sensation that the body I own was more than just a body, that it was also a vessel. A vessel that can turn life on, or turn life off. Realising that the power behind that vessel was based on *the way that I am*, and the actions that I chose to take, was breathtaking.

Coming back to work after a six-week recovery, we had a new branch manager. Sandy had been with the bank for as long as I've been alive. She started her banking career when she was sixteen and she was intuitive and astute in making executive decisions. She recognized the skills that I could put to better use than simply counting money as a bank teller and offered me a promotion as a full-time customer service specialist. A job that I'd always coveted since I started four years ago, where I would have the ability to speak to clients not just about their banking, but also their future goals and dreams. The bank referred to this conversation as the "needs analysis". For me, it was an opportunity for deep and meaningful discussions.

I accepted the position with a grateful heart and immediately began working on my mindset. I wanted to be more approachable to all of our bank patrons, including the forty-something, pervert customers that I used to avoid like the plague.

I decided that I would hold myself and all of my clients in high esteem. And if I ever felt creeped out by anyone, I would simply use highly professional language so that they would want to stay professional themselves. My back up plan was to ask a colleague for intervention, should I ever feel too uncomfortable.

But it turned out that I never had to worry about pervert customers ever again. The moment I decided to hold myself and all of my clients in the highest regard and esteem, all of my conversations became fruitful, meaningful and productive. Those that I judged to be perverted were transformed, and became just like everybody else, friendly and harmless.

I may not have become sagacious after a near-death experience, but something had definitely shifted in me. As I changed the way I viewed myself, the people around me, and things in general, also started to change.

I discovered a passion for deep and meaningful conversations that allowed people to be candid and even vulnerable without feeling unsafe. My self-confidence and sense of self-worth increased with every interaction I had with my customers, on the phone, or in person. They would share stories of their lives along with their financial goals and challenges with me, and then when they asked me about my own life and upbringing, I always just put it down to, *"I was born and raised in Southern Philippines."* I never offered any more details, but instead I regaled them with fun stories from my travels and adventures.

I never talked about my real past to any of my colleagues or clients during my twelve years at the bank because it was the one place where I could be normal just like everyone else, and I didn't want any past memories to taint that experience. The bank was my daily dose of safe haven, and I was determined to keep it that way.

Chapter 34
Showdown

In the winter following my shoulder surgery, my daughter and I began feeling strangely ill. We were so tired for no apparent reason and could hardly eat anything. Some days we slept for hours on end, only to generate half an hour of energy and then lay back down again.

A series of blood tests showed that we have both contracted glandular fever. An illness with no medical cure other than rest and recovery. I asked Pedro to take our son while I took time off from work to recuperate with my daughter. In the meantime, Luke hung around like a ticking time bomb, waiting for the right moment to blow up. He had been seething through my detached attitude and lack of interest in his usual dramas.

I was so weak from the virus that I could hardly lift a finger, my house was a mess and it was a herculean effort to keep my daughter and myself hydrated and breathing. And just when I thought things couldn't get much worse, I received a message from my brother Larry saying that his wife had been diagnosed with stage three breast cancer.

Remembering the loss of my dear friend Merri, an overwhelming sense of fear came over me. I called my brother to give him some support, only to be confronted by his incoherent sobs and out of control wailing. From what I could hear, he was trying to tell me that my sister-in-law was in the operating room undergoing a mastectomy, and he feared that she might not come out of the operating room alive.

I felt distraught. My big brother, the only man that I ever truly loved and respected, the strong, courageous, super smart and kind brother that I knew, was not there. All I could hear was a man gripped with the insurmountable terror of losing the love of his life. His voice was unrecognizable, his sobs came from a place so dark it reminded me of something so familiar, and his breathing was an aberration of highs, lows and sideways howling. As I listened to him, it struck me that my brother was losing his mind in a state of pure, unadulterated, fear.

Fear breeds fear. And fear spreads into fifty different shades of annihilation.

Knowing that my mother would do anything for my big brother, I wasted no time in calling her to report Larry's mental and emotional state. I wanted to see how we could collaborate to help Larry and his wife. But the phone rang out. I tried calling her three more times, knowing that she had caller ID, but nothing.

So then I called my aunt Ellie and asked her to tell my mother to pick up the phone, to which she kindly obliged. But then she called me back very quickly and reported, *"I have spoken to your mother and she knows you've been trying to call her, but she said that as far as your brother is concerned, she has everything taken cared of. And there will be no need for you to get involved."*

I was enraged by my mother's dismissal. A ball of heat coiled inside my gut, then it shot through my chest and up to the centre of my brain. Anger rose from the pit of my stomach and Pandora came out in all her fire and glory.

The only thing I could feel was hatred. Hatred for a woman who never allowed me to love. Hatred for a woman who put a cork in the outflow of my heart. Disgust for the way she treated me and absolute vile for her glaring narcissism. It was like my heart had frozen once again, and my body was on fire. Pandora was wide awake and incensed. Sleep eluded me that night.

The next day I was still sweltering from Pandora's emancipation when Luke came by and began demanding, for the nth time, that I allow him to move-in to my house. Since the early stage of our relationship, he had been pressuring me to let him move into my house so that he could save money on rent. And each and every time he brought it up, I said no. The argument would usually end with him calling me a *"selfish c*_t"*.

On this particular day the heat was on and *I* was conditioned for it. Pandora was awake and ferocious, like a predator waiting for her prey. When Luke started yelling, I outmatched him by screaming like there was no tomorrow. Possessed by fury, I walked around the house grabbing every random item that he owned and left at my place, throwing them at his face as I screamed that he will never, ever move in with me, over my dead body.

My anger was unstoppable. I just wanted to unleash. And Luke was the absolute, perfect prey. He had invoked a psychotic territory that no one had ever been privy to before this moment. I walked ever so slowly toward my prey, my body was so light I felt like I could pounce on him and pin him down like an ant. I felt so strong that I could imagine Luke's bones breaking into pieces when I crush him in my bloodthirsty hands. I heard a hoarse, alien voice come out of my mouth, *"I'm going to kill you."*

Suddenly, I was jolted out of my demonic trance when I heard a loud crash and a big bang that came from the hallway. I was zapped right back into reality. Feeling alarmed, I ran to my daughter's room and there I found my little girl, sitting by her door. Totally spent and exhausted after throwing her toys against the wall and the mirror. "What happened?" I kneeled next to her and looked at her face. She looked up to me, tears in her eyes and said, *"I can't live like this anymore mum. I can't live like this anymore. Please, mum. Stop it."*

"Please, mum. Stop it." It took all of my daughter's strength so she could cast the spell that I had been unconsciously waiting for. I felt a vacuum force suck away the diabolic energy of my personal protector. Pandora vanished and I felt awash with relief, feelings of self-forgiveness came over me like a bucket of cold water. My daughter's unconditional love permitted me to exit the trappings of madness and abomination.

I heard a gentle but firm voice coming from a woman, inside my mind. *"Leave."* I knew at that moment that it was going to be the last and final time that I will ever face Luke again.

I scooped my daughter up and grabbed my car keys. Luke screamed *"Where the f*ck do you think you're going?"* He chased us to the car, but I managed to get inside and lock it before he could keep up. I wound the window two inches down and calmly said to him *"I don't care what you* do, but I want you to be gone by the time I get back here tonight, and never return. If you do, you will have to deal with the police."

I drove straight to my ex-husband's house and dropped my daughter off. In the meantime, I had some business to take care of immediately.

I pulled over in front of the Tweed Heads Police Station on August twenty-four at five thirty in the afternoon. I sat in my car to gather my wits, closed my eyes and took a few deep breaths. I was exhausted and trembling from the stress of fighting for my peace whilst battling glandular fever.

I was startled by a sudden banging on my car window, I opened my eyes and it was Luke. He had the nerve to follow me to the police station, thinking that he could threaten me one more time and make me change my mind. He signalled for me to roll down the window with such belligerence in his eyes. I moved my hand as if I was reaching for the window button, while secretly turning the video on my phone. I raised my hand with my phone in it and captured his face right next to my car window, berserk and riotous. When he realised I was filming him, he gave me two rude fingers and then walked away briskly back to his car.

As soon as he was gone, I ran into the police station, shaking and trying so hard to compose myself. The woman's voice came to me again and said, *"Don't worry in here, they know how you feel. You can trust these people."*

A police officer came to the desk and said, *"What can I help you with."* Not a question, but a statement. I took a deep breath and surprisingly felt calm enough to explain, *"I would like to file a restraining order on* my ex-boyfriend please." I looked the officer in the eye. He gave me a half nod in acknowledgement, then another statement, *"Can you let me know what happened."*

I explained our four-year dating relationship as condensed as I could. I told the officer that I did not want to be contacted by this man ever again. Then I broke down crying in a state of sheer physical and mental exhaustion. I apologised profusely for my tears and said, *"I'm sorry for crying, I'm just a little overwhelmed because he was just here."* The officer said, *"What do you mean he was just here?" "There. Outside."* I pointed to the street. *"He followed me."* The officer looked incredulous, so I opened my phone and showed him the video.

From there the police gave me their full sympathy and walked me through a written apprehended violence order against Luke, with the tightest conditions stipulated: no contact permitted in any way, shape or form. I signed the order and the police promised that they would have it served to Luke by the end of the night. I gave them every information I knew on where they could find him.

After checking that my kids were safe and secure at their Dad's, I went home alone feeling a little scared but determined to hold my space. I looked around the house and there were pieces of white paper lying in every corner. Luke's handwriting splattered all over them:

"If you dare go to New Zealand without me... you might as well stay there."

"Payback is a bitch."

"Tell your cop boyfriend that you were a druggo."

"Say goodbye to your job at the bank."

My heart sank with every word he wrote, not because I was scared of his threats but because I felt sorry for him. Luke had so much fighting spirit that if only he shifted all his energy from trying to control other people, to his own healing and health, he would be a very happy and successful man.

Grateful for the bed under my body, I slumbered like a log until I heard the banging on my bedroom window. I sat up, it was five o'clock in the morning and almost light outside. Panicked, I grabbed my phone and called the police. *"I filed a restraining order last night, but he is here again, right now, he is banging on my window as we speak!"* The police could hear the banging and they said, *"We have men around your area, and we will send them to your house right away."*

Luke was now at the front door shouting and demanding for me to open. My mind raced. I needed to stall him for time. I opened the wooden door, leaving the screen door locked between the two of us. Luke kicked and shook the screen door violently, harassing me to open it for him.

He knew that the police were on their way and he wasted no time to tell me his ultimate message: *"If I can't have you, then no other cunt will. But if you really want me to go away, I will take fifty thousand dollars."* And then he fished his phone out of his pocket and flashed his screen saver at me, which was a picture of myself. I felt a shiver crawl up my spine.

Luke had been gone for twenty minutes when two police officers arrived. They entered my house and instinctively picked up one of the odd, white pieces of paper strewn around and said, *"This is his writing isn't it."* I nodded my head and stupidly asked *"How did you know?"* They ignored my question, *"Is there any more of them?"* I gathered all the white pieces of paper and muttered, *"I used to have many more, but I just throw them in the bin. He writes these things a lot."* One of the officers prodded, *"Anything like these on text message?"* I was fascinated by their questions. It was as if they knew what was going on.

After briefly scanning all of Luke's text messages on my phone, they started scouring my house looking for something else. First, they found a missing steel handle from the screen door. It had broken off when Luke once tried to force himself into my house. *"Where is the broken handle?"* I fished it out of a drawer and handed it over. They looked at it for two seconds and said, *"Broken by force."* Then they looked at my laptop and saw its severed wire charger and fiber-optics hanging loosely. *"Force."* One officer placed his palm on a jagged surface on the wall. He found a patch with fresh gyprock that was painted over with white enamel. The patch did not quite match the rest of the ecru coloured wall. The officer then clenched and framed his own fist against the patch, where there used to be a hole, punched by Luke himself. *"Force."* Again, the officer said.

They have identified several incidents of force and violence caused by Luke, without even asking me. I was gobsmacked. I had been living in a hellhole, and I didn't even know it. And then they left to find Luke.

I got a call by noon. Luke had been taken in custody for unlawful intimidation, malicious damage, stalking, and harassment. The police asked me to come by the station for a 'witness affidavit'. I told them honestly that I wasn't interested in going to court to punish this man, I just wanted him to leave me alone. But the police assured me that the case was being filed *by the police* and I would not have to attend any court proceedings. They just needed my help to put the story and evidence together.

I was still frail and fraught from the glandular fever and all I really wanted was peace and quiet. For a moment I was tempted to decline the police's invitation to talk with them, but just as quickly I thought about other women who could be suffering, just as I have. Women who were being abused, beaten and oppressed; who may not have as good a chance as I did, to get out of their situation.

If I backed away and let people like Luke continue to inflict malice and abuse, what kind of a woman would I be? If I walked away from my responsibility to reveal this kind of chronic, toxic, subliminal injustice, what does that make me? When my daughter will be old enough to ask me if I ever did anything to stop bullies, what kind of answers will I have for her? These questions ignited a visceral kind of energy from deep within me. I jumped out of bed and drove to the police station.

It was surreal. I felt no shame, guilt, or fear, as I sat in an office talking with police, recanting the dark side of what was supposed to be my romantic life.

The case took a life of its own and true to their word, the police never asked me to stand in court.

Chapter 35
Personal Revolution

A couple of weeks after that life changing day, I was due to fly to New Zealand with my kids and Luke. I had purchased the tickets earlier that year and we originally planned to hire a campervan for a few days of skiing in a place called Queenstown, in the South Islands. Since things have changed drastically in the last couple of weeks, I wasn't too sure if I could manage travelling alone with my little kids. My daughter and I hadn't fully recovered from glandular fever yet and I also worried that Luke would show up and have the nerve to board the plane with us.

However, my New Zealand born doctor insisted that a quick trip to the Land of the Long White Cloud won't hurt us. My ex-husband also volunteered to be our bodyguard and make sure that his children (and ex-wife) would board the plane un-accosted and safe.

With the ex-hubby extraordinaire and my Kiwi doctor cheering me on, I decided that New Zealand was destined to be my first trip as a capable, single mother of two super cute little ones.

I re- configured my trip and rented a car instead of a campervan. I cancelled the skiing altogether and decided to explore and cross the country from East to West starting from Christchurch to Greymouth and then to Fox Glaciers. I would then veer downwards via Haast Road, bypassing Queenstown to cross the country back towards Dunedin, and finally back upwards to Christchurch. In total, I would drive a trapezoidal direction of two thousand kilometres in nine days, in a country I've never been to before. It was a short but busy adventure, and I was up for the challenge. I felt like I have suddenly woken up to my freedom and power as a single mum!

Our first stop was a place called Orari bed and breakfast in Christchurch, which was located right in the heart of the city. It boasted some fancy, Victorian furniture and the breakfast was sumptuous with loads of bacon, pancakes and maple syrup. So far, my kids were loving every minute of our trio adventure.

Their joy and excitement brightened up the entire galaxy and expanded my heart infinitely. I felt so blessed to be able to create beautiful memories with them. We spent the entire day exploring the Canterbury museum, browsing through some retailers at Quake City, and lazing around the Botanical gardens.

On day two we were up bright and early, and ready to hit the road. Within ten minutes of driving away from the city of Christchurch, I checked the GPS for some directions. It indicated that I had six and a half hours of driving to get to Fox Glaciers. Reality sunk in and a feeling of overwhelm came over me – I had never driven more than two hours on my own before, let alone cross a new country, with my little kids in tow – was I crazy?

I had an *"Oh Shit"* moment on the wheel and I was about to panic when my daughter squealed *"Oh my God! Look!"* She pointed to the distance where we could see snow-capped mountains ahead. I gasped and completely forgot about my panic. *"Oh my God! That is so pretty! Let's go there!"* I squealed back at my kids as adrenaline and excitement charged through all three of us. *"This is fun!"* My son said and I couldn't agree more.

The rest of the drive was a giggly exchange of snacks, water, jokes and sing-alongs as we traversed the Great Alpine Highway. The kids took turns reading road signs and keeping me updated on how far we had left to go. We stopped at a town called Arthur's Pass to stretch our legs and touch the sleet gracefully falling from the sky.

By mid-afternoon we arrived at Fox Glacier, and I was amazed at the whiteness of the entire village. The sky, the trees, the mountains, and even the road was white. The atmosphere gave me an intense feeling of purity, like white fire burning through the depths of my stomach. A kind of energy that was so quiet, yet so powerful. For the first time in my life, I *felt* peace. Tangible, all-consuming and beautiful, peace.

I welcomed the air into my lungs, savouring the pureness that seeped into my veins. I gratefully surrendered to the universe and said a simple prayer, *"Thank you God."*. The minute we stepped into Fox Glacier, my daughter and I completely recovered from the remnants of glandular fever. Weeks of chronic chills and painful coughing had completely vanished within moments of coming into this twilight zone of decontamination.

That evening, we found Café Neve, *"where they make the best banana and chocolate milkshake in the world"* according to my children. The kids ordered pizzas while I settled for the house special, pumpkin soup. We ate our meals next to a glass window where we could see more sleet falling from the sky. *"What an unreal experience."* I thought to myself. Only a few weeks ago I was shackled in a distorted relationship and now I'm here with the loves of my life enjoying a peaceful meal, in a different world, a thousand miles away from home. It was magical.

Fed and spent, I watched my cherubs slumber peacefully in our warm and super comfortable hotel. I stayed up for a bit just listening to the peace. Getting to know peace. Getting to know me. And then finally I dozed off holding the view of a beautiful glacier in my mind.

The next morning, I woke up and said to the kids, *"We are going to climb to the base of Franz Josef today."* They looked at me with excitement and said, *"Yaayyyy! But what does that mean, mum?"* I couldn't help but laugh at their contagious exuberance, then hurried them along. *"You'll see!"*

We hiked without a guide, nor did we have proper hiking shoes, but we were armed with high spirits and in absolute awe of our paramount surroundings. The tracks were moderately easy, with funny little dwarf bridges and ice-cold streams. But as we ascended closer to the base it became steep and tricky. The rugged allure of the glaciers kept us going, and when we finally reached the base, we felt exhilarated and breathless.

I stared at the terrain for a little while, and then it dawned on me that the higher I climbed, the humbler I felt. Even though I felt my world beacon under my feet, I knew that I was at nature's mercy, no matter what.

The magnitude of the glacier felt like a doorway to a time warp, and suddenly I felt closer to God. I closed my eyes and inhaled a deep, grateful breath. Then I released it slowly and prayed sincerely, *"Thank you for keeping us safe."*

The following day we received news that the storm from Christchurch had travelled further south and caused an avalanche at the Haast Mountain, shutting the Haast highway for an entire week. Which meant that we had to deviate to a new plan very quickly. With such short notice and small amount of time left in the country, I was a little stumped for new ideas and didn't really know what else to do.

Ever so intuitive of their mother's emotions, my kids sensed my dilemma and asked, *"What's wrong, mum?"* "We're kind of stuck. There's been an avalanche and we can't proceed down Haast highway." I told them. *"We're not really stuck, are we? We can just hang out here and then go back the way we came from!"* My daughter mused. *"Yeah, let's do that. Let's climb some more glaciers!"* My son volunteered.

The kids looked at me with such innocence and unconditional love, and then it occurred to me that the mileage we would cover in this trip did not matter so much as the memories we would create together. I was too hung up on reaching our destinations with military precision that I've forgotten how much fun it would be to let loose and hang loose, just because we can. And so we did.

For the next couple of days, we simply explored.

One sunny morning, we drove southwest looking for a track that led to a place called *Lake Matheson*. The GPS led us to a forest with an isolated, empty car park. I was taken aback by a sudden feeling of insecurity. *"What if something bad happens to us inside that forest?"* A cautious voice in my head. I pondered the thought and weighed my feelings carefully, and then I looked at my children who were bouncing with contagious energy and happiness, talking and laughing with each other. I took a breath and allowed my gut to rule, it was telling me to go and create memories with my children. *"Trust that the world is a good world."* I told myself. Aloud.

So we began our walk which led us to interesting, skinny tracks that looped around the foot of the mountain. They walked together with their arms wrapped around each other's shoulder and began to hop and skip singing to the tune of *"Hi ho, hi ho, off to the lake we go, hi ho! Hi ho!"* I took videos and photos of almost everything they did, feeling such a blast of mommy joy for this very private, very isolated, and very peaceful day.

Finally, the lake was there. Lake Matheson was so serene that the mountains and the clouds reflected on its crystal-clear waters. There was no sound except for the little voices of my kids. We were completely alone in the wild and disconnected from the world. A feeling of delicious surrender came to me and for once in my life, I was completely present in the moment. All that there was were the beautiful lake, peace, and my kids exploring happily without a care in the world. It was such a spiritual experience.

By the time we drove back to Christchurch, I felt like I've grown two inches taller and five years wiser. I was grateful for the confidence that my kids had in me, more so than I had in myself at the beginning of the trip. It was a humbling experience to see how much I've doubted myself in so many ways for so long, and exalting to realize that I have the power to build myself back up again. Our trip to New Zealand was more than just an adventure, it was a personal revolution.

Chapter 36
Strip me bare but my dignity

Back in Australia, the battle to completely expunge Luke from my life was far from over. To protect myself from financial ruin, I made a stressful but legally sound decision to move into the rental property that we bought together. This was the only way to ensure that Luke wouldn't move into it himself, which would've given him the power to drag us both down into the dumps of bankruptcy.

By the time the kids and I moved into the rental property, I had lost track of eating and sleeping, and I began to steadily lose the baby weight that I'd carried since my son was born eight years ago. I plummeted down to forty-eight kgs. The irony was I've never had so much energy in my life. I was operating on a torrent of adrenaline, constantly trying to think one step ahead of Luke's games. I felt light in my body and strong in my actions.

The next surprise was a letter of demand from his lawyers. The letter said that I had an *"obligation to disclose all of my assets, subject to be considered as, and divided between, Luke and Grace, under the Australian laws of de facto relationships"*. I looked at the letter dispassionately, almost with disdain for these lawyers who agreed to represent such a lowlife. But having been a law student myself, I understood their legal responsibility.

"*Let the games begin.*" I could almost hear the click of the seatbelt buckle as Pandora took the driver seat, ready to do what she's best at. Fighting my battles for me.

I hired a lawyer who had the same personality as my Kiwi doctor, totally composed, slightly compassionate, and generally pragmatic, with a dry sense of humour. His name was Gary Mallett, and after perusing through the case, Gary squarely said, *"We have a gold digger boyfriend."* To which I had nothing to add. Then he asked what I wanted to do about the situation. My answer was, *"Absolutely nothing. Tell them to try and prove that Luke and I, did indeed, have a de facto relationship. If they succeed, then I will disclose my assets."* Gary warned me, *"That process could take years, even decades, and it could cost you all of your money on legal fees."* I looked him in the eye and said, *"No it won't. They can't 'begin' to prove anything if there is nothing to prove in the first place. Trust me."* Albeit I knew I was being arrogant and proud, something in my gut told me that I had to back myself on this one.

Every move I made regarding my breakup with Luke was intuitive and instinctive. Something divine and primal was awakened in me and we have reached a point where the truth about our relationship was about to be unveiled. That, was empowering. In all of my life's experience, the truth, no matter how hard, no matter how ugly, had always set me free.

Meanwhile, life went on as I tried to make myself and my kids comfortable in the rental property. It was a two-storey townhouse located in a busy road facing the Tweed river, in a mid to low socioeconomic neighbourhood. We missed the peace and familiarity of our main house, which I had temporarily rented out to a lovely, pregnant, single mum.

My kids and I soldiered on. That summer, my daughter started high school while my son went through a massive growth spurt and growing pains on his hips and thighs. I worked hard during the days, and found myself writing again, during the nights.

Writing became my solace. When the kids went to bed, I sat in front of my laptop and poured my soul out, over a glass of Moscato. I discovered iTunes and began to play soft, soul music, and wrote aimlessly. Every now and then I would get up and simply move my body. I poured out my unrequited, undirected love, from the fire in my belly, out through my limbs as I swayed, and whirled, and turned, and tumbled on the carpet. I found myself unable to contain passion. I had to let go, through my writing, and the music, and the wine. Loneliness was the mother of my personal introspection.

I found out later on that Luke pleaded guilty to all of the charges pressed by the police against him. And as for his court antics, his lawyers eventually ran off steam as I have predicted, and their letters of demand died a natural death.

The last and final fish there was for me to fry was selling the rental property, and it wasn't a simple feat. Luke still had the power to refuse to sign the sale of the property, despite having stopped his share of mortgage repayments a long time ago.

I hired a real estate agent who was locally known to be a great negotiator, Jay Elliott. Jay was in his early thirties, he was stoic, efficient, and highly experienced. Jay did not enjoy being caught in the middle between Luke and myself, but he was determined to stay professional. Which was why I had full faith in his tenacity to get Luke to agree and sign the sale of the property.

Sure enough, after a short seven weeks of harrowingly abusive conversations and negotiation between Luke and agent Jay, the investment unit went on the market for sale. To say that I was relieved was the understatement of the century. Somehow, somewhere, someone had given Luke a sound advice and convinced him to do the right thing for his own sake. Jay started to show the property on open house inspections.

While waiting for a buyer, it occurred to me that I was never going to get out of this whole mess completely unscathed. Having failed to punish me using the legal system, Luke resorted to slandering my personal reputation. He had accosted some of my colleagues and neighbours in public places, and they were forced to listen to his stories. Stories to insinuate that I used the bank as a front for drug dealing, that I slept with the police officer who filed a case against him, that I was a conniving, money grabbing, manipulative, evil witch.

Although his onslaught didn't surprise me, I was astonished by how hurt I felt after a few of my Filipina friends ostracised me, based on what they've heard. Luke was excellent at begging for sympathy, and it would take a discerning mind to see behind his angelic facade.

Despite the pain of judgement and losing a few friends, I stood my ground and kept my silence. Never one to wash my dirty linen in public, I had no interest in getting involved with Luke's childish games of Chinese whispers. I had nothing to prove and nothing to defend.

I grieved the death of my friendships over my trusty Moscato during the evenings, while I pored over my keyboard and created epistles from my broken heart. Watching Luke slay my character one toxic rumour at a time, was like looking at a heavy downpour of rain. Relentless, and cleansing. Unpleasant, but purifying. And all I had to do was let it be.

In life, our biggest blessings come not from the great experiences, but from the ones that break us open and vulnerable, invoking our courageous selves and unbreakable spirits.

Chapter 37

Opening up to my higher self

I asked myself, *"What else could I do to become fully unchained from toxic relationships?"*

I reminisced the New Zealand trip with my kids just a few months earlier, and remembered its empowering effects on my mind, body and soul. And then the answer came to me. A big adventure with my kids, somewhere so far away that we could gracefully unplug and reinvigorate.

I have always dreamed of seeing Europe, and twelve months earlier, I would have thought that a trip to the other side of the world was still ten years away in the future. But after everything that had recently transpired in my life, it was no longer about the perfection and grandiosity of my dreams, than the strength of my intentions to manifest my dreams into reality.

Resourcefulness is the number one secret weapon of a kickass, single mum. I couldn't simply afford a trip to Europe for one adult and two children on my single household income. So I had to think outside the box.

One evening when the kids were in bed, I opened my laptop, this time without the wine, looking for a way to make our Europe trip feasible for my pocket. I began by tallying my Qantas frequent flyer points, which totalled almost three thousand dollars in value. Then I logged into my share portfolio for the first time and found that the bank had awarded me some shares, as a Key-Performance eligible employee. From there I sold a few thousand-dollars-worth of shares. Finally, I lodged my tax return on e-tax, and it yielded a refund of almost six thousand. Overnight I found almost fifteen thousand lazy dollars. I could see our trip coming up in time for summer in Europe. I had an expectation of selling the rental property in the fall, so a three-week Europe trip would be the perfect way to celebrate the dawn of a new era.

Tears fell through my face as I felt that the universe was conspiring to send me and my kids to this celebration adventure. Through a new and avant-garde experience, I could enhance and grow my perspective. And what beautiful perspective to be had by stepping into some of the oldest and most beautiful places in the world. I quietly sobbed, folded my laptop away and crawled into bed, whispering, *"Thank you God."*

Driving to school the following morning, I casually asked the kids, *"Hey, do you guys want to go to Europe?"* They screamed, *"Yesss!"* Within fifteen minutes, we came up with a rough itinerary. We wanted to see Disneyland in Paris, the Colosseum in Rome, say a prayer at The Vatican, and also try to visit the Queen in London. *"How about Venice? I heard it's sinking. Should we check it out before it's completely submerged?"* I said. The kids yelled out, *"Sure, Mum!"* as they went off to school with a skip and a hop.

Momentum builds when you build on it. As I began to visualise a drama-free, new way of life, I could feel the subtle shifting of energies both inside, and outside of me. I woke up one day to a serene, almost soundless, rainy morning. I could see the rain drops but I couldn't hear any sounds. No birds chirping, no rain falling on the roof, no cars driving past. It was like a silent movie unfolding before me. I stared at the traffic free road from my loungeroom, and across to the river on the other side. Everything was so still, except for the rain. Then a voice came to me *"This townhouse will sell today."* I listened for more but that was the only message. I took a deep, grateful breath and said, *"Yes."*

That night, the agent called me to say that a buyer came forward with a pleasing offer, which I immediately accepted. As I put the phone down, I thought of the voice that spoke to me earlier that day. It was my sixth sense, my intuition, God, the Supreme being, my guardian angel. I wished that I could be with that voice always and everywhere, so that I can feel safe and loved, always and everywhere. For now, I simply whispered *"Thank you."*

When the property settlement summary was drawn, it showed a bottom-line loss of three thousand six hundred and seventy-two dollars. I looked at the document and my heart skipped in gratitude and excitement. I was willing to cop a loss twenty times over for this final deliverance. A tiny three grand loss for the price of my freedom was THE best gift ever.

Moving back into our home at Lilly Pilly was like eating chocolate coated vanilla icy pole underneath a palm tree in a tropical island. It was a very laid back, easy going process. The kids and I were just so relieved to be back in our real home, and grateful for an exciting future that lay ahead. Life, had a way of working things out for you, when you are willing to work it out for yourself, against all odds.

Chapter 38
London – Resilience and Teamwork

We landed at Heathrow airport on the eighth of June 2014. The customs officer looked at the three of us with expert eyes and said in her crisp, British accent: *"First time in London? What are you looking forward to doing?"* *"We are going to the London Dungeon!"* My son exclaimed. *"Mum said we're going shopping at Harrods!"* My daughter volunteered. I rolled my eyes and the lady officer laughed. *"We're going to see the queen!"* They finally recited in unison.

My heart brimmed with pride to see my munchkins so energetic even after thirty-two hours of zigzagging from Gold Coast, to Brisbane, to Melbourne, to Dubai, and then finally to London. Lucky for us, our Qantas points afforded us to fly with Emirates, which made everything so much more peaceful and luxurious for me and the kids.

Summer in London was so much better than I imagined. Hardly any rain and the skies were blue almost all of the time. There was order to the chaos of the city and elegant symmetry in its otherwise diverse population.

One day at eight o'clock in the morning, the kids and I bumped into a conglomeration of guided walkers around the Bayswater Road and

Hyde Park area. We weren't quite sure where they were headed to, but the robust, tour guide lady seemed like she had something real important to show everyone.

Curious, I looked at the kids to see if they were thinking what I was thinking. We just looked at one another, shrugged our shoulders and said, *"Well, let's walk and see, shall we?"* So, we walked with this group of twenty adults, plus me and my two little kids, led by the tour guide lady with a loud voice. After a few cuts and corners, we realized that she was guiding us to Buckingham Palace. *"Why, that is exciting! Do we get to see the Queen?"* I said out loud. A woman who was walking with us smiled and said, *"I doubt it, but you never know, do you?"* "Surely we couldn't be this lucky to get an invite inside the palace?" I bantered. The woman said, *"We're not going inside, but we will be getting a front row spot to watch the changing of the guards."* *"Oh!"* I said, *"Sounds rather official, let's do it!"*

The kids and I were overcome with a renewed vigour and breezed across the bustling corners around Marble Arch, totally oblivious to the fact that we have effectively crashed a private, guided walking tour to the Buckingham Changing of the Guards. Some things you get away with when you have two cute little ones in tow.

The lady tour guide led us to stand across the rear gates of Saint James Palace, where the soldiers inspected their gear and artillery before getting the show on the road. The troops seemed to communicate in official, halting words that I could only guess was royal military lingo.

Then finally, the entourage was ready for the parade. The gates opened as hundreds of horses with knights in armours, band players, and soldiers on foot, cascaded gracefully into Buckingham Palace, in all its flair and flamboyance.

The pomp and circumstance reminded me of the *Kalilangan festival* in my hometown Gensan. *Kalilangan* would be just as grand as the *Changing of the Guards* in Buckingham palace, except without the horses and the fluffy hats. But unlike the Changing of the Guards, which took place *daily* during summer in London, *Kalilangan* was an annual ceremony.

To think that this type of grandeur was commonplace in one part of the world and rare in another, shifted my perspective on life transitions. It occurred to me that no one can dictate my timeline, and I can do things as fast or slow as I wish. The power to live my life as simple or as complex as I want, at any given moment, was totally up to me.

My daughter grew up with Harry Potter. She was five years old when she first saw The Philosopher's Stone movie. She lived the world of Harry, Ron Weasley and Hermione Granger, and at the age of seven, she had mastered her British accent. Naturally, our biggest London mission for her, was to see the Harry Potter Studio at Watford.

But our Harry Potter day went off to a rough start when my son had an excruciating attack of growing pains on his left leg while we were on the train, fifteen miles out of London. His growing pains were consistent and intense earlier that year, but they seemed to have subsided in recent weeks. I then wrongly assumed that his growth had stabilized, and the pains had gone. Hence, I didn't have anything for its surprise onset on the train.

My boy was in tears. Silent, agonizing tears that begged me to make his pain go away. I felt utterly heartsick that I didn't have anything for his pain. The three of us sat in the moving train, and my daughter and I held our boy, whispering words of strength in his ears. When the train finally stopped, we slowly helped him limp out and sit on one of the benches. I massaged my son's leg and prayed that we could at least make it back into the train and to the hotel.

When my daughter heard my prayer, she started to object, *"Mum, no, we have to pray that we will make it to the Harry Potter Studio, it's just there across the road from here, and we already have our tickets!"*

"But your brother is in pain." I protested.

"He'll be fine! Won't you brother? Please don't forsake me of Harry Potter!" She begged her brother.

My son looked at me desperately and whispered, *"I don't want my sister to miss this."*

I looked at them both and said firmly, *"You know, sometimes things happen outside of our control. Even though we already paid for the tickets, we must ask, what is the most important thing at this moment? I think it's fair to say that your brother needs us right now, more than you need to go and see Harry Potter. We would do the same for you, my child."*

As I said this, my kids looked at one another, and without consulting me, they made a pact together. My son said to my daughter, *"I will do my best for you if you promise that one day you will do your best for me too."* My daughter nodded and gave him a tight hug and a kiss, grateful for his willingness to sacrifice.

I looked away to hide my tears. Tears of pride and joy for the troupers that my kids were. I wiped my face as I turned to them and said, "Okay, let's do this! How about we try and get up, walk one step at a time until we see something where we can place our bums on, otherwise known as chairs. Then we sit down and take a rest, get up, and then do it again until we reach the queue. And then God help us once we get to the queue!"

Where focus goes, energy flows. Three human beings emitting clear intentions of gaining strength and energy for our growing boy with growing pains. As we limped and hopped our way across the street, our spirits lifted, and then just like the red sea parting for Moses and his men, a man approached us to inspect our pre-ordered tickets. I asked if they could allow us to jump the queue, for my little boy who was in a lot of pain. The English man unclasped the bollards, let us through and wished us well.

Inside, a world of Magic and Wonder greeted us. My kids' faces were a picture of pure awe. My son's pain vanished, and my daughter was in Harry Potter heaven. I felt their little hands slip out of mine, as they quickly got lost into the fantasy world of wizards, muggles and spells.

Towards the end of the day we found an outdoor cafe where they sold the legendary *Butterbeer* from *The Goblet of Fire*, which tasted like an infusion of liquid butter and caramel with some gooey cream on top. And then finally it was time for my favourite part of every theme park, the souvenir shop. This meant that we were nearly on the home run, and I could buy a fridge magnet to commemorate the day's adventure.

Altogether, our Harry Potter day was more than just a visit to a theme park, it was an exercise of resilience and teamwork, with a side of mystery and magic.

The most animated part of our London trip was hanging out and having dinner with some old friends from high school, Jake and his wife Connie, as well as my dear friend and former Jollibee boss, Jenny, with her husband Paulo. Jake and Connie lived and worked in London. While Jenny and Paulo were visiting Paulo's mother who lived in the city.

We spent a few hours sitting under a huge tree at Hyde Park, just talking, laughing out loud and reminiscing. The memories and jokes we shared were hilarious and my stomach hurt from the belly laughs. I felt so light, so happy and so carefree. There we were, sharing a day in London and speaking in our native tongue without a care in the world. It was surreal. It was beautiful. Life felt so amazing.

After dinner at a Chinese restaurant and then some late-night dessert at a French patisserie, my kids were exhausted, and we started heading home by midnight. I half carried my son while my friends held my daughter's hand as we walked the streets of London back to our hotel. When we said our goodbyes, my heart felt billowy and I was so grateful for old friendships, that I felt like I was in cloud nine.

Chapter 39
Rome - Becoming the woman of my dreams

Rome was a flurry of ancient Roman architecture, and my kids were overwhelmed by the parade of endless ruins and copious history behind the Colosseum, Pantheon, Trevi and Piazza Navona. It was a lot of information to appreciate in a short span of three days, especially for little surfie grommets like my babies.

Italian cuisine, however, was a completely different story. Italian food, cooked by Italian people with fresh Italian produce, was simply divine, and my kids couldn't get enough of the authentic pizza and gelato, while I tucked right into my favourites, carbonara and vongole.

Indulgence aside, I had a personal affair that I needed to address while we were in the ancient city.

Growing up as a Catholic child, I used to think that The Vatican was the church of all churches, where your prayers would be closer to God, and stronger in its essence. But then as a woman, I didn't believe that my prayers would be heard by God, anymore in The

Vatican than if I was at the top of Machu Picchu. Yet I couldn't deny the magnetic pull of this city within a city.

So, with my wavering faith and curious mind, I shamelessly marched my kids along St Peter's Square towards thousands of people that gathered outside of St. Peter's Basilica. There were half-a-dozen giant TV screens mounted at the top of the museums surrounding the Basilica, plus hundreds of security on foot, and stationed up high by the windows, in every corner of the city. Coincidentally, it was a Sunday and the Pope was due to deliver a sermon in the next hour.

Although it was exciting for me and the kids, the intense tension in the atmosphere was almost on the verge of an uproar. The Basilica itself was at the dead-end of a large, round enclosure, filled with thousands of tourists and locals alike. It wasn't an ideal crowd to take children to, but I reminded myself that seeing and hearing Pope Francis in the flesh may be a once in a lifetime experience.

To everyone's delight, the Pope came out and as he started to address the crowd my nerves settled down, even though I couldn't understand a word he was saying. He was speaking in Latin, and for an old man, he was a dynamic and purposeful speaker. His presence made me feel reassured, and I even let go of my kids' hands to stream the Pope's sermon live on Facebook. Afterwards, the kids and I queued to go inside the Sistine Chapel. It was a long forty-five-minute wait, while each and every person went through sophisticated technology checking for arms and explosives.

But it was worth it, and as we stepped inside the Sistine Chapel in the Basilica, nothing could have prepared me for it. Michael Angelo's art that covered the walls and ceiling were spiritually graphic and heart stopping. It moved me in ways that no priest nor their sermons ever have, in my years of listening to the Holy Mass back in my hometown. This, was something else.

The chapel spoke, and it screamed, and it wailed, and it pondered, and it lulled, into my soul. It was an all-encompassing, spiritual, emotional, sexual and mental invasion. I wanted to touch, but we weren't allowed. I wanted to cry, but the kids had no idea what was happening in me, so I stayed composed. I wanted to lay there in eternity to think about life, but it was a church, not the Garden of Eden. So instead I did the one thing I could, I prayed.

First, I thanked God for keeping us safe. Then I prayed that my kids would have the greatest fun for the rest of our holidays. And finally, I thanked God for keeping me alive in spite of all the risks I've taken in my life, and that I hoped to find clarity and joy in my own little fragile heart. Out of habit, I finished my prayer with "Our Father" "Hail Mary" and "Gloria Patri".

After checking out old Michael Angelo's artwork, the kids wanted to climb to the Dome of the Basilica. Their boundless energy was contagious as we hopped and skipped upward to the slanting floor. But then my hop and skip halted when the floor quickly shifted into a claustrophobic, one-meter wide, steep, spiral staircase. So much so that when another person was on their way down, we had to shimmy sideways with our backs against the wall to make enough room for each other. I found only one small window on the way up which was barely enough to stop me from fainting. The journey to the top was oxygen poor and definitely not for the faint hearted. *"This better be worth it, kids!"* I said out loud. *"Don't worry mum, almost there!"* My little boy assured me.

We finally reached the dome, which, after seeing Sir Michael's masterpieces down at the chapel, was pretty standard. However, the view outside was a sight to behold. The Vatican country sprawled before our eyes, giving us a glimpse of a world like no other. A dazzling maze of ancient architecture, potentially holding the deepest secrets and stories of devouts and pagans from a half-forgotten era. It was absolutely breathtaking to see from the vantage point of the dome.

The whole Vatican experience was more profound for me than it would have been for my kids. But being there with them, took the experience to the next level. Up until that very moment, on the balcony of the highest point of Sistine Chapel, I never thought of weighing the integrity of my religious faith, against the fortitude of my spirituality. Yet there I was, thinking, *"What do I really believe?" "Who am I in this universe?" "Why, am I here?"*

I wasn't just some lost Christian wandering aimlessly in the limbo of theological conundrum, I was a mother and a woman, searching for her higher self, to *become the woman of her dreams.*

Chapter 40
Venice - Prophecy

Finally, it was time for a brand-new experience, a land crossing from Rome to Venice on board the luxurious Le Freece high speed train. The kids had so much fun playing cards and ordering food during the three-hour transit while I happily sat and stared at the glorious countryside.

I loved the fact that I orchestrated this entire trip all on my own, including all our European cross-country flights, buses, trains, hotels, restaurants, excursions, places and people to see. As my friends from the bank would put it, I did a *wing-it-dot-com* type of itinerary, and it's been absolutely amazing so far.

I allowed my wandering mind to daydream of a life full of love, and to meet a man who would see me for who I am and love me no matter what. I imagined the warm sensation of someone taking me into their arms and whispering how beautiful life is. As I stared out to the beautiful landscape of Florence, I let go of any expectations on who, where, when and how my true love would happen. *"There will be time for everything."* I heard a voice that caressed my heart, very gentle, almost inaudible.

The lack of roads plus the clustering of old buildings, both Gothic and tenements in Venice, threw me completely off of my geographical compass. Within ten minutes of navigating through hundreds of skinny passages that were intimately lined with boutique shops, it all became a trance. I lost my bearing and completely relied on a porter, who, after asking half a dozen locals, took a painful forty-five minutes to find our accommodation.

We stayed in a 17th Century Venetian style hotel called Locanda Correr, which we could only locate after a twenty-minute labyrinth hunt from St. Mark's Square. Locanda was quaint, the walls in our room were covered with beautiful damask, and their service was warm and friendly. The wi-fi password was a sixteen-character, alpha numeric, meaningless phrase, much to my son's chagrin. *"Who does that?"* He wondered. *"Italians."* My daughter muttered under her breath. I couldn't help but laugh whenever I heard my kids talk as if they were adults. If only they knew what it's like to be a grown up.

The following day I've decided that the best way to get my bearings back, in the floating city, was to get used to the canals. And what better way to do so than ride the gondola. For one hundred and fifty euros per half hour ride, it cost me an arm and a leg. But then again, sailing through the grand canal and watching the hub of the city from a distance, was surreal.

The subtle art of people watching from the gondola allowed me to not only recover my sense of geography, but more importantly, it widened my perspective just a little bit more. As we sailed past crowds of people dining, honeymooning, talking, laughing, living, the uniqueness of every scene was like little snippets of movies from a different world. A magical world. My kids loved the gondola and I loved seeing them experience these rich textures of life. A privilege that I would never, ever take for granted.

By the end of day two I was forced to let go of the need to know exactly where we were. It was impossible, what with a million mini alleys all conjoined together somehow.

Forty-eight hours of disorientation had loosened my brain and put it out of its usual arrangement, and then that night, I dreamed of one of the most prophetic dreams in my life.

It was midnight in my dream. I was standing across the road from a building that I used to admire as a kid, before my mother abandoned me. *The Yap Mabuhay*. The building was well lit all around, as if a party just wrapped up and all the guests have just left. I felt pulled to cross the road for no apparent reason and as I stepped off of the bitumen and on to the front of the building, I saw rows and rows of long, black bags lying parallel next to each other.

There was something inside each black bag. I crouched down to the one closest to me, turned the bag over and found a dead body in it. I was taken by surprise, but I felt no fear, nor danger. If anything, I was curious. So, I turned the bodies over one by one, hoping that not all of the bodies were dead. But they were all corpses wrapped in body bags, hundreds of them, placed neatly in a row from one far end to the other.

I was alone with my kids in a sinking island, fifteen thousand kilometres away from home, so that even though the dream did not have the quality of a bad dream, I had to find out what it could have possibly meant, for the safety of my kids.

The first thing I did upon waking up was google the meaning of death and dead bodies in a dream. Most of the resources I found suggested that a dream of a dead body or a corpse, where there was no danger or fear, meant birth, or the beginning of something new.

But I didn't just dream of *A* dead body. There were hundreds of them. That was what really intrigued me. It was obvious in my recent life events that I was going through new beginnings, so to dream of a dead body or two was no big deal. But hundreds? I spent hours poring over the internet for more answers, but I simply could not find any more information to satiate my curiosity. I had to settle for the generic suggestion that my dream simply meant the birth of something new.

Six years later on, as I write about this experience, I finally see the manifestations of that dream in my life at present, and its ongoing ripple effects.

The death in my dream symbolized the loss of some friendships, as a result of my break-up with Luke. The number of dead bodies in the dream symbolized the abundance of new friendships that would open up to me. My lack of fear in the dream was a message from my deeper consciousness, that if I learned to love and trust myself enough, I would make beautiful friendships, in abundance.

We left Venice at three-thirty in the morning, taking only five minutes to navigate through the labyrinth from the hotel to the pier in front of Doge's Palace.

The city slept in a dark slumber. Unadmired and unattended, even the ancient buildings had a quality of resignation to them. A rogue speedboat whizzed by, with people singing to the top of their lungs, happily drunk from the night's frolic. My daughter watched them with intensity, paying close attention to the women in the boat. *"Don't do that when you grow up."* I whispered to her as we boarded the ferry. She whispered back, *"No Mum, we don't have ferries at home, only taxis."* I rolled my eyes and started to say *"Oh dear Lord! That's not what I meant...."* But the ferry driver's happy voice boomed through the tiny vessel *"Buongiorno! Benvenuta!"* I sighed as I resigned to the fact that this was always going to be a multi-dimensional education for all three of us.

Chapter 41
Paris - Razzle Dazzle

We flew from mainland Venice in Treviso, to Orly in Paris. The sun was high when we finally emerged out of Charles de Gaulle-Etoile metro station, and the first thing we saw was the imposing, aristocratic Arc de Triomphe. Its imperial presence was like a vortex of energy emitting grandeur and overflowing with strength. It was impossible to stand there and not look at it. *"Whoa!"* My son's reaction. *"Mum what is that?"* My daughter said. *"It's a monument. One of the biggest in the world. Welcome to Paris, kids!"*

As we drove away from the arc in a taxi, I felt very chic. Paris was contagiously stylish. We turned left from the Palais Garnier towards a mall called Galleries Lafayette in the ninth district, and into cobblestoned alleyways that showcased a collision of neat, old buildings with shiny French balustrades outside of every window. Our room at Hotel Aida Opera was contemporary French. It had white, red, and brown hues, mahogany-coloured furniture, and small, delicious chocolates on the pillows.

Our view overlooked more of those beautiful balustrades from the buildings across the street, and we were high enough on the seventh floor to get a glimpse of the glorious, cloudless blue sky. It was a hot day in Paris, and for once, we were happy to hang out in our beautiful room.

I sank into the fluffy bed as I looked at the two angels that have shaped my life in the last eleven years. The gift of motherhood is the best thing that's ever happened to me, and my greatest dream is to become the matriarch of a big family that love, cherish and protect one another.

The most anticipated day of our Europe trip has finally arrived – Disneyland!

We arrived half an hour before the gates opened, and there were already thousands of people waiting to enter. At this stage of our trip, we've become used to feeling like a speck of sand in an ocean of pebbles. Our tolerance for big crowds was high, and we were always mindful of looking out for one another at all times.

Once inside, I realized that one full day would not be enough to see everything in Disneyland. From what I could make, there had to be at least fifteen thousand human beings in the park. The park itself had four or five different sections, and they were at least four kilometres apart from each other!

I looked up from the map to check the beautiful pandemonium happening right before my eyes, and then I looked down to the map again to shake the overwhelm off of my system. We made a plan and picked our top three must see rides and attractions. My son picked the pirates ride inside of Adventureland, my daughter wanted to see the Cinderella castle and then the Main St. USA, while I was keen for the two hundred feet drop in the Tower of Terror. *"Great! Once we get through this top list, then we know we can wander aimlessly and see what else awaits."* I said with relief. And then we walked, and rode, and ate, and took photos, on a magical summer day in Disneyland Paris.

I was in heaven. When I was a child I never dreamed to be in Disneyland. To me it was a fantasy world reserved for children and parents who loved each other and were happy together. Even though I knew Disneyland was real, I was convinced that it was only real for other people. Much like the sun and moon, and the planets. I knew they were there, but "there", was not my world.

But on this day, I was in real Disneyland, in my own flesh and bones. I dreamed of the undreamable, and now I didn't just make it real for me, I made it real for me and my babies. It was like the childhood I've never had, on steroids. I cried in silence, hiding my face behind my cotton candy. When my tears abated, I hugged my kids so tight to stop my heart from bursting out of my chest. *"Let's go ride Buzz Lightyear!"* I squealed.

The day rolled with no mercy as Disneyland pulsated on a high note, every minute, every hour. At seven o'clock in the evening, the sun was still beaming high, and the kids and I were beginning to feel tired. We knew we needed a good break when hunger, thirst, and sore feet began to cloud our enthusiasm.

We found the Plaza Gardens Restaurant near the park entrance. It was set in the Victorian era and much fancier than the fast-food hamburgers we had for lunch. The sign said that children ten years and younger would only pay half-price. My daughter was eleven, but she ate like a six-year-old, and she was almost the same height as my son, who was only eight years old.

"Bonjour Madame!" The lady said. *"Bonjour!"* I smiled back. I pointed to the two heads standing next to me and gleefully said, *"Twins!"* My kids rewarded her with their sunniest smiles. She smiled happily back at my partners in crime and said, *"Yes, this way please, children, and Madame!"* She ushered us to the door and charged me for one adult and two kids, before showing us to a table in the middle of the restaurant.

The carpet was so thick and fluffy that I couldn't help but remove my shoes and massage my aching toes on the padded floor. My daughter did the same while my son vanished into the enormous array of food.

As fate would have it, the restaurant served an international buffet, including Filipino dishes. I ate my fill of *Embutido*, my son tucked into the Escargot, while my little lady helped herself with some cherry tomatoes and salami. My daughter had always been a delicate eater. And it amused me to ponder the contrast between her eating mannerisms and mine when I was her age, when I used to have to eat really quickly before anyone could pinch the food off of my plate. Different times, different worlds.

Back to the park, the evening was getting chilly as we continued to explore. At nine-thirty, the crowd started to gather around the castle to watch the final show and fireworks, at eleven o'clock. We decided to do the same and sat amongst a couple of thousand people waiting and chatting with one another. The crowd was far smaller and much more subdued than it was earlier that day.

The sun began to set nicely behind the castle by ten o'clock at night. Most of the kids in the park were yawning by then, while others were fast asleep. Then finally at eleven o'clock, the castle came to life with breath taking cinematography featuring Peter Pan and Wendy, looking for Tinkerbell and her magic pixie dust.

The story of Tinkerbell and her pixie dust being held hostage by Captain Hook, had drained the magic and life out of the castle, making it grey and desolate. But then it all became well when Peter Pan came to the rescue and defeated Captain Hook and all his cohorts, releasing Tinkerbell and her magic dust. Then she went to work and sprinkled faith and light back into the castle. Magic! The castle sparkled and shone like a giant rainbow tiara. Then the fireworks came, along with singing, celebrations and happiness. And then everyone lived happily, ever after.

Exhausted but totally enthralled, the three of us held hands as we walked out of Disneyland. While waiting for the train, I overheard my kids having a conversation in the sea of movement and noise. My daughter said to her brother, *"When I grow up, I will take you back here to Disneyland."* My son replied to his sister, *"Me too. When I grow up, I will take you back here to Disneyland."* It was the sweetest thing I have ever heard in my entire life. And this time, I just let the tears roll down my face, proudly.

The next day we went to see the most famous landmark in the world.

"I reckon we can climb that tower on foot, in thirty minutes time." I said to the kids, as we ogled Eiffel Tower from the gardens of Champs de Mars. It was a warm, windy day and the crowd at the bottom of the tower was a little hectic, so we decided to sit on the grass and wait for the queue to settle down.

An hour passed, and we still weren't in a hurry to start climbing, when suddenly a woman in her mid-forties with an Eastern European accent, approached us. She was wearing a smudged white shirt tucked in a pair of blue jeans, worn sneakers and a white turban to contain her long mane of black, wavy hair. Carrying a canvass bag across her chest, she held out an A4 sized writing board with pieces of paper that showed a list of people's names, their residential and email addresses, signatures, and monies they've allegedly donated to this woman.

She spoke in brusque, pidgin English, explaining that she represented a movement that fought for the good of the Eiffel Tower community. She shoved the manifesto in my face and pointed at people's names from different countries and the monies they donated to her cause. I quickly scanned the poorly staged fraud that she presented to me. Amounts between thirty Euros, up to one thousand Euros. I scanned right down and silently calculated the median of her modus operandi, which was approximately two hundred Euros. Then I looked up and scanned the vicinity for her cohorts, assessing how dangerous she might be, and what our safety would cost. Not very dangerous at all, she was a solo worker.

I was wearing a cross body bag with two separately zipped compartments inside of it. The back compartment was where I kept my real money, and the front compartment was where I kept very little, in case I would be confronted by hustlers like this woman. And for a second, I thought of telling her to go away, but then I decided that I wanted to give her at least just a little bit of money, to say that even though I knew she was a con artist, that I cared about her as a person anyway.

I smiled at her and wrote a made-up name and address on her list of benefactors and pulled out everything from the front compartment of my bag, all of Five Euros, while apologizing that I was poor, and spreading my bag wide open so she can see that I had no more money.

Then I grabbed my kids' hands and started walking to the Eiffel Tower. The look on her face clearly showed that she was highly offended by my Five Euros. She started to follow me and my kids, and began to hurl abuse at us loudly, in her own native language. My kids were half confused, half terrified. *"Why was that lady angry at you for giving her some money, mum?"* They prodded. *"Just keep walking and don't look back."* I said to the kids with absolute certainty, and so they kept walking and never looked back.

I was furious at myself for even thinking that she might appreciate my gesture. She was a con artist, after all. *"Next time, don't be a pussy and just tell them to go away."* I heard a familiar voice in my head, from someone who had been in absentia for a little while, Pandora. I was even more infuriated and blurted, *"You, tell them to go away!"*

"Huh, what mum?" My kids looked at me, even more confused. *"Nothing. I said we have to go up!"*

We reached the ticketing office at the base of the tower, which was manned by a non-English speaking man. The queue had died down to fifty or so people, but I was so flustered by my encounter with the hustler that I got our tickets all mixed up, or perhaps more accurately, I got my French all mixed up. I grabbed our tickets thinking that they were valid from the second floor all the way to the top.

We walked up for forty-five minutes to the second floor, with our hearts pumping nicely from the steady climb, and then presented our tickets to the elevator man to take us up for the rest of the way.

The French man said, in crystal clear English, *"Madam, these were your tickets from the bottom to here, the second floor."*

"Oh, my mistake. May I buy tickets from here to the top then?"

The French man kindly said, *"You have to go back downstairs to do that."*

"Huh?!?" The three of us exclaimed in unison. *"But that's crazy, we're already here!"* We protested.

The Frenchman said *"I'm sorry Madam, we have no tickets for sale here. Perhaps you want to walk, it is breezy on the way up."*

The kids and I looked at each other, then I shrugged my shoulders and said, *"Oh well, either we go down or we go up, eh?"* I cajoled the kids as they rolled their eyes at me and said *"Mmmuuummmm… What did you do!"*

"Sorry kids, I guess my French isn't up to scratch! But I will buy you ice cream!" I pleaded as they rolled their eyes some more.

Everything happens for a reason. Albeit the full climb to the top of the Eiffel Tower was brisk, it was so beautiful and very refreshing. The exercise was the antidote to the toxicity of our little confrontation with the mad woman at the gardens of Champs de Mars.

The kids and I stopped every now and then to catch our breath and take in the views. It was progressively stunning. *"Wait till we get to the top!"* My son yelled out, while my daughter was carefully quiet, as she tried to manage her fear of heights. She was doing an exemplary job and I never once let go of her hand. My heart swelled with so much pride for her fighting spirit. *"I musn't be such a bad person, because someone Up There had decided that I deserve to mother these two amazing little people."* I silently thought.

As we reached the very top, suddenly all that there is, was Paris, in all its three hundred and sixty degrees of glory. The view was spectacular, as I expected. The thing about progressively climbing to the top, is that I already had a fair idea of what I was about to see.

Victory has no element of surprise. Instead, it comes with a heightened sense of purpose and an enormous dose of self-appreciation.

The rest of Paris was an interlude of ease and finesse. We cruised through the River Seine under the evening sky, window-shopped along Champs Elysees, climbed the top of Arc de Triomphe, explored Luxembourg Gardens, and took fun photos outside of The Louvre.

I may have absolutely no idea what it's like to live an everyday life in Paris, but I found the city to be endlessly seductive and spellbinding. It's easy to see why people call it the city of love. I think of it as the city of blazing passion with a side of razzle-dazzle.

The trip that I designed to transform me from feeling sorry for myself, to feeling empowered in myself, did its job, and so much more. The kids and I bonded together in a very special way. They were my super-heroes, as I was theirs.

Chapter 42
Strong

Shortly after coming back from Europe, I turned thirty-nine, and as I eased into my newfound self-contentment, I found my own drug of choice. The drug of Growth. I was hooked on the feeling of being Enough as I am. The joy of Emotional Freedom. The liberty of making fearless decisions. It was an energising experience.

It was my kids' weekend away with their Dad when I woke up from an indulgent nap on a Saturday afternoon. I stretched my arms ever so slowly as I sat up on the bed, gingerly moving my ankles in clockwise motion under the doona. I took a deep *Ujayi* breath, one that I haven't done in a long, long time, when I felt a surge of heat from the base of my spine up to the crown of my head. It took my breath away and suddenly a thought shot through my mind *"I want to be strong."* It was a welcome thought as I had been sickly in the last few years, living a sedentary life and making no time for my fitness and wellbeing.

Without hesitation, I grabbed my phone and searched up *"Pole Dancing"*. I've always been fascinated by the beautiful art of spinning and dancing, with your feet never touching the ground. The strength and elegance of women in pole dancing was something I've always admired, yet the stigma and association of pole dancing to stripping for money, had stopped me from ever looking into it. But the good thing about going through harrowing experiences in the last twelve months was, it stripped me of my inhibitions, no pun intended. I felt like I couldn't care less about people's opinions.

My eyes popped out of my skull when I found a pole dancing school five minutes from my house. I spoke to the owner, Sharmila, and told her, *"I'm not strong. But I want to be strong. That's why I want to learn this."* She was very supportive and even coy, *"Yes I understand. Strong, you will become. That I can guarantee."*

My first class was on a Wednesday evening after work. I took a brand-new leap of faith as I decided that my kids were old enough to be on their own for ninety minutes, while I did Pole. I walked into the studio and was surprised when I met Sharmila. She was diminutive in stature, but what she lacked in height she absolutely made up for with her spunk and no-nonsense temper. You did not want to mess with Miss Sharmila.

I was the only beginner in the class, which was a bonus because it meant that I could learn and watch from the others. Sharmila walked me through a warm up which included six sets of arm lifts, where I would stand with the pole facing the middle of my chest, hold the pole with both hands just above my head, and then lift my body using my arms, as I take my feet off of the floor. That wasn't too bad.

Then she showed me a basic walk holding the pole with my right arm and walking around it like a ballerina, toes always pointed. Next she showed me how to do a *"fireman's spin"*. Walk three steps around the pole, swing my body out as I hold the pole with both arms, simultaneously wrapping my entire body around the pole and then bringing my knees and feet together on the pole to complete the fireman's spin. Very pretty. She told me to repeat these simple things for the entire sixty minutes which I was very happy to do, as they felt easy and simple.

I went home in high spirits and told the kids that my new sport from now on was Pole Dancing. They looked at me with their mouths open, at a loss for words for once in their lives. *"What are you looking at me like that for?"* I asked. *"Mum, that's for strippers!"* They protested. *"Who told you that?"* I challenged. *"Everybody knows that."* They insisted. *"Well kids, you'll be surprised how everybody knows not much at all. So just trust me okay. This is good for me."*

The next morning, I woke up unable to move. My entire body hurt like hell.

I was still semi immobile when I showed up for my second pole class a few days later, but I was determined to align the strength of my body with the strength of my mind. My classmates were a mix of young and old. Some of them were stay-at-home mums, a couple of them were sixteen-year-olds, while others were working women like me. What we had in common was our passion to combine physical strength with graceful movement. Pole Dancing is an expression as much as it is a discipline. A transmutation of energy into art.

Generally, there are three levels in pole dancing. Beginner, intermediate and advanced. The beginner has a set of relatively achievable moves and poses, and it goes on to progress into more powerful poses that require inversions and aerial transitions. Each dancer is unique. Some dancers are feminine, some are masculine and robust, while others are playful. Facial expressions are fascinating when you watch a woman on a pole, as they are often raw and confronting. Whether she is serious, playful or seductive, her eyes would say, *"This is me. Watch me, love me, or leave me. I don't give a damn."*

By the end of my second session, I had pressure bruises on my inner thighs and shins, which my classmates said were a sign of good progress. In no time, they said, I would be swinging on the pole like a monkey.

True to their word, I learned the *inverted crucifix* pose within two months. I got hooked on inversions from there and learned to transition between moves like waterfall, superman, scorpio, leg hooks and suspended butterflies, without my feet touching the floor.

As my body became stronger and my self-esteem sprouted like Jack's beanstalks, I started to open up to other women in the class. Through our candid conversations I learned that it was necessary for me to have lost the friends who turned their backs on me, so that I can grow and become the woman that I've always known I can be.

The process of becoming, required a process of letting go. It was a concept that I struggled to understand at first. But as I became more confident on the pole, I realized that the idea of letting go of the past so you can become someone new, was much like pole dancing itself. To create the full expression of the pose, you must let go of the fear of falling, and become the epitome of gracefulness and strength.

Chapter 43
New Friendships

The speed with which I discovered my pole dancing school on google had got me thinking, what else can I find? One day when the kids were once again at their Dad's for the weekend, I typed *"I want to make new friends for me"* on my phone. The first thing that showed up was the *MeetUp* website. Something that I have never heard of before, but quickly became fond of. In MeetUp, you can configure the type of people you would like to meet, based on your common interests and the distance you would be willing to travel to meet up with them.

I found an active MeetUp group that instantly piqued my interest. *The Gold Coast Single Parents Meetup* had over two thousand members, with some fifty highly engaged participants. They held fun weekly get-togethers with all their kids, as well as weekend getaways to beautiful coastal towns.

My heart was singing with excitement, while my mind was completely blown away by their lack of regard for the social stigma of being "single parents". Quite the contrary, they celebrated being single parents, and I loved it.

That same weekend, the group had a meetup at Burleigh Tavern. It was easy to register my interest to become part of The Gold Coast Single Parents Meetup, but when it came time to show up in person, my nerves were wrecked. The event description said that there would be a jumping castle for the kids, and some al fresco tables for the parents to share a bite to eat together. I punched the address of the tavern in my GPS and told the kids about the group that we were about to meet. They were intrigued. They have never seen me seek out strangers before, especially not for the purpose of making new friends.

I was hoping to settle my nerves on the drive to the meetup, but to my dismay, the meetup venue was only eleven minutes from my house. I parked my car inconspicuously and sat there for fifteen minutes, making the kids bored and impatient. I watched the group from a distance, mingling, talking and socializing. Thoughts of self-doubt came racing in my head.

"I don't know these people.
What am I going to say?
How will it feel like?
Is it worth trying to see what happens?
Should I just leave and take the kids to the park instead?
Why am I so nervous?
I don't think I can do it."

I was petrified. The feelings of rejection and abandonment from the friendships I've lost have lingered far longer than I was consciously aware of. I thought I had moved on, but now the fear of potentially going through the same process was blocking me from truly moving on.

"C'mon Mum, what are we doing?" My daughter.
"I'm hungry can we have something to eat now?" My son.
"Are we staying or going, just make a decision!" My daughter.
"I'm bored.. Look, there's a jumping castle over there." My son.
"Okay, okay. Just give me one more minute, we will do something." I said.

I took a deep breath and looked out to the space in front of me. I visualized a boulder. So big and immoveable that there was no way I could get through it. Fear. *"But you know you can walk around the boulder."* The voice in my head said. *"Aaahhh... Yes, I can walk around the boulder."* I said out loud to no one in particular. *"Boulder? What boulder?"* My son asked. *"Nothing. Let's go and get this show on the road kids!"* I declared with renewed vigour and started to move before I could change my mind again.

We hopped out of the car and I ushered my kids to the tavern. Approaching the group, I put a small smile on my face and shyly eyeballed a couple of the women there, looking for a look of acknowledgement. To my relief they all had smiles on their faces and a few of them almost simultaneously greeted me and my children.

Drawn to the positive energy of the group, I felt a rush of warmth in my chest as I held my hand out to one of the friendly faces and said *"Hi, I'm Grace, I'm here with my kids and we're new to the group."* As I uttered these words it was if I cast a spell on myself. The spell of taking responsibility for the friendships that I so choose to make. The spell of being grateful for other people's time and efforts. The spell that opened the gates for healthy and positive relationships.

Meanwhile, at work, I was promoted once again, this time as a business banker. Witnessing the growth and evolution of my uncles'

TV Repair business back in the '80s, I've always been fascinated by the different psyches that drove each of them to succeed or fail. One business, six uncles, six different outcomes.

Naturally, my interest in becoming a business banker was inclined towards the people inside of their businesses, rather than the businesses themselves. Entrepreneurs I found, were in a league of their own. They had an insatiable drive for freedom, even if it cost them their sense of security.

On the personal side, I began to form meaningful friendships with a few people from the Single Parents Group, and my physical health was at its peak. I was halfway to my fortieth birthday and feeling like I was on top of the world.

But then it would seem, that my personal war was far from over. I had yet to face the biggest, and most important spiritual combat of my life, so that I could heal the oldest wound in my heart. The scar of Pandora.

Chapter 44
Inner Child

It began one Saturday morning. I was home alone lying in bed when I started thinking about my daughter who just turned twelve years old. I recognized that she was beginning to change into a young teenager. I have been warned by some friends that this phase would happen, and then it would pass. So, I prayed, *"God, please give me the strength and wisdom to be the mother that my daughter needs in this time of her life. I am blessed to have her, and I pray that I could be worthy of her."*

I lied very still, listening to the palpable silence, when a slight breeze whiffed past my bedroom door. I sat up on the bed involuntarily, feeling like I was summoned to do so, and then I saw a ghostlike figure. A little girl with black hair and skinny arms, about four or five years old. I blinked my eyes and stopped breathing, wondering when the illusion would fade away. But it didn't. She stood there, looking lost, alone and suspended in time. Suddenly I realised she had been waiting for me, all this time, to love her, nurture her, and tell her she's worthy.

It was me, the wounded child, standing before my eyes, reaching out to be loved, accepted, and made to feel that she was worthy. My heart overflowed with compassion as I opened my arms and walked around the bed to give her a hug.

I knelt on the carpet by my bedroom door, the early morning sunrays peeping through the bathroom window, as I hugged myself, whispering, *"I love you. I love you little Grace. I will nurture you and make you happy and strong. We will grow together. I love you. You're so beautiful. You are worthy."*

Maybe I was finally going nuts after all that I've been through, talking to some ghost from the past promising her the future. But then again if not for that half nuts, half spiritual encounter, I would never have known how to bridge the gap between the powerless, abandoned child, and the self-confident, go getter adult. Both of them lived in the same body, the same mind, the same heart, and yet they lived in very different realities. One was a victim while the other was a victor. Two polarized people living in a mind that had been forced to live in split paradigms, so that life can go on, no matter what.

It was through this self-reunion that I had finally recognized the voices within myself. There was the voice of Pandora, with the scared shitless and defensive paradigm; and then there was Grace, with the fearless and unstoppable paradigm. My job was to integrate the two and make them love each other.

This self-assigned purpose of being whole again was a radical ambition. But I was ready.

Like most women do, I spent a little time reflecting on my life when my fortieth birthday was fast approaching. I created a mental VCR in my mind and hit the fast rewind button, starting with my recent victories in my career, my personal life, and my health. I worked backwards from there, reflecting on the decisions I've made that seemed catastrophic at first, but turned out to be my greatest source of education.

I thought about the men that graced my life, and I thanked them for the lessons I've learned, through them and from them.

I thought about my kids, and the joy and hope they give to me, and to the world. How blessed I am to have been assigned as their mother.

I also thought of other kids, whose mothers and fathers left them by choice and by will. For them, I made a promise that I will do everything I can, to try and stop whatever it was that caused the heinous epidemic of child abandonment.

Then finally, I focused on one child. Little Grace. *"What can I do to love you?"* I asked her. She said, *"Take me back home."*

The plane landed Ninoy Aquino International Airport on a humid, June afternoon. We checked in at Diamond Hotel overlooking Manila Bay for two nights before heading south to my hometown. My children were bursting with excitement for another adventure, while the child in me was thoughtful and reserved, insecure of where she would fit in this trip.

I organized a 40th birthday party for myself and invited my old friends and family members, plus my favourite cousin Skye who now lived in Germany was travelling back home especially for my birthday.

On the outside, it looked like the trip was designed for my womanhood, but my secret intention was to go back in time, so that Little Grace can see where she began and how far she had come. I wanted to mother the child in me, in a way that she was never mothered. I wanted to give her an overdue loving and nurturing experience, in her very own hometown, with the protection of the woman she had become.

That night, as my kids lay peacefully asleep, I stared out to the bustling scene down Roxas Boulevard, remembering fifteen years ago when I used to live in this city. A lot has changed since then, yet everything seemed to be fundamentally the same. I've become a woman of the world, yet I was the same girl with the same dreams: To love and be loved.

In the midst of my reverie, I became very conscious of a presence standing right next to me. There she was again. The child. My inner child. Her presence was stronger by the hour and I was forced to snap myself out of my musings and pay attention to her in the moment. I looked down to the space next to my right hip and said, *"It's going to be okay. I am going to be there with you."* My daughter stirred in her slumber, thinking I was speaking to her, and murmured *"Yes mummy."*

While the heart of Manila was filled with traffic and pollution, where people slept on sidewalks and beggars roamed the streets at all hours, my kids slumbered like logs up in the twenty-third floor of a five-star hotel. The contrast between deprivation and provision made me feel even more determined to be a better person. I wanted to give to the world what I was able to give to my children. But first things first, I must love and nurture the first child in my life. My inner child.

Arriving in General Santos, my aunt Ellie welcomed us into her home with open arms. It was good to be back. The first person I called was my father, whom I have only seen and spoken to twice in the last thirty-five years.

"*Hello Pa!*" I said on a high note when his voice rolled on the other end.

"Kinsa ni?" *(Who's this?)* He said.

"*Si Ging-ging.*" *(It's me, Ging-ging)* using my nickname when I was a child.

"*Oh! Ging! Anak! Bertday nimo next week!*" *(My child! It's your birthday next week!)* He exclaimed.

A lump caught in my throat, the warmth in his voice was a kind of warmth that I have never, ever felt from anyone before. "*My Papa loves me.*" I whispered quietly not so much to myself, but to the child that was in me. "*Papa loves me.*" I told myself again, as if saying it more could make the love sprout out of the phone like a beautiful vine.

We talked for a while, and I invited him to my birthday party even though I knew he lived seventy-five kilometres away and would be unlikely to attend. It was my way of saying that I loved him in spite of his absence in my life.

I had four days to get everything ready for my birthday bash, and in spite of my apprehensions, I decided that no relatives were banned from my party. I wanted to celebrate me, and if anyone didn't like being at my party, they would be most welcome to leave. Besides, I knew I was going to have a great time no matter what, as I had been speaking to my old friends quite regularly, and we were all looking forward to being together again. I had mentally prepped myself thoroughly, and felt quite invincible, so that I didn't even think much about what I would do if my mother decided to come to the party.

So invincible that when she turned up, I could literally see the battle she was having in her mind whether she should hug and greet me, or bypass the niceties altogether. And perhaps I should have acted more compassionately and helped her out of her discomfort and hesitation, after all, she made the effort to be there. However, at the time, I was clearly still in the egoic level of my healing, and in a moment of pride and prejudice, I left her to suffer in her uneasiness and ignored her altogether.

In hindsight, my haughtiness was a necessary step. After all the pain that my mother had consciously and unconsciously inflicted on me as a young person, I needed to arrive at a neutral ground, before any real healing could even begin. And that neutral ground was the realisation that my mother and I, were total strangers. And as strangers do, I let her be and she let me be. We were at the same party, but we didn't party together.

It was a fun night. I ordered a three-tiered, exaggerated cake with big numbers four and zero at the top, and my kids helped me blow the candle.

As far as my relatives were concerned, they loved the excuse to have a drink or two, and perhaps so did I. My girl cousins whom I love dearly, brought some tequila and wine, and when all the guests have gone home, we turned the karaoke on and started the real party. I had a couple of shots, my auntie had a few, while my cousins don't count their shots.

My daughter stayed up with us for a while and sang Avril Lavigne songs, while my son played computer games till the wee hours. At one-thirty in the morning, I called it a night, noting the beautiful grin on my drunk aunt's face. I loved seeing her lose her inhibitions. She had been through so much with her son Mark's issues, not to mention her siblings fighting around her all the time, ironically because of her own generosity with money.

I bid all good night as the kids and I resigned into our quarters. *"I love you my babies."* I whispered to them. Then as I heard the magic words *"G'night mum, love you."* I slumbered like a log. Forty years young and feeling like life was unfolding at a new dimension.

We stayed at my aunt's place for a couple of weeks enjoying the pilgrim that it was meant to be. I drove all over the city during days and nights, visiting, looking, and reminiscing the sense of awe it used to bring me; going out for dinners and lunches with my friends, and simply being a Gensan girl once again.

I made sure that I came by my grandmother's house one more time before I left, to see both my grandmother and my mother. I wanted to leave my grandmother some money and also to exchange courtesy with my mother. I gave her a day's notice on the phone that my kids were coming with me.

In a gesture of love and kindness, she made some mango smoothie for my kids plus some home-made pan de sal for me to taste. We exchanged a few generic information as a way of conversation, and I made sure the kids expressed their gratitude to her for the delicious and refreshing mango smoothie.

I took time to look around in my grandmother's house, careful to see it with fresh eyes, guarding my Little Grace against any trigger points, yet curious to see her reactions. I went upstairs to see my old sanctuary, the room where I slept with my aunt when she came to visit, the floor where I slept with the maids, my grandfather's old books and his reading chair. My grandfather passed some years ago, and I could imagine that he would have had a big, Chinese style funeral, none of which I heard about until months after he had been dead. Nobody remembered to tell me.

In spite of a few refurb jobs, the whole house seemed to have shrunk, and more stoic than ever before. Like an old tree that had seen generations come and go, standing still and eternally mum.

I checked in on Little Grace, but she was so self-preserved that I couldn't reach into her. It was as if she hid herself inside of my adult body, refusing to be part of *the tour*. So I didn't force anything, and decided that it was time to leave. There was nothing in this house for me now, nor did it ever have anything for Little Grace.

Altogether considering, it was a pleasant visit, and my grandmother was so happy when I slipped a fat wad of cash into her hands. She then offered me some soft drinks from the fridge in her sari-sari store, something that she would only have offered to my cousins back when I was a kid.

I smiled in gratitude of her offering and then I heard a childish voice come out of my mouth, *"Wala ko gainom soft drinks Mommy, pwede skyflakes?"* (I'd love to, Mommy, but I don't drink soft drinks, so can I please have some skyflakes biscuits instead?)

I was taken aback by the sound of my shallow, high pitched voice. And then I knew. There she was, finally, Little Grace. Tears welled up my eyes as I felt the spirit of my inner child step out of my chest and walk over to the jar of individually wrapped skyflakes, and reached inside the jar with ginger hands, ever so slowly, almost wondering if she was indeed, allowed to do this.

It was a brief but intense out of body experience that left me choking with emotions. I had to face away from my grandmother to take a couple of breaths and gain my composure.

Taking a bite of the crunchy skyflakes, I could hardly taste it. That's when I knew my inner child had gone back into her safe haven, a little spirit incubating inside of its adult version.

From then on, she developed a habit of randomly coming out into the surface, but more often than not she is safely ensconced in my heart. My special Little Grace that I love just the way she is.

My last and final pilgrimage was to see my father. It had been almost twenty years since I saw him, and I wanted my children to meet their grandfather. Knowing that my children may not visit the Philippines as often as I would, this could be the only time that they would meet my father. They were excited because they had never had a grandfather, their own father's father having died long before they were born.

Larry kindly offered to drive for us to the town of *Marbel*, where our father lived. My Papa was wearing a blue collared shirt, brown pair of slacks and black rubber slippers. Standing out the front of *KCC Marbel* waiting for us, with a hunched posture and a canvass bag on his shoulder, he looked rather short, a stark contrast to the tall and strong man that I remember of him as a child.

In his late 70's he now looked frail and subdued. Nonetheless I was so happy to see him and gave him a tight, long hug. A gesture that he reciprocated with intensity. Unexpressed emotions and affection between father and daughter came flooding through between us and I didn't want to let go. I stayed in the hug for as long as I could until Papa let go so he could hug the rest of the troop. My heart beamed to see my kids welcome their grandfather with instant love and affection, while my big brother gave Papa a tight but curt hug, just like typical men do with each other.

We found a quiet restaurant and shared a meal together. My Papa said to me, *"Ang akong anak, salamat sa Ginoo nga nagkita gyud ta."* (My child, I thank the Lord that you and I are together now.) I felt like a child again being in his company, beaming like a pig in the mud, yet unable to say too much with my emotions just bubbling around the surface of my throat. I was in seventh heaven, being with a parent who loved and accepted me.

I asked what's been keeping him busy, and his eyes lit up. He had been appointed as Bishop of a non-catholic religious sector in the Southern Philippines region. He proudly showed us his certificate of appointment and ID card with his name and title on it. I was so proud of my Papa and especially that my kids were there to see and hear of his passion, directly from him.

Knowing that this was not the first time that my father had changed his religious association, I took solace in knowing that at least he had an active pursuit of faith. It didn't matter how many more religions he would explore in his life, for as long as he was exploring. It wasn't so much about finding a perfect destination, as much as it was about being joyful in the journey.

Then he gave me a gift. A herbal remedy cream for mosquito bites and skin related ailments, which he had been manufacturing from home. I opened the tiny, round canister and rubbed some between my forefinger and thumb, relishing the organic feel of the ingredients, creamy but slightly coarse.

My kids were so impressed by their grandfather's talents. I encouraged my Papa to keep pursuing the things that were dear to his heart, as I listened between the lines of his stories, catching on his inconsistent resources to support the development of the herbal cream. I said to him that I hope I could help even for just a little bit, and handed him a wad of cash that I knew would be more than he would have seen for a while.

By mid-afternoon it was time to say goodbye. We took my Papa to the jeepney station where he would take the local ride to a small *Barrio* called *Banga*, insisting that he didn't need my brother to drive him all the way home.

As we bid farewell, I could no longer hold my tears and I sobbed quietly, mindful that we were in public. I held my Papa tight and said goodbye. *"Love you Pa."*

On the ride home my family left me in peace to shed some tears. Tears for the relationship I've never had with a parent who loved me. Tears for the joy of starting that relationship again. And then the tears for not knowing when, or if ever, I would see him again.

It was such an emotionally intimate afternoon for me, my father, and my big brother, so much so that on the drive home, Larry and I finally begun a conversation that's been a long time coming. For the last thirty minutes of the trip, we started talking about our childhood. And although we didn't have a lot of time to talk, I felt like we had a breakthrough as brother and sister.

As we both reflected upon the lives that each of us had chosen to live, including me, my big brother, and the cousins that I grew up with, I realized that the tables have turned. I've since learned that my cousins Mark, James, and Carlo, the cousins whose parents showered them with spoils and favours, have done time for very similar, drug-related crimes. While here we were, my big brother and I, the oppressed and wretched ones have ended up becoming fully functioning, thriving adults.

The irony was inescapable, and as Larry and I concluded the day's journey, I couldn't help but wonder, was our suffering pre-requisite for our success?

On the day of our flight back home, I felt a sense of graduation from my old home. While it is true that nothing will ever substitute the place where I've experienced the kiss of God on my cheeks for the first time, playing in the open fields as a child, caressed by the breeze and feeling connected to my soul; I know that there is a better place than home – and that is the home that I had finally begun to create inside of myself, for myself. A new home that's not borne from a tangible environment but borne from a spiritual place and deep sense of self-acceptance.

At forty years old, I could feel a brand-new paradigm of self-love growing inside of me, a fearless, paradigm of self-love.

Chapter 45
Kindred Souls

It was the middle of winter in Australia and the kids and I have been back for two weeks. Life was humming rather uneventfully, which I found to be a beautiful thing. Something had changed ever since my pilgrim to the Philippines. Where I used to feel alone and lonely when my kids were away at their Dad's, I started to find joy and contentment in my solitude.

My weekends used to be packed to the brim with things to do, places to go, and people to see; and even though I told myself that in doing those things, going to those places and seeing so many people, that I was giving myself some *me-time*, it dawned on me, that there was no me in the time. In fact, I was avoiding me, by putting my attention to everything outside of me.

I realised that my old paradigm of self-love was largely based on fear. Fear of missing out. Fear of being by myself. Fear of not belonging. Fear of not being loved. Fear of being lonely. Fear of leaving the herd. Fear of getting my voice heard. Fear based paradigms of self-love that hindered me from being truly me.

One day my life was turned upside down and inside out, in a good way. I was out to dinner with a few friends from the bank and having so much fun chatting with everyone when two of my girlfriends, Julie and Jess, turned their attention to me over dessert.

"So Grace, are you dating anyone?" Julie quizzed.
"No." I muttered with a plastic straw in my mouth sipping my lemon lime bitters.
"Still single huh!" Jess butted in.
"Yeah." I said, putting my drink down, unsure where the conversation was headed.

Knowing this cheeky pair, I smiled and braced myself for what would come of the subject, especially that they have had a drink or two by then. I'm used to my friends' antics and in fact I missed that, so I was more than willing to play along.

"Well, what are you doing then?" Jess challenged me.
"About what?" I was perplexed.
"Dating!" she exclaimed.
"Oh." I was starting to feel a little stupid for my short answers. "Well, I'm waiting! I'm ready. If it's there that's great, otherwise it's all good." I said.
"That's it, I'm putting you on *eharmony*!" Julie declared.
"Putting me where?" This time we were all laughing.
"Eharmony! The dating app! Here, give us your phone!"

Having known and worked with Julie and Jess for many years, they were some of the most trustworthy and caring people I have known, and I knew that they only had my best interest at heart. I handed my phone obligingly, curious about what was going to happen, as Julie downloaded the eharmony dating app and signed me up on it in lightning speed.

With borrowed inspiration and courage from my friends, I went home that night and made a decision to be proactive and carry on with the eharmony app. I had to pay to become an active member, which I begrudgingly did, for a special one-month trial price of thirty-three dollars.

Next, I answered the dating questionnaire that was designed to match people together. At first it was just something to do out of boredom, but then the questions became more interesting, and I became more curious. Curious about myself and the answers that I wrote.

It was thought-provoking and covered aspects of life like religion, money, career, children, ex relationships, physical looks preferences, dating experience preferences, and a whole lot more. After completing the questionnaire, I felt like I got to know myself more than I ever have, especially in terms of my own personal values. Never mind meeting men, to me, that in itself was worth paying thirty-three dollars for.

It took me ninety minutes to complete my eharmony profile and be fully ready for online dating. I wasn't trying to present perfection, far from it, but I took my time thinking about my "preferences" and seriously contemplated on what my true intentions were.

That night, I went to bed exhausted, but settled. Yes, I was once again open to a new relationship, but this time only with a person who made me feel respected, cared for, adored, and desired. A person who shared important personal values with me, such as creating a peaceful family, continuous personal growth, no alcohol, no gambling, no lying, no cheating, no smoking, no swearing, and no abuse.

Was I looking for the perfect man? I asked myself. Absolutely not. There were things that weren't too important for me, such as good looks, ethnicity, and type of profession. It wasn't about the way they looked, where they came from, or what they did for a living than it was about who they were as a human being, and how they made me feel.

This kind of intentionality turned my life upside down and inside out in a good way, but not before I could prove to the universe that I was worthy of what I was asking for.

Dutch said hello to me on the dating app with a cute photo of himself sitting across from a woman in a restaurant with the caption, "Me and my sister." They were both smiling to the camera, but it was Dutch's eyes that pored directly into my soul. My first reaction was, *"Oohhhh…. There you are."* I felt like I've known him for a long time. I could visualize his stance, and there was an invisible energy that made me feel we had somehow connected before. I was mystified.

I swiped my phone to see more photos. The next one was of his super cute, four-year old gorgeous little boy wearing a man's singlet and steel capped boots, smiling to the camera. Dutch's "hunky Dad" score had just gone up gazillion points more. The last photo was of him sitting next to an old woman. The caption said, "My Nan's 80th. One of the most beautiful women in the world." Again, I swooned *"Ooohhhh…"* and ogled him some more.

Butterflies fluttered in my chest like no one had ever done to me before. I was smitten by this man, and we started writing long, deep and soulful emails for a couple of weeks which was so much fun for me.

Dutch had been single, all of his life. He was a Brisbane restaurateur turned serial wanderer after a business partnership with his father folded in the early 2000's, which, not so much ruined him financially, but broke his heart and wiped out his relationship with his father altogether. With the business gone and his spirits in shambles, Dutch spent time in Western Australia where he bounced back through timely and wise real estate investments, during the mining boom.

In spite of his financial comeback, he felt that something important was missing. So he inched forward looking for some kind of meaning in his life, travelling to places like Spain to learn a new language, Philippines to teach kite surfing, then India and Thailand to study Yoga. Along the way, he had sired his beautiful son from a relationship that ended rather briefly, which catapulted him to an unexpected, full-time single fatherhood.

A self-confessed former egomaniac, all of Dutch's lessons through Yoga and life itself, allowed him to develop the awareness he needed, to scrutinize his life and re-engineer his future. By the time I met him, I couldn't see a trace of the society induced stress head that he used to be. Instead he was calm, softly spoken, very thoughtful and perpetually charming, making him ultra-seductive in my eyes.

Chapter 46
Self-love

Our courtship was sweet and straightforward. Like two kindred souls who spent a few eternities waiting to be together, we didn't waste time in dating games by trying to guess if we liked each other or not. We simply fell into a rhythm of loving every minute we had by deepening our connection with conversations that could rock the entire galaxy. He paid attention to my mind and cared about how I felt in everything that we did together.

His physical affection was both nurturing as it was abandoned, morphing me from being shy about my body, to a mature and sensuous woman. At times it almost felt like I was under a spell that I didn't want to end, but then I thought, if the spell was making me discover and love myself more, then perhaps it wasn't so much a spell, as it was a gift of life.

Inevitably, we fell in love. This was a big thing for me to acknowledge, because it wasn't something that I expected. Even though I knew I've always wanted to fall in love with the right one, I didn't expect that the *experience* of falling in love, can be so beautiful and amazing. To say that I was caught off guard was an understatement. I had been so used to relationships that gave me stress and heartbreak, that I thought I might have missed something in what I had with Dutch. Our love just felt so good in my heart that my little brain could not begin to comprehend.

One evening I came home from a big day at work feeling exhausted, when Dutch called just to say that he was thinking of me, which lifted me and put me in an energised mood. But then just as quickly after the phone call ended, I realised that I was starting to get used to his regular phone calls, and then I worried, what would happen if he ever decided that he didn't want to make those phone calls to me anymore? I couldn't help but wonder, *"Is this for real?"* Then another voice in my head said, *"Could this really be love?"* Before I knew it, a mental pandemonium had broken in my head, and the voices had gone bananas.

"He's so good, what's wrong with him?"
"There's gotta be somethin' up with him, aye."
"He never gets angry, that's sus."
"What's the go with this bloke?"
"So he doesn't smoke, doesn't drink, doesn't gamble, that's a little too good to be true, don't you reckon?"
"He likes talking about your feelings? Yeah right."

The voices were relentless and making me crazy, I covered my ears and screamed, "Shut! Up! Shut up! JUST. BE. QUIET!"

The voices halted and then there was a deafening silence. Much like the dead silence when my cousin whacked me in the cheek as a little girl. I looked around me and I saw my children sitting on the couch with bewildered looks on their faces. They thought I'd gone completely demented. I shook my head and shifted my body to bring me back to the present, then I took a deep breath and apologised to them. *"I'm sorry kids. I was just talking to myself."* They nodded their heads and suspiciously said *"Oooowwwkaayyyy…"*

Before they could say another word, I ran to my room and burst into gut wrenching sobs. Dutch made me feel things that my heart loved to feel, but my mind hated to accept. According to my brain, he was highly unusual, and therefore highly suspicious.

Nagged by the fear of *"What if I make another catastrophic mistake?"* my self-sabotage system kicked in full swing. Pandora's mindset, originally designed to protect me, has now turned into a prisoner's mindset. One who was not prepared to let go and let live.

Exhausted from my inner battles, I fell asleep that night with no victories except for the knowing that my heart and my mind did *not* want the same thing. I may have won the battle against people who tried to destroy me in the past, but I was so far from having won the battle against my old self: The ageless warrior that was Pandora, born not from a linear perspective but from a pain perspective. The more pain she was subjected to, the stronger she became.

But since my life had shifted radically from manifestations of pain to manifestations of love and joy, Pandora was not only hungry for pain, she was also angry for not having it. You could just about say that she was one *hangry alter ego.*

Most of the insanity I've had in my life, I survived through sheer test and learn. But as a forty-year old woman I didn't want to live a test and learn existence anymore. I wanted to consciously become the woman of my dreams. With this in mind, I woke up the next day basking in the catharsis of last night's nervous breakdown, while pondering a quote from some Greek philosopher called Socrates: *"The secret to change is to focus all of your energy, not on fighting the old, but on building the new."*

I relished this quote over a mug of black coffee, gingerly reading and re reading it until it was embedded in my brain. And then the idea came to me. I'm going to have to *"adopt and raise all of me"* just like I did with my Little Grace, so that one day all my broken parts would be glued back together. Like a beautiful mosaic, with each piece telling a unique story, so that the entirety becomes a beautiful creation of tranquillity and love.

"That's it!" I stood up from my morning musings and made a decision that I was going to *"put me back together"* so that my heart and my mind will come to an agreement and want the same thing.

"How?" A familiar, dubious voice in my head. *"We'll get started with you, my darling!"* I responded out loud to no one in particular, laughing at my crazy, beautiful self. For the first time in a long time, I felt the unconditional sense of faith and hope that I've always had as a child. A kind of faith that lives in the beauty of the unknown, untethered by self-sabotage.

My self-therapy was powerfully amplified because of the presence of Dutch in my life. He re-ignited my love for Yoga, and I loved being his student in meditation and breathwork. We spent many hours on long walks along the beach, holding hands and talking about anything, everything and sometimes nothing. Silence with Dutch yielded just as much as talking with him. We spoke often with words, but we communicated even deeper with physical touch and acts of kindness. After a short but exquisite courtship of three and a half months, we took the plunge from being a couple and moved in together to a loving, blended family of five.

EPILOGUE:

It was daylight in my dream. Slithers of feathery clouds laced the blue skies in a nostalgic and tranquil fashion. I was in my great grandmother's house where my mother and my big brother used to live, and I felt no sense of hunger, no sense of sadness, and no sense of fear.

Everything was clear, pronounced and vibrant. I could see the grains of the wooden posts that held the tin roof above a makeshift kitchen in the backyard, the richness of the soil under my feet was as coarse as it was hot, keeping my body alive.

I started to wake up in my dream, feeling the familiarity of the surroundings but also recognizing that I was looking at it from a new set of eyes, the eyes of the woman that I've become. As I awoke in my dream, things became even more alive, and then my mother was there. She was sitting in a squat position next to me, and together we observed the sprouting of ferns and yellow African Daisies next to my great grandmother's outdoor bathroom. There was an air of ease and camaraderie, and my mind was so quiet, so calm, and so present in the moment.

In a flash, a giant, shiny, slithery, black, reticulated python with white spots on its skin, started to swirl all around me and my mother. It was three times the size of the house and it swirled on the outer edges of the property in a joyous, rather excited fashion, like an eel in a tiny fish tank.

It was a beautiful snake, and I was in a beautiful dream, fully awake and enjoying every moment that I had in it.

I opened my eyes and came out of my lucid dream, and the first thoughts that came to me were: Love and Abundance. It has been five years since I've made the decision to *"put me back together"* and create a mosaic life of tranquillity and love.

I eagerly stepped out of the covers while Dutch was still sleeping, as well as our three kids who were now at the vibrant ages of eighteen, fifteen and ten. It was time for my morning meditation and there is so much to be grateful for.

Shortly after I met Dutch, I received a personal challenge from my then mentor, Sam Cawthorn, to *"complete an incomplete"* and have a *"forgiveness conversation"* with the one person who held the key to my inner healing.

Although she wasn't expecting the call, I could tell that my mother was happy to hear from me.

"Ma." I said
"Ging!" She said.
*"Ma, I apologise for holding you accountable for my personal happiness, all these years. I just want to say that I'm sorry for making you responsible

for the circumstances in my life. I know now that my life is up to me. I love you." I said.

"I understand, Ging." She said.

Although my mother is unable to fully express herself and show the depth of her emotions, I know now that she is perfect as she is. Exactly as my late friend Merri had said to me, my mother did her very best, each and every time, and for that, I am who I am today.

My greatest gift was my greatest pain, and I would never swap them for anything in the world. My life is an all-encompassing gift of learning to love myself unconditionally, unapologetically.

In order to heal, I had to forgive. And the biggest forgiveness conversation that I had to have was the one with myself, and cleanse myself of all the fear, guilt, and shame that marred the purity of my heart. Because forgiveness, is the ultimate act of self-love.

In the last five years, I've transformed the landscape of my life by making fearless decisions and bold actions. Starting with leaving my sterile, secure, corporate job and finding my voice as a writer and speaker. I have since shared my stories and lessons to a collective audience of over half a million people globally, and in doing so, I find myself in a blissful trajectory of consciousness expansion.

As I allow myself to be vulnerable and share my story with the world, I am also taught and enlightened by those who shared their stories with me, and some of the most significant lessons I've learned are:

~ It is our birthright to become fully aligned mentally, emotionally and spiritually, so that we can unveil our life's true purpose.

~ Every living thing in our planet has an assignment. And as a human being, it is our calling to work towards living a life of love, peace and abundance.

~ Only those who feel the pain are truly alive; and if you ever find yourself numbing the pain and dying a slow death, reach for your divine power of transcendence, by simply asking for help. Simple and consistent acts of self-love create the most transformative outcomes.

~ One of the deadliest psychological tools that the human race had ever invented is comparing oneself to others. It is biologically and spiritually sacrilegious.

~ To live the life of your dreams, you must first become the woman of your dreams.

~ True self-love is not about creating an experience of joy, it is about being the experience of joy.

~ "Family" is a reflection of your personal power. Honour the power of your divine soul by accepting that your family goes beyond your bloodline. Your family is everything that is in your consciousness, including, and especially those, who gravitate to your wisdom and guidance.

~ YOU: Are the observer of your thoughts and the curator of your belief systems. Choose carefully and wisely.

~ There are no right or wrong decisions. Only fear based and fearless ones. From there, you can either destroy or create, and you have the sovereign power to make the choice, each and every time, no matter what.

~ Fear, guilt and shame are life suckers. Try gratitude, affirmation and intention instead.

~ In dire straits, close your eyes, take a deep breath and just whisper, "Thank you."

At the time of publishing this memoir, my grandmother passed away. While the *covid* pandemic prevented me from flying into Gensan and *see her* for the last time, I found myself traveling back in time and reminiscing my childhood in a way that I never have before. And the one thing I found is this: No matter how heartbreaking my life was as a child, and in spite of all the psychological warfare that Pandora and I went through together, I loved my family, and I still do.

Loving them was hard, and the difficulty to express and receive love was the most painful part. But they did the best they could, with the knowledge that they had and the basic belief systems and values that they possessed, at that time.

My uncle Roy, the genius behind the TV Repair business, has now moved on to passive real estate revenue stream. My cousin Mark is currently doing time for a crime that he had remorsefully pleaded guilty to. My cousins James and Carlo have done time and are now free again, getting back into a clean, drug free life path. My favourite cousin Skye now lives in Europe and recently released her first single. My aunt Ellie's husband passed away and she now lives in the Philippines, surrounded by nature and her animals. My uncle Cris and auntie Lorna have separated and are happily remarried with other people. My uncle Andy and his wife raised two amazing children who have given them three amazing grandchildren. My father is ailing in his old age and has his current life partner taking care of him.

My brother Larry holds an executive job and has a beautiful family. In our recent conversations, we have finally come to a safe and open space to share each other's heartaches and experiences as children; and he referred to my grandmother's house as the *House of Hell*. He is proactively acknowledging his own demons and bravely doing the work to liberate himself from anxiety and depression. And I am so grateful that I have done the work on my healing so that now I can assist in his. My mother lived with my grandmother all of this time while running her own internet hub business with the help of my younger brother.

But now that my grandmother had passed away, her children will divide her estate, and the House of Hell will be demolished, sealing all of its secrets and stories into oblivion. From ashes to ashes and dust to dust.

The dawn of a new era is always unfolding. For you, for me, for all of us. When you learn to see every brand-new day as a brand-new era, you can think, feel and act with wonder, curiosity, and fearlessness, regardless of what happened yesterday and what awaits tomorrow.

Each and every day that you heal yourself with tender, unconditional self-love, you are creating an energy that will inevitably explode into unprecedented transformation, beyond what you had ever imagined you could do.

Trust Your Divine Power. Become the woman of your dreams.

www.ingramcontent.com/pod-product-compliance
Lightning Source LLC
Chambersburg PA
CBHW030252010526
44107CB00053B/1677